UNIVERSITY OF NORTH CAROLINA AT CHAPEL HILL
DEPARTMENT OF ROMANCE LANGUAGES

NORTH CAROLINA STUDIES
IN THE ROMANCE LANGUAGES AND LITERATURES

Founder: URBAN TIGNER HOLMES

Editor: CAROL L. SHERMAN

Distributed by:

UNIVERSITY OF NORTH CAROLINA PRESS

CHAPEL HILL
North Carolina 27515-2288
U.S.A.

NORTH CAROLINA STUDIES IN THE
ROMANCE LANGUAGES AND LITERATURES
Number 269

MANNERISM AND BAROQUE IN
SEVENTEENTH-CENTURY FRENCH POETRY:
THE EXAMPLE OF TRISTAN L'HERMITE

MANNERISM AND BAROQUE
IN
SEVENTEENTH-CENTURY
FRENCH POETRY:
THE EXAMPLE OF
TRISTAN L'HERMITE

BY

JAMES CRENSHAW SHEPARD

CHAPEL HILL

NORTH CAROLINA STUDIES IN THE ROMANCE
LANGUAGES AND LITERATURES
U.N.C. DEPARTMENT OF ROMANCE LANGUAGES

2001

Library of Congress Cataloging-in-Publication Data

Shepard, James Crenshaw.
   Mannerism and baroque in seventeenth-century French poetry: the example of Tristan L'Hermite / by James Crenshaw Shepard.
   p. cm. – (North Carolina studies in the Romance languages and literatures; no. 269).
   Originally presented as the author's thesis (Ph. D.)–(University of North Carolina at Chapel Hill, 1997) under the title: Mannerism and Baroque in the poetry of Tristan L'Hermite.
   Includes bibliographical references.
   ISBN 0-8078-9273-4
   1. Tristan L'Hermite, François, 1601-1655–Criticism and interpretation.   2. Mannerism (Literature)   3. Baroque literature.   I. Title.   II. Series.

PQ1929.Z8 S53 2001
841'.4–dc21   2001027174

Cover design: Heidi Perov

ISBN 0-8078-9273-4

IMPRESO EN ESPAÑA

PRINTED IN SPAIN

DEPÓSITO LEGAL: V. 2.377 - 2001

ARTES GRÁFICAS SOLER, S. L. - LA OLIVERETA, 28 - 46018 VALENCIA

To
JUDITH

CONTENTS

ACKNOWLEDGEMENTS

I would like to thank the administration of Talladega College for the financial support they have given to this project. The Provost, Dr. Arthur L. Bacon, and the Dean of Humanities, Dr. Trellie Jeffers, have been especially helpful. Also I would like to thank Professor Frederick W. Vogler of the University of North Carolina at Chapel Hill for his many valuable suggestions and his careful reading of the text. Special thanks are due to the editor of this series, Professor Carol Sherman, whose guidance made this project a reality. The staffs of the Davis Library at North Carolina and of the Alabama Public Library Service have been instrumental in gathering the materials needed for this study.

Finally, I would like to thank the scholars who have been pioneers in Tristan studies: Claude K. Abraham, Amédée Carriat, Charles Mackey, Catherine M. Grisé, Jean-Pierre Chauveau, Gisèle Mathieu-Castellani, and, of course, Napoléon-M. Bernardin whose work started the Renaissance in Tristan and his works.

CHAPTER I

INTRODUCTION

THE application to art and literature of the terms "mannerism" and "baroque" is of relatively recent origin when one considers them in relation to more accepted appellations such as "Romanticism" or "Classicism." Indeed, the very existence in literature of mannerism and baroque has been, and still is, a matter of great controversy–especially when applied to French literature. The first part of this essay is a survey of the history of scholarship in the two areas, followed by an examination of the validity of the two terms as they apply to literary history and criticism. It is hoped that this inquiry has defined mannerism and baroque, as the two designations apply, generally, to French literature, and, specifically, to the poetry of Tristan L'Hermite. The discussions of baroque and mannerism will conclude the first part of the study and will provide the definitions that will be used in the remainder of the work.

The second part of the study, introduced by a survey of Tristanian criticism, is an analysis of mannerism and baroque in the poetry of Tristan L'Hermite. As will be shown in the next chapter, Tristan is one of the most versatile writers of seventeenth-century France, and his works reflect both periods and styles under consideration, as well as the pre-classical or *baroque dompté*. I have examined all the published collections of his poetry, as well as other poems, which were published individually or in the many anthologies that appeared during Tristan's lifetime. Since a chronology of his poetry is virtually impossible to establish, I have studied his poetry in the order in which he published it. I have saved the religious poems, thirteen previously unknown amatory poems, and a long heroic poem that does not appear in any of his collections, for the penultimate chapter. The rich variety of subjects and styles in the poetic output of Tristan L'Hermite provides fertile fields for a study such as this one. It is also hoped that, seen from the perspective of my analyses, the poetry of this, the outstanding lyric poet of the XVIIth century, will be further elucidated.

The study is organized as follows: A preliminary chapter discusses Tristan and his works, especially those which are relevant to this investigation, and justifies the choices of both Tristan and his poetry for an analysis of the two styles. The next chapter deals with mannerism and its history as a literary and artistic term. The chapter concludes with an attempt to define the term and enumerate its characteristics. A subsequent chapter contains a similar discussion of baroque and ends with a comparison of the two concepts. The final chapters contain analyses of the two terms as they apply specifically to the poetry of Tristan L'Hermite. A final, brief chapter serves to summarize the conclusions reached during this study. A comprehensive bibliography of baroque, mannerism, and works by and about Tristan L'Hermite concludes this effort.

CHAPTER II

TRISTAN L'HERMITE

IN April of 1870, Ernest Serret published an article in the *Correspondant*,[1] which marks the beginning of over a century of study that has led to "un regain de faveur"[2] of Tristan L'Hermite. Serret's study was soon completed by N.-M. Bernardin, whose doctoral dissertation,[3] published in 1895, remains the standard literary biography of Tristan.[4] Amédée Carriat has contributed to Tristan's reputation as one of the foremost lyric poets of the seventeenth century[5] and has provided us with a comprehensive bibliography of the poet's works.[6] He is also the founder of a journal devoted exclusively to Tristan, the *Cahiers Tristan L'Hermite*.[7] Within the past 30 years, critical editions of Tristan's theater,[8] *Lettres meslées*,[9] *Vers héroïques*,[10] and *La Lyre*[11] have appeared to compliment Marcel Ar-

[1] "Un précurseur de Racine, Tristan L'Hermite," *Le Correspondant*, 46 (Nouvelle série, 25 April 1870): 334-354.

[2] C. K. Abraham, J. Schweitzer, J. van Baelen, eds., Introduction, *Le Théâtre de Tristan L'Hermite* (Tuscaloosa: UP of Al, 1975), 1.

[3] N.-M. Bernardin, *Un Précurseur de Racine, Tristan L'Hermite* (Paris: Picard, 1895).

[4] C. K. Abraham, *Tristan L'Hermite* (Boston: Twayne, 1980), 138.

[5] *Tristan ou l'Éloge d'un poète* (Limoges: Rougerie, 1955); cited hereafter as *Éloge*. See also his anthology, *Tristan L'Hermite: Choix de pages* (Limoges: Rougerie, 1960).

[6] *Bibliographie des oeuvres de Tristan L'Hermite* (Limoges: Rougerie, 1955).

[7] Mortemart: Rougerie, 1979-present.

[8] See note 2.

[9] C. Grisé, ed. (Geneva: Droz, 1977). All quotations from the *Lettres meslées* will be from this edition. The reader is also referred to the biographical work of Grisé in her dissertation: "The Poetry of Tristan L'Hermite" (Diss. U of Toronto, 1964).

[10] C. Grisé, ed. (Geneva: Droz, 1967).

land's edition of *Le Page disgracié*[12] and P. Camo's edition of *Les Amours.*[13] A search of the *MLA Bibliography* (1963-1999) reveals over a hundred titles devoted to Tristan L'Hermite, sixteen of which are doctoral dissertations. Professor Claude K. Abraham has written a book on Tristan which is a part of the Twayne's World Authors Series,[14] and Tristan has been included in virtually all anthologies of seventeenth-century French literature published in the second half of this century.[15]

The renaissance of interest in Tristan has been almost simultaneous with the re-discovery of the baroque in literature. Now Tristan, along with Théophile de Viau and Saint-Amant, is regarded as one of the three best French lyric poets of the first half of the seventeenth century.[16] More recently, as mannerism has become a part of our critical vocabulary, many of the traits that were considered "baroque" are now thought to be mannerist. The works of Tristan L'Hermite contain both styles, as we shall see later in this study, because he was very much under the influences of both currents. Tristan, student of Scévole de Sainte-Marthe, page to the royal household at Fontainebleau, Luxembourg, and the Louvre, was exposed to all the architectural and artistic treasures of the finest of both styles. Furthermore, he was a member of the entourage of Gaston d'Orléans, whose mother, Maria de' Medici, brought Marino and mannerism to France. He was thus exposed to both currents almost from infancy.[17] His friendship with Théophile de Viau, Voiture,

---

[11] J.-P. Chauveau, ed. (Geneva: Droz, 1977).

[12] Paris: Stock, 1946. All quotations from this work, hereafter cited as *Le Page* will be from this edition. J. Serroy has published a critical edition of *Le Page* (Grenoble: UP of Grenoble, 1980).

[13] Paris: Garnier, 1925.

[14] See note 4.

[15] Among the many anthologies of XVIIth-century French literature published since 1950 which include Tristan are: A. Lagarde and L. Michard, *XVIIe Siècle* (Paris: Bordas, 1963); Alvin Eustis, *Seventeenth-Century French Literature* (New York: McGraw-Hill, 1969); Jean Rousset, *Anthologie de la poésie baroque française* (Paris: Armand Colin, 1968); Jean-Pierre Chauveau, *Anthologie de la poésie française du XVIIe siècle* (Paris: Gallimard, 1987); Gisèle Mathieu-Castellani, *Anthologie de la poésie amoureuse de l'âge baroque, 1570-1660* (Paris: Livre de Poche, 1990); and Claude Puzin, *Littérature, Textes et Documents, XVIIe siècle* (Paris: Nathan, 1987)–a volume in the prestigious Collection Henri Mitterand. An edition of his complete works is in preparation.

[16] Antoine Adam calls Tristan the greatest poet of the age of Louis XIII (cited in Abraham, *Tristan* 123).

[17] According to the poet's brother, Jean-Baptiste L'Hermite, Tristan became a

Saint-Amant and the aging Alexandre Hardy put him very much in the midst of the prevailing style of the age of Louis XIII which is, depending on one's viewpoint, either baroque or mannerist or both. A look at the life and works of Tristan L'Hermite will serve to demonstrate the fact that he underwent both mannerist and baroque influences. The biography of Tristan presented here makes no claim to be complete–the reader is referred to the works already cited of Bernardin, Grisé, and Carriat for as complete a life of Tristan as has been written. The purpose of this short biography is to introduce the life and works of Tristan and to emphasize those events and influences that might have led to the mannerist and baroque elements that we find in his poetry.

François L'Hermite, who later assumed the name of Tristan, was born, according to most students of his life, in 1601 at the family château of Soliers in the Haute-Marche between the towns of Guéret and Bourganeuf. At the age of three, perhaps because of the financial difficulties of his father, Tristan went to live with his maternal grandmother in Paris. She presented the child at court, and he was selected as a page to the young Duc de Verneuil. During his childhood, spent at the royal palaces, Tristan received the same education as the young duke and his brothers, Gaston and Louis. He was also able to meet Théophile and was permitted to attend plays at the Hôtel de Bourgogne. Thus, by the time of his adolescence, he had already acquired his loves of poetry and the theater. Around 1615, Tristan, who had succumbed to "les mauvais examples que me donnaient beaucoup de jeunes gens libertins que je voyais dans la maison," [18] was forced to flee the court for having wounded someone in a fight. He claims to have spent some time in England where, given his love for the theater, it can be assumed that he was exposed to the Elizabethan and Jacobean "baroque/mannerist" theater.

In 1618 Tristan returned to France and entered the service of Nicolas de Sainte-Marthe, a minor poet and dramatist. Nicolas' uncle, the renowned Scévole de Sainte-Marthe, needed a reader and librarian, and Tristan was given this position of service to one of the

---

page of the Duc de Verneuil at the age of three and lived with the royal family until age 15. He returned to the royal household in 1621 and became closely allied with Gaston d'Orléans and the Queen Mother, Maria de' Medici (Carriat, *Éloge* 23).

[18] *Le Page disgracié* 56. Most of the information that we have about the early years of Tristan is gleaned from this novel.

"mannerists" of the Pléïade. Carriat describes Tristan's education at Loudun with Scévole:

> Le poète octogénaire lui fait un accueil magnifique. Tristan devient son lecteur et jouit de ses conversations avec son entourage de poètes et d'érudits. Scévole a connu Vauquelin de La Fresnaye; il a connu Ronsard et se rappelle avoir reçu du grand poète une lettre assez vive au sujet d'Hélène de Surgères qui, par le truchement de Scévole lui-même, s'était plaint au maître de voir dans les Amours diverses ses rivales côtoyer son nom. Tristan avec délices entend parler poésie chaque jour [. . .] Il s'initie, dans la vaste bibliothèque, non seulement aux oeuvres des Anciens, mais à celles de la Renaissance et de ce dix-septième commençant [. . .]. [19]

It is significant that Tristan's first twenty years included life at the court of Henri IV and Maria de' Medici at Fontainebleau, a center of baroque and mannerist art and architecture. He also was in Jacobean England and had a close association with a member of the Pléïade, whose circle of admirers included many luminaries of contemporary letters. The next step in his literary education was to come, again, at court.

In 1620 Tristan was recognized by Louis XIII during a royal visit to Blaye and rejoined the king's household as "gentilhomme à la suite du roi." It is interesting to note that, immediately before rejoining the royal entourage, Tristan, if we can believe the *Page disgracié*, had fought a duel with a scholar who had insisted on the superiority of Virgil to Tasso. [20] He later became a member of the "Illustres Bergers"–a society of poets who claimed to emulate the lifestyle of the *Astrée* while encouraging the study of poetics. [21] After a year in the suite of Louis XIII, Tristan entered the service of Monsieur, Gaston d'Orléans, the younger brother of the king and the favorite of the Queen Mother, Maria de' Medici. The next twenty years saw Tristan in constant turmoil as he depended on this rebellious and unreliable patron who did not always pay his followers and often abandoned them without any explanation. The inner

---

[19] *Éloge* 25; see also *Le Page* 239-242.
[20] *Le Page* 296.
[21] A. Adam, *Histoire de la littérature française au XVIIᵉ siècle* (Paris: Dorat, 1949), I: 343.

struggle of Tristan the poet with Tristan the courtier is the subject of both poems and letters written during this period.[22] In a letter, he laments:

> [. . .] je ne suis coupable que du vice qui est naturel à tous ceux qui se meslent d'écrire [. . .] Comme il est difficile d'embrasser la vie active et la contemplative tout à la fois, il est mal-aisé de se rendre grand courtisan et grand écrivain tout ensemble. L'art des Muses demande trop de repos, et celuy de la Cour trop de reverences. Celuy qui se levera du grand matin pour aller voir quantité de gens, feindre espouser beaucoup d'interests, et se mesler de beaucoup d'intrigues, ne reüsira guere grand poëte; et celuy qui tiendra presque tousjours les yeux attachez sur un livre, et qui ne fera guere autre chose que penser à representer la grandeur des passions, ou les beautez de l'univers, amassera peu de richesses. Ce sont deux champions qui ne courent pas en mesme lice, et qui ne se proposent pas un mesme prix. Ils suivent deux sentiers fort divers, et ne sont pas également batus; l'un se rend au temple de la Fortune, et l'autre à celuy de la Gloire.[23]

His frustration at being a man of letters in a society where he was forced to depend on others for his livelihood is expressed in the very touching lines from his "Ode à Monsieur de Chaudebonne" (1623) in which he implores Chaudebonne to intercede with Gaston, who has apparently abandoned him:

> Il est vray que loin du grand Prince
> Dont mon esprit est amoureux;
> Je serois tousjours malheureux
> Eussay-je acquis une Province;
> Le sort auroit beau m'obliger,
> Il ne pourroit jamais purger
> L'humeur dont je serois malade:
> Et le Ciel n'a point de liqueur
> Dont la douceur fascheuse, et fade,
> Ne me fit tousjours mal au coeur.[24]

In the course of his service to Gaston, Tristan followed him in exile to Brussels to the court of the Infanta Isabella, who had also

---

[22] See letters LXXIX and LXXXVI and "La Mer" and "La Servitude."
[23] *Lettres meslées* 199-200.
[24] Camo, ed., *Les Amours et autres poésies choisies* (Paris: Garnier, 1925), 174.

granted asylum to Maria de' Medici. The Queen Mother sent Tristan on a mission for her to the court of Charles I, where he dedicated his "Eglogue maritime" to the English king and queen. There, Tristan, who had learned English as an adolescent, was perhaps exposed to the "baroque" theater and the mannerist and baroque poetry of Donne, Herbert, and Crashaw. The court at Brussels, quite naturally, had many Spaniards in attendance, and Tristan had ample opportunity to discover Spanish literature there. His only novel, *Le Page disgracié*, is heavily influenced by Mateo Alemán's *Guzmán de Alfarache*,[25] and he very probably had access to the works of the Spanish baroque–Góngora, Quevedo, Lope de Vega, and Pedro Calderón de la Barca. Spanish *conceptismo* and *culteranismo* were important influences on the French baroque. The atmosphere at the court of the Infanta was one of *galanterie,* and many of Tristan's love poems and "Lettres amoureuses" were written during his stay there.[26]

Gaston, as Claude K. Abraham has shown, claimed to be a Maecenas and, indeed, did provide some patronage to men of letters.[27] There were representatives of many literary currents in Gaston's suite: Voiture, Besançon, Le Compte, R. Passart, Mareschal, and Grandchamp reflect to varying degrees both mannerism and baroque. It must also be remembered that when Maria de' Medici and Concini brought Marino to France, he was welcomed by Gaston "comme un frère."[28] It was in this milieu that Tristan composed most of his works–a milieu marked by intense rivalry among writers for the favor of their patron and by constant intrigue–an environment conducive to both mannerist elegance and baroque intensity.

During the years of his service in the suite of Gaston (1622-1645) and in spite of the uncertainty and turbulence of those years, Tristan composed and published many notable works. A great many of the poems later published under the titles *Les Amours* (1638), *La Lyre* (1641), and *Les Vers héroïques* (1648) were written between the year 1622 and the year of their inclusion in a published collection. The same may be said of the *Lettres meslées* (published in 1642), some of which were written perhaps as early as

---

[25] Abraham, *Tristan* 21.

[26] For a thorough account of life at the court of Gaston, see C. K. Abraham, *Gaston d'Orléans et sa cour: étude littéraire* (Chapel Hill: UP of N.C., n.d.).

[27] *Gaston,* ix.

[28] Antoine Adam, as cited in Abraham, *Gaston* 17.

1617. [29] His great theatrical success, *La Mariane*, with Tristan's friend Mondory in the role of Herod, appeared in 1636 and rivaled the *Cid* in popularity. His very unique picaresque novel, *Le Page disgracié* (1643); a tragi-comedy, *La Folie du sage* (1645); a comedy, *Le Parasite* (1653); and four more tragedies, *Panthée* (1638), *La Mort de Sénèque* (1643), *La Mort de Chrispe* (1644), and *Osman* (1647) are among the diverse production of Tristan L'Hermite.

One can observe throughout the literary output of Tristan a steady swing of the pendulum from mannerism to baroque. The Tristan of the "Promenoir des deux amants," an ingenious conceit contained in the Marinistic trappings of the conventional love lyric, and the Tristan of *L'Office de la Sainte Vierge*, the *Vers héroïques*, and the *Exercices spirituels* are two different people. Weary from the struggles of life at court, Tristan began to change in the 1630's and became more serious and, as, will be seen later, more baroque. At the time of his death in 1655, Tristan resembled very little the gallant of *Les Amours*.

---

[29] Some of the "Lettres amoureuses" may date from the days spent with Scévole (1618).

Chapter III

MANNERISM

F OR many years the period in French literature between "Renaissance Classicism" and the *Grand Classicisme* of the Age of
Louis XIV was regarded by most French critics as either an era
of decline and decadence or as simply a period in which the seeds of
Classicism germinated–a "pre-Classical" period.[1] The individuality
and poetic gifts of such artists as d'Aubigné, Théophile, or Tristan
went virtually unnoticed by most early twentieth-century scholars
of French literature, who simply ignored these "inferior" artists because they did not fit into the neat schema of the progress of
French literature from one Classicism to a greater one. Since virtually all Western European literatures had a similar gap in their his-
tories, the problem of terminology for this period of approximately
a century was common to all of them. *Préciosité, conceptismo, culteranismo, Gongorismo, Schwulststil, marinismo, Euphuism,* and
Metaphysical are but a few of the terms used to describe the literature of the era. The fact that three of these terms come from Spain
and that none of them even comes close to describing the poetry of
d'Aubigné or La Ceppède betrays their insufficiency. A term or
concept was needed that would describe this period in European

---

[1] Nitze and Dargan, in *A History of French Literature* (New York: Holt, Rine-
hart and Winston, 1938), state: "It was principally in the development of social
form or etiquette that the Pre-Classical period was fruitful" (220). Lanson, in his
Manuel (Paris: Hachette, 1953), ignores all writers of the period between Montaigne and Malherbe, save Régnier. In his *Histoire*, 12th edition (Paris: Hachette,
1912), he refers to such writers as d'Aubigné, Théophile, Voiture, d'Urfé, Racan,
Saint-Amant, Georges and Madeleine de Scudéry, and Scarron as "attardés et
égarés" (366-390) and ignores Tristan in that part of his book.

literature as well as the terms "Romanticism," "Realism," and "Naturalism" had described the literary production of the nineteenth century.

Two terms, "mannerism" and "baroque," have been proposed to serve this purpose–both have been very controversial since the late nineteenth century, when Wölfflin, in his *Renaissance und Barock*, used the term *Barock* to describe Roman art of the High Renaissance and suggested that the term might also be applied to literature and music.[2] The interesting, though controversial and confusing, history of the two concepts in art and literary history and criticism is the subject of this and the following chapter. Also, a definition of these terms as they apply generally to literature and specifically to Tristan L'Hermite and his poetic output has been undertaken in the same two chapters, which serve as preludes to the analyses in the final ones. Since mannerism preceded baroque chronologically, and since mannerism is Tristan's dominant style in his first two volumes of poetry, it will be discussed first.

The use of the word *maniera* to describe the plastic arts and architecture may be found as early as the *Lives* of Vasari, which first appeared in 1550.[3] The term was rejected by critics of the seventeenth through the late nineteenth centuries but began its long journey toward acceptance in the present century–especially after World War I.[4] It is generally agreed that mannerism flourished in the period 1520-1600 as far as the arts and architecture are concerned, and that Michelangelo, in his late period, Pontormo, Rosso Fiorentino, Il Parmigianino, Tintoretto, El Greco, Bronzino, Beccafumi, Cellini and Bruegel are its best representatives.[5] In France, Fontainebleau was the center of mannerism: "centre italo-français

---

[2] Heinrich Wölfflin, *Renaissance und Barock: Eine Untersuchung über Wesen und Entstehung des Barockstils in Italien* (Munich: Ackermann, 1888).

[3] James V. Mirollo, *Mannerism in Renaissance Poetry, Concept, Mode, Inner Design* (New Haven: Yale UP, 1984), 10.

[4] Mirollo 21. For a more detailed treatment of mannerism in art criticism, the reader should consult: John Shearman, *Mannerism* (Baltimore: Penguin Books, 1967), Arnold Hauser, *Mannerism, Crisis of the Renaissance* (London: Routledge and Kegan Paul, 1965), and Frederick Hartt, *History of Italian Renaissance Art, Painting, Sculpture, Architecture*, 3rd ed. (New York: Abrams, 1987), 538-670. An excellent web-site devoted to mannerism can be found at *http://lonestar.texas.net/~mseifert/mannerism.html*.

[5] Roy Daniells, *Milton, Mannerism and Baroque* (Toronto: UP of Toronto, 1963), 6.

par son esprit, international par son rayonnement et sa clientèle; 'une nouvelle Rome' (selon Vasari)," whose Italian artists-in-residence included Rosso Fiorentino, Primaticcio, Cellini, and Serlio.[6] Following their lead were the French mannerists such as Jean Goujon and Germain Pilon, sculptors; Jean Cousin and Antoine Caron, painters; and Philibert de Lorme and Pierre Lescot, architects; the latter known for his designs for the Louvre and the Hôtel Carnavalet.[7] Among the "classic" works of the period in architecture and sculpture are Michelangelo's Medici Chapel and its tombs of Giuliano and Lorenzo de' Medici, the Entrance Hall of the Laurentian Library, also by Michelangelo; Cellini's *Perseus and Medusa*, and Giovanni Bologna's *Rape of the Sabine Women*. In painting, Michelangelo's *Last Judgment*, Tintoretto's *Crucifixion*, Titian's *Rape of Europa*, Vasari's *St. Luke Painting the Virgin*, El Greco's *Burial of Count Orgaz*, Il Parmigianino's *Madonna with the Long Neck* and his *Self Portrait in a Convex Mirror* are but a few of the masterpieces of mannerism. Perhaps the best-known mannerist *objet d'art* is the exquisite *Saltceller* which Cellini crafted for François I–acknowledged by virtually all as the archetypal mannerist work of art, even if it is interpreted in many different ways.[8]

The rehabilitation of *mannerism* as the term for a period and style in art history and criticism has been a long and controversial process. It was first employed to designate the period in art history between the Renaissance and that other controversial period, the Baroque.[9] As the baroque had been discovered by the Romantics and others of the nineteenth century, mannerism was rediscovered by the Dadaists and others of the early part of this century. Walter Friedlaender, Max Dvořák, Nikolaus Pevsner, and Erwin Panofsky are among the vanguard of art historians who undertook the reevaluation and rehabilitation of mannerist art. Mannerism's anti-classical, grotesque, and bizarre features, plus "the mannerists' expressive content, spiritualization, subjectivity, and willful rejection of both material nature and established artistic norms, must have

---

[6] Marcel Raymond, *La Poésie française et le Maniérisme 1546-1610(?)* (Geneva: Droz, 1971), 8.

[7] Raymond 8.

[8] See Mirollo 30-31 and 85-89.

[9] There is a great deal of inconsistency in the capitalization of *baroque* and *mannerism*. I shall capitalize them only when referring to the specific periods in art or literary history. They will be used in lower case for all other designations.

made the style appealing to the period of expressionism, dadaism, and nascent surrealism. The mannerists of the sixteenth century, like the poets of the seventeenth century, suddenly seemed modern." [10] Raymond describes mannerism in the plastic arts under five categories while emphasizing that, in mannerism, "Le temps est venu de la promotion de l'homme avec ses caractères distinctifs, le temps où la *phantasia* tend à l'emporter sur la *mimesis*." [11] Following Shearman, he sums up the style under five general categories. Mannerism contains:

1. [. . .] un ensemble de figures instables ou mobiles [   ] D'où la prédominance des symboles du feu, de l'air, de l'eau mouvante, et des thèmes ou des motifs du mouvement: le vol et l'enlèvement, la danse, la fête, la chasse, la bataille. Les scènes religieuses [. . .] sont animées par un souffle orageux.

2. L'attention de l'artiste se détourne de la nature [. . .] pour se concentrer sur le corps humain, sur la nudité de l'homme et de la femme, [. . .]. Ici triomphe l'art du caprice dans les proportions, du contraste, de la dissymétrie, de la syncope, du contraposto. Et tout naturellement la sensualité et l'érotisme. Certains schèmes formels conditionnent de nouveau le choix des thèmes: les dieux, les déesses et leurs amours, célestes ou terrestres, la dame au bain, la dame à sa toilette, parfois vêtue de ses bijoux, les jeux de nymphes et de naïades.

3. [. . .] Les toiles à figures nombreuses manifestent des symptômes de désintégration. L'oeuvre est décentrée, ou même compartimentée; on croit glisser du principe de l'unité multiple des Classiques, intérieurement organisée, à une sort de morcellement [. . .] la composition [. . .] doit susciter l'étonnement.

4. [. . .] la plupart des maniéristes, fidèles au dessein linéaire, même lorsqu'ils cultivent le sfumato, et quelle que soit l'audace de leur chromatisme, ne frayent aucune voie en direction du Baroque. Mais ce qui importe avant tout c'est leur attachement au principe de la ségrégation des plans, qui caractérisait la peinture de la Haute Renaissance. Il s'ensuit que le mouvement, dans les toiles maniéristes, ne se propage ni ne rayonne librement, comme il sera chez Rubens.

5. [. . .] l'espace existe à peine hors des corps et des volumes qui rendent sensible sa présence. Il deviendra après lui de moins

---

[10] Mirollo 27-28.
[11] Raymond 18.

en moins saisissable, au travers de figures entremêlées jusqu'à
l'encombrement. Il sera montueux, hétérogène. Espace plein [. . .]
parfois espace vide, ponctué, parsemé de petits personnages
dont le rapport aux personnages principaux est presque impossible à fixer, et qui sont comme posés sur un autre sol, une autre
terre. [Les] grandes figures [. . .] paraissent s'avancer vers le
spectateur, descendre jusqu'à lui [. . .]. Espèce de proéminence
qui engendre une relation inattendue du spectateur à la peinture,
de l'espace réel à l'espace imaginaire. Un gros plan en saillie,
avec lequel on se croit de plain-pied, s'établit fortement à la
manière d'un trompe-l'oeil.[12]

The application of mannerist art criticism to literature has been
both difficult and questionable. Probably the best treatment of the
subject is in the comprehensive review of most books and articles
on mannerism, which is in James V. Mirollo's 1984 study, *Mannerism and Renaissance Poetry*.[13] Two articles by Robert N. Nicolich[14]
and a dissertation by Pierrette-Monique Denzler[15] supplement
Mirollo and provide a comprehensive review of the history of mannerism in literary criticism. In his exhaustive study of "Renaissance,
Mannerist and Baroque in Literature," John M Steadman gives an
insightful analysis of studies in both baroque and mannerism before
1990 and contributes to our understanding of both.[16] In her introduction to her *Anthologie de la poésie amoureuse de l'âge baroque
1570-1640*,[17] Gisèle Mathieu-Castellani provides us with the most
relevant analysis of the two concepts as they apply to French litera-

---

[12] Raymond 19-21. See also Jacques Bousquet, *Mannerism: The Painting and
Style of the Late Renaissance*, trans. Simon Watson Taylor (New York: Braziller,
1964), in which is contained an excellent description of mannerist style in the visual
arts.
[13] See note 4.
[14] "Mannerism and Baroque: Further Notes on Problems in the Transfer of
these Concepts from the Visual Arts to Literature," *Papers on French Seventeenth
Century Literature* 9 (1983): 441-457 and "The Baroque Dilemma: Some Recent
French Mannerist and Baroque Criticism," *Oeuvres et Critiques* 1 (1976): 21-36.
See also the bibliography of Richard Studing and Elizabeth Kruz, *Mannerism in
Art, Literature, and Music: A Bibliography* (San Antonio, Texas: Trinity UP, 1979).
[15] "Mannerisms in Marinism, Gongorism, Preciosity, Euphuism and Mannerism: A Rhetorical Analysis" (Diss. U of New Mexico, 1987).
[16] *Redefining a Period Style* (Pittsburgh: Duquesne UP, 1990). This work provides excellent summaries of recent scholarship in mannerist, baroque and metaphysical literature. It is especially important for students of English literature.
[17] Paris: Livre de Poche, 1990.

ture in the late sixteenth and early seventeenth centuries. Relying heavily on these and other works, I have surveyed them and discussed the history of literary mannerism. I have also posed and answered many of the questions that are pertinent to the present study.

As one examines the many articles and books which attempt to define mannerism, several questions stand out as essential to an understanding of the concept. Most of those who have worked in the area of literary mannerism have been concerned with one or more of the following: (1) Does mannerism refer to a single period in the history of literature and art? Is it rather a recurring phenomenon that began in Ancient Greece with Asianism, and has reappeared as "anti-classicism" many times throughout literary and art history? What exactly is the periodization of baroque and mannerism? (2) How does one, or, indeed, can one transfer a term of art history to literature? Is it of any value to do so? What is the place of rhetoric in the discussion of literary mannerism? What figures or tropes are indicative of mannerism? (3) Do the two concepts of baroque and mannerism overlap? If so, what distinguishes one from the other and how does one confront the two? (4) What are the consequences of the inclusion of mannerism in the history of French literature? Is *préciosité* mannerism or baroque? (5) What exactly are the mannerist characteristics that we will be looking for in the poetry of Tristan L'Hermite?

Just as Eugenio d'Ors [18] saw the baroque as a recurring phenomenon in the history of art, many have seen mannerism as a reappearing tendency in artistic and literary style. Ernst Robert Curtius, in his *European Literature in the Latin Middle Ages*,[19] maintained that *mannerism*, which he would substitute for baroque, is a stylistic mode that appears episodically in the literature of Europe. Gustave René Hocke, echoing Curtius, saw mannerism as a stylistic inclination that began with Asianism in Greece and has reappeared throughout history (its most recent incarnation being the poetry of Rimbaud). [20] René Bray, in his study of a type of mannerism, *pré-*

---

[18] *Lo barroco* (Madrid: Aguilar, 1943).

[19] Originally published as *Europäische Literatur und lateinisches Mittelalter* (Bern: Francke, 1948) and translated into English five years later by W. R. Trask (New York: Pantheon Books, 1953).

[20] See the two works by Gustave René Hocke: *Manierismus in der europäischen Literatur* (Hamburg: Rowohlt, 1959) and *Die Welt als Labyrinth: Manier und Manie in der europäischen Kunst* (Hamburg: Rowohlt, 1957).

ciosité, finds it regularly manifesting itself in French literature from Thibaut de Champagne to Jean Giraudoux. [21]

That there are two antipodal currents in literature, which may be called "Classical" and "anti-Classical," seems self-evident. The former style has appeared in the literature of France as Classicism, Realism, and Naturalism while the latter has seen incarnations as baroque, mannerism, Romanticism, and Surrealism. In antiquity, the Attic style was the clear, intellectual, simple, polished and witty style; while the Asiatic style was emotional and made abundant use of rhetorical decoration in seeking the grandiose and the ornate, often declining into what is called today "mannerism" in the pejorative sense of the term. Since Mannerism, like Romanticism, refers more to a specific period of time than to a recurring mode, and since Asianism is the first manifestation of it, the latter term would seem far more appropriate for this general tendency than mannerism, which has been accepted by art critics as a single period in the history of art. [22] Let us, therefore, accept the terminology of art criticism and define Mannerism, in majuscules, as a period in the history of art and literature between the High Renaissance and the Baroque. It and "Baroque" will be capitalized when referring to chronological periods. It should be noted that many who have studied literary mannerism believe that baroque and mannerism are the two aspects of the Baroque, the period. [23] The question of the feasi-

---

[21] René Bray, *La Préciosité et les Précieux, de Thibaut de Champagne à Jean Giroudoux* (Paris: Nizet, 1948).

[22] As will be shown later, many would say that mannerism and baroque occurred simultaneously in the period between 1550 and 1650. Frank J. Warnke, who considers mannerism as an aspect of the baroque, says that mannerism and baroque appeared at the same time outside of Italy; see his article: "Mannerism in European Literature: Period or Aspect?," *Revue de Littérature Comparée* 56 (1982): 255-260. Richard Sayce has also extended mannerism into the seventeenth century in his essay "Maniérisme et périodisation: quelques réflexions générales," in *Renaissance Maniérisme Baroque, Actes du XIe stage internationale de Tours* (Paris: Vrin, 1972), 43-55. This is not the position traditionally held by art historians. "The term 'Mannerism' is normally understood to refer to the artistic style prevailing in Italy and northern Europe for the greater part of the sixteenth century. Its beginnings coincide approximately with the death of Raphael in 1520, and the disintegration of the High Renaissance; it was in turn superseded by the early Baroque from c1590 onwards." Sir Lawrence Gowing, ed., *The Encyclopedia of Visual Art*, I (Englewood Cliffs, NJ: Prentice Hall, 1983), 676.

[23] See the discussions of Warnke and Mathieu-Castellani, which follow in this chapter.

bility of using mannerism to describe a style of literature requires a
more detailed answer than do the questions of chronology.

When we look at a mannerist work such as Il Parmigianino's
Madonna with the Long Neck, we are struck by the serpentine figures of the Virgin, the Christ child, and the leg of one of the on-
lookers. The elongated proportions, especially the Virgin's fingers,
the rounded shoulders, the unfinished column and the ambiguous
figure at the lower right demand our attention and cause us to pon-
der the intentions of the artist. There is an unmistakable eroticism
that pervades the painting, but there is no logical focus for the composition. There are allusions to various painters in the work—the
child "lies asleep across the Virgin's lap, in a pose suggestive of
death, his left arm hanging as in Michelangelo's Rome *Pietà.*" [24] In
short, the painting reveals most of the characteristics described by
Marcel Raymond in the passage quoted on pages 25-26. The question to be answered now is how can the traits of visual mannerism
be applied to literature? To answer that question, a short history of
the last fifty years of mannerist studies is in order.

Though Curtius, Hatzfeld, and Hocke had begun the stylistic
approach to mannerism in the 1940's, the first real attempt to see it
as a cultural panorama was made by Wylie Sypher in 1955. [25] He
saw mannerism as the recurring style of Curtius but with an important difference: to Sypher, mannerism was psychological as well as
stylistic. There was a mannerist state of mind marked by "unresolved tensions," which manifest themselves in six categories: disturbed balance, techniques of accommodation, the dramatic artifice, the revolving view, unresolved tensions and shifting planes of
reality. The turmoil of the religious wars led to mannerism, which
Sypher saw as a period of decline. In his view, the stability brought
about by the Council of Trent led to the much superior baroque. [26]
Literary manifestations of mannerism are primarily psychological
and are expressed in terms of irresolution and instability. [27] Though
Sypher's study of mannerism is important from a historical perspective, his rather limited view of literary mannerism was insufficient

---

[24] Hartt, 578.
[25] *Four Stages of Renaissance Style, Transformations in Art and Literature
1400-1700* (New York: Doubleday, 1955).
[26] Sypher 162-171; 180-185.
[27] See 180-185.

and his emphasis on the mannerist state of mind failed really to serve the needs of literary criticism.

John Shearman, in his 1967 book, *Mannerism*, attacked Sypher's concept of an anguished mannerism and did much to establish the modern idea of a "stylish mannerism." *Maniera*, he said, was a term that denoted elegance and refinement of style in sixteenth-century Rome and should be used to describe works of art that contain this type of stylistic opulence. For Shearman, Mannerism was a period in the history of the arts that bridged the gap between the High Renaissance and the Baroque—a period when *maniera* was the primary concern of style. [28] He accepts the rhetorical definitions of Mannerism that had been advanced by Curtius, Sypher, and Hauser and adds his interpretation of *contraposto* as antithesis in literature. [29] The real importance of Shearman's work lies in his limiting mannerism to a specific period in history, even if he narrowed it a bit too much by limiting it to the sixteenth century, and in his placing great emphasis on style rather than on the search for a mannerist state of mind.

The next important step in the evolution of contemporary thought on the subject of mannerism is the "Introduction" by Marcel Raymond to his anthology of mannerist poetry published in 1971. [30] In it, he attempts, as Mirollo has succinctly stated: "to sketch out a poetic fusing rhetorical, anguished, and stylish mannerism, applicable especially to the lyric yet related to the figurative art." [31] Thus, he attempts to synthesize the concepts of mannerism represented by Curtius, Sypher, and Shearman. His great success, it seems, is his very logical transfer of terms of art criticism to literature. As was the case with his description of visual art, his analysis of literary mannerism's adoption of some of the terms of art criticism deserves extensive quotation:

> Parmi les caractères ou les critères soulignés, convertibles sans distorsion des arts figuratifs à la poésie, je retiendrai:
> 1. L'idée du mouvement, entraînant certains choix thématiques. Ce mouvement a besoin d'une expression excessive, il va aux extrêmes opposés, jusqu'au paradoxe.

---

[28] Shearman 20-22.
[29] Shearman 91-95.
[30] See note 6 *supra*.
[31] Mirollo 49.

2. L'idée d'une structure décentrée, compartimentée. Quantité de poèmes, élégies, discours, etc. de Ronsard et de ses disciples semblent "mal composés". Jugement négatif et sommaire. Un principe de composition fuyant, des développements faiblement coordonnés, sans articulation rigoureuse et apparente, peuvent ne pas être involontaires.

3. L'idée de la proéminence des figures et des formes, les choses étant rendues "animées et vivantes par un style tout en action" ou "sensibles aux yeux par un style tout en *images*". Il s'agit de ce que Denys d'Halicarnasse appelle *enárgeia*, soit des deux formes contiguës de ce qui est pour Du Bellay *l'énergie*, rangée par lui parmi les "figures". L'énergie du second genre équivaut à *l'hypotypose*, mais il est patent qu'elle rejoint celle du premier, s'il est vrai que les images des choses sont généralement "en action".

(La notion de profondeur, en littérature et en poésie, n'est pas d'une application aisée. Il est certain toutefois que le style riche en énergies ou en hypotyposes, qui fait voir et toucher la réalité, relève d'une catégorie générale: le style des choses proches, s'opposant au style des choses lointaines, lesquelles s'offrent sans reliefs ou particularités. Les premières heurtent les sens, les secondes s'adressent plutôt à l'intellect ou à l'affectivité.)

4. L'idée d'un style à la fois "énergétique", suivant la définition précédente, et "floride". Le mot floride revient à tout instant, en Italie comme en France, sous la plume des artistes, des poètes et des théoriciens. La "naïve facilité" d'Homère est préférée à "la curieuse diligence" de Virgile [. . .].[32]

Among the many figures of rhetoric mentioned by Marcel Raymond in his Introduction as mannerist are epiphonema, repetition, chiasmus, hypotyposis, antithesis, asyndeton, oxymoron, the *pointe,* and the conceit. In broad terms, we have here a basis of looking at mannerism that makes every effort to "translate" visual mannerism to poetic mannerism. To this rhetoric of excess, Raymond adds two very important elements. First, he stresses the fact that the mannerist work can be simply a "fiction"–the poet seeks *vraisemblance* rather than *vérité*. Second, and very important, is the doctrine of imitation, which was retained from *Pléiade* poetics. These concepts make room for two very important groups of French poetry not la-

---

[32] Raymond 25-26.

beled as mannerist by Raymond, the Petrarchist, and the *précieux* poetry of the seventeenth century. Raymond hints at both of these in a paragraph on the "aspect ludique" of many mannerist poems but nevertheless confines mannerism in French poetry to the sixteenth century, plus the first decade of the seventeenth. Very significant is his placing mannerism in the tradition of the French love lyric: "Cette activité ludique est un des aspects de l'invention, chez les troubadours et les trouvères déjà, comme chez Pétrarque. Les poètes de l'époque maniériste ne sont pas d'une autre lignée."[33]

Another critic, Claude-Gilbert Dubois, devotes considerable space to the mannerist use of tropes as reflective of a general mannerist style. In his 1979 book *Le Maniérisme*,[34] his outlook on mannerism had changed considerably from that of his 1973 study, *Le Baroque: Profondeurs de l'apparence*.[35] He now considers mannerist many works and stylistic traits that he had called baroque, but the importance of his study lies in his re-emphasis of the importance of "imitation" in the literature of the period. Nicolich sums up Dubois' ideas on the subject as follows:

> Mannerist imitation, according to Dubois, implies the artist/writer's production of a work with reference to a model by varying, deforming (distorting), subverting, digressing, multiplying repetitions of select elements while reducing others, richly displaying rhetoric (in literature) while obscuring essential structures or content, all of which is an assertion of the individual, subjective, expression of the artist/writer, addressing his work to an elite audience preferring to unravel complexity rather than contemplate transparent simplicity.[36]

Dubois carries his discussion of "imitation" to its logical conclusion when he calls *préciosité* a late mannerist manifestation.[37]

With the work of Dubois taken into consideration, we have a picture of literary mannerism emerging that includes several items of importance. As the decade of the 70's closed, the state of man-

---

[33] Raymond 27.
[34] Paris: PUF.
[35] Paris: Hachette.
[36] *Mannerism and Baroque* 444-445.
[37] *Le Maniérisme* 224. This same conclusion of Petrarchism and *préciosité* as mannerism had been expressed by Robert M. Burgess, "Mannerism in Philippe Desportes," *L'Esprit Créateur* 6 (1966): 270-281.

nerist studies had reached the point where some general conclusions could be drawn. First, we have a definition of Mannerism as a
period in the history of the visual arts and literature between the
High Renaissance and the Baroque, with some overlapping in the
first half of the seventeenth century. Second, we see mannerism as
more of a literary game in which the doctrine of imitation is most
important. Usually the work to be imitated will be by Petrarch–especially in the domain of erotic literature. The imitation will be
brought about by the clever use of *maniera* or style and rhetorical
devices are all important. By nearly unanimous agreement, most of
the literary output of the last half of the sixteenth century in France
is considered mannerist, but there is still great confusion between
mannerism and baroque in the early part of the seventeenth century. Frank J. Warnke writes convincingly that:

> It would seem that, outside Italy, Mannerist and Baroque im-
> pulses made themselves felt at almost the same time as modifica-
> tions of the Renaissance literary sensibility. Martz remarks that
> "[. . .] All the styles and stages of the European Renaissance
> were compressed and recapitulated in England during this brief
> time [i.e. the earlier seventeenth century]." I would basically
> agree, adding, however, that the same thing is true in Europe
> outside Italy, that the Renaissance appears as a distinct phase
> prior to the others in Spain, France, and England, and that it is
> rather Mannerism and Baroque that appear as simultaneous phe-
> nomena in those lands. [. . .] European literature during the time
> span 1550-1700 presents us with a waning Renaissance followed
> by a powerful, extravagant, and highly varied period of Manner-
> ism and Baroque, yielding eventually to the very different synthe-
> sis of Neoclassicism. [38]

Also, there was still much debate over just what figures of rhetoric
were mannerist and which were baroque, or if indeed there was a
difference. The trend in mannerist studies, influenced by Dubois and
Raymond, began in the next decade to center on rhetoric and style.

The decade of the 80's has seen these questions answered in a
very satisfactory manner. The two works that have done much to establish a mannerist poetic are those of Mirollo and Denzler. [39] Mirol-

---

[38] "Mannerism: Period or Aspect?" 258-259.
[39] See notes 3 and 15.

lo concludes his extensive history of mannerist criticism with a
short section entitled "Toward a Mannerist Poetics" in which he
states that mannerism is a useful term as an instrument of research,
description, classification and criticism (66), which should be "mul-
tidisciplinary" in scope and requires "inter-disciplinary or interme-
dia criticism." He believes that much work remains to be done in
the area of confronting mannerism with the baroque (69) and that
the thematic approach is not as useful as the rhetorical. Mannerism
is "a particular artistic sensibility," expressed in a certain style
which occurs "whenever and wherever the Renaissance artist has to
imitate both nature and art, and in the case of art, to contend with,
to quote but not ape a predecessor whose achievement in a particular genre or form has been declared supreme or unsurpassable, or
simply *the* norm" (68). To him, the most important consideration in
classifying mannerist poetry is the type of imitation involved–he
names three results or products of artistic imitation:

> First, there is the *mannered*, analogous to *di maniera* or to
> *manierato*, which I would define as exploitation [. . .] of the
> normative tradition [. . .]. An example [. . .] would be the liter-
> alizing of a Petrarchan metaphor and its use, by extended con-
> ceit, as the witty subject or point of the whole poem [. . .].
> Another example would be the image-by-image and argument-
> by-argument parody of counter-Petrarchism, as in the well-
> known poems by Berni, du Bellay, and Shakespeare. A second
> possible outcome would be [. . .] a version of the model that
> echoes its purity of language, its polished form, its serious
> tone, its sententious statement, its total artistic finish [. . .].
> What with its social and linguistic as well as aesthetic implica-
> tions–it being intended to purify [. . .] language [. . .] manners
> [. . .] even the morals, of a cultivated society–it promotes a
> community of taste. [This *stylized* imitation] [. . .] has *maniera*
> in the sense of elegance and refinement; but unlike the man-
> nered [. . .] it is not content with mere literary reminiscence,
> the titillation of recognition, or clever virtuoso display [. . .]
> (The term) *mannerist* [. . .] is for only a third product of literary
> imitation, since it is the least *mannered* of all [. . .] because
> mannerist imitation so defined dwells completely in but can
> also talk about the realm of art, because the poet is totally ab-
> sorbed in but also self-conscious about this creative situation,
> he can include complex perspectives and meanings, and even

allow strain to show, whereas mannered or stylish works cannot. He may sacrifice some *maniera* to do so, but he is thereby less likely to create merely *di maniera* (69-70).

The first two products of imitation are clearly mannerist: the first may be seen in the imitations of Petrarch and Marino by seventeenth-century poets such as Tristan, [40] and the second seems almost a description of the early *précieux* of the Hôtel de Rambouillet. The third, with its more serious side, is, in French poetry of the period, baroque, as will be seen in the next chapter. The poetry of Tristan L'Hermite contains all three styles and will be discussed in this context in the final chapters. With Mirollo, our definition of mannerism is almost complete. It is necessary now to define the mannerist rhetoric and then to answer our final questions regarding *préciosité* and mannerism.

In her excellent dissertation, Pierrette-Monique Denzler answers our inquiries regarding mannerist rhetoric and *préciosité*. Writing in 1987, she analyzed rhetorically two hundred poems (forty each belonging to Gongorism, Euphuism, Marinism, *Préciosité* and *Schwulststil*) for mannerisms; i.e. rhetorical ornamentation. In her analysis, she presents convincing evidence that each of the five styles contains enough common figures of rhetoric to be included under the general heading of Mannerism (the period and the style) (448). The elements of rhetoric studied are the conceit and twenty other figures, the definitions of which she places in an Appendix. [41] Analysis of forty poems, including some by d'Urfé, Théophile, Saint-Amant, Voiture, Tristan, Georges de Scudéry, Sarasin, Conrart, Montausier, Benserade, Ménage, Brébeuf, Segrais, and the abbé de Pure, reveals that: "Compared with *Marinismo* and *Gongorismo*, *Préciosité* is a rather tame and modest literary phenomenon. Relatively few mannerist rhetorical figures adorn *précieux* poetry, but for French taste, which has been classicizing since

---

[40] See, for example, Tristan's "La Belle Esclave Maure" which is an imitation of Marino's "La Bella Schiava" and his imitation of another Italian in the sonnet which he frankly admits in the title, "Imitation d'Annibal Caro" in *La Lyre*.

[41] The phrenic figures studied are anacoluthon, antonomasia, apothesis, catachresis, dissimile, hyperbaton, metaphor, metonymy, oxymoron, periphrase, prosopopoeia, solecism, syllepsis, synaesthesia, synecdoche, synoeciosis, and zeugma. She studies two aural figures: annominatio, which she contrasts with paronomasia, and antanaclasis.

the Renaissance and even more so after Classicism, these few peculiarities were the source of much ridicule and contempt" (458).
While it may be true that the poems studied reveal fewer mannerisms than their Spanish or Italian counterparts, most of the figures
listed above can be easily found in the French poetry of the period
1550-1650. [42] Furthermore, many critics have included the French
poets of the first half of the seventeenth century in the tradition of
poetry that Denzler is studying. If she had been able to include the
pastoral and the pre-Cornelian theater in the study, an abundance
of these figures would have been found. Perhaps in addition to the
"classicizing" in France, the tradition of the love lyric lends itself to
less rhetorical excess than is found in Italy and Spain.

The thematics of the love lyric originated in Provence and soon
spread to the north by means of *troubadours* who inspired imitation
by the *trouvères*. Dante and Petrarch were greatly influenced by the
French poets and kept the traditional themes alive until they were rediscovered by the members of the Pléiade and reached an apogee in
the sixteenth century with Desportes. [43] This tradition, augmented by
the influence of Marino and encouraged by the *ruelles*, led to a re-
vival of the love-lyric in the early seventeenth century. The rhetoric of
the troubadours was more marked by metrical and rhyming skill than
rhetorical decoration. The images and metaphors of a Bernard de
Ventadour, for example, "ne se présentent pas comme le fruit de
recherches laborieuses mais comme l'expression immédiate d'une ex-
périence intérieure, d'une émotion intense, d'une âme tourmentée." [44]
The mannerist and baroque French poets are not quite as extrava-
gant in rhetorical display as some of their European counterparts,
but nevertheless could hardly be called restrained when compared to
the classical ideal. As will be seen in subsequent chapters, Tristan can
be very restrained in his poetry but succumbs to the excesses of mannerism in some of his least successful efforts.

In the introduction to her *Anthologie de la poésie amoureuse de
l'âge baroque*, Gisèle Mathieu-Castellani prefers to both the themat-

---

[42] See the detailed rhetorical analyses of many seventeenth-century French
works in the anthology by Eustis cited above.

[43] An excellent treatment of this literary tradition can be found in: Lu Emily
Pearson, *Elizabethan Love Conventions* (Berkeley: UP of California, 1933).

[44] Moshe Lazar, ed., Bernard de Ventadour, *Chansons d'Amour* (Paris: Klincksieck, 1966) "Introduction," 23.

ic and the psychological analyses of mannerism, an examination of
the baroque and the mannerist *discours*. She seems to agree with the
assertion of Warnke that baroque and mannerism were both aspects of the same style. She therefore attempts to establish "un ensemble de critères qui permettraient de mieux 'situer' les différents
types de discours." [45] Among the poets of the period 1570-1640 Desportes, Durand, Théophile and Tristan are considered more mannerist, while d'Aubigné, Sponde, Nuysement and Beaujeu are more
baroque. No poet is one or the other entirely; most show traits of
both styles in their works and even within the same work. For the
purposes of this study, it should be noted that the anthology stresses the poems written before 1640 and does not include any of Tristan's later poetry.

In order to separate the mannerist discourse from that of the
baroque, Mathieu-Castellani proposes a system of criteria (linguis-
tic, literary and rhetorical) which would question the text to mea-
sure its "réaction." The mannerist text is skeptical of universal
truths and reflects the doubt and skepticism of its author. It is non-
judgmental and it may well contain elements of *libertinage*. The
mannerist never seeks to convince because he lacks conviction and
shows very little true emotion. The mannerist poet is, according to
Mathieu-Castellani, melancholy, non-didactic, and self-effacing; the
je, so important to the baroque artist, is unimportant to him. He
suggests reality but constructs only "objets-simulacres" whose sole
existence is in language. Nature is mythicized because the poet does
not really believe in what he is writing and he has no real desire to
make his audience believe him. The world is presented as fragment-
ed because the mannerist is more interested in imitating parts
rather than the whole. Professor Mathieu-Castellani concludes her
very perceptive analysis by assigning symbolic characters to represent mannerism (Narcissus) and baroque (Pygmalion). She too
refers to the ludic nature of mannerism, which she contrasts with
the more serious baroque:

> Dès lors que dominent dans un texte l'intention ludique, le goût
> de l'artificiel, le doute et l'incrédulité, quand la relation au
> lecteur, qu'il s'agit moins de persuader que de séduire ou de

---

[45] Mathieu-Castellani 9.

troubler, se maintient dans une espèce d'indécision, lorsque la parole est douteuse, on tiendra ces traits pour des indices du maniérisme; si s'affiche au contraire la volonté d'emporter l'adhésion intellectuelle et affective du destinaire, de l'émouvoir à tout prix, de lui délivrer un message de vérité, on tiendra pour représentative du baroquisme cette parole magistrale, donnant leçon.[46]

The question of baroque versus mannerism is indeed the most difficult to answer. A detailed discussion of the baroque will be necessary before the two periods and styles can be compared and contrasted. Therefore, that discussion will be postponed until the next chapter, as will be the question of Classicism in seventeenth-century French literature. A more detailed discussion of *préciosité* as mannerism will be found in the chapters dealing with Tristan's love poetry. The other questions that were raised above on page 27 have been answered. Mannerism is a distinct period that connects the High Renaissance with the Baroque in the literature and arts of many western European countries, with some overlap. As we have seen, the style, mannerism, is one of rhetorical and stylistic ornamentation that has, in the past, been called Gongorism, *préciosité*, Marinism, Euphuism, *Schwulststil, conceptismo, culteranismo,* and Metaphysical. The concept is of value in the study of literature, because the artistic style of mannerism can be translated into literary terms that enable us to recognize and discuss works written in France and other European countries from a more informed perspective than that of Lanson and his followers who had no appreciation of these works and confined them to a long period of neglect.

Some of the salient characteristics of mannerism are its anti-Classicism, its fondness for imitating parts of a whole, its profuse use of rhetorical ornamentation, and its ludic nature. Sypher's "anguished mannerism" has been largely discredited and has been replaced with the epithet "stylish style" which reflects more accurately the nature of mannerism. [47] Just as allusion plays a role in *The*

---

[46] Mathieu-Castellani 10; her equally perceptive discussion of the baroque will be treated in the next chapter.

[47] James V. Mirollo, in his "The Mannered and the Mannerist," in *The Meaning of Mannerism,* ed. Franklin W. Robinson and Stephen G. Nichols, Jr. (Hanover, NH: UP of New England, 1972), says: "A third theory of literary mannerism, popu-

Madonna with the Long Neck and in many other mannerist paintings and sculptures, imitation is of paramount importance in the literature of mannerism. Petrarch, Marino, Bembo and other Italian
masters were considered as models to imitate by the French poets
of the sixteenth and seventeenth centuries, and this imitation, coupled with French literary tradition, gave us a toned-down mannerism that, in the lyric, lacked the excesses of Marinism and
Gongorism but nevertheless reflects the same style or *maniera*.
Mannerist imitation is described by Daniela dalla Valle as follows:

> Le principe d'imitation se trouve ainsi mis en crise, mais d'une
> manière oblique, indirecte, il s'agit moins d'un refus du modèle
> que d'un rapport problématique avec le modèle lui-même, dont
> la présence s'impose d'une façon péremptoire à l'artiste
> maniériste. Mais celui-ci l'élude à travers une imitation partielle,
> déformante, qui cherche à atteindre et à créer le nouveau et
> l'original. En fait ce n'est pas seulement le principe relatif à l'imi-
> tation des classiques qui est remis en question, mais aussi le
> principe relatif à l'imitation de la nature: L'artiste maniériste s'ef-
> force de rendre concrètement l'idée–intellectuelle, fantastique,
> de toute façon intérieure–que lui suggère son moi, et il cherche à
> la réaliser de la façon la plus personnelle possible, selon la
> manière qui lui est propre. Cela le conduit à poursuivre non pas
> un idéal de beauté absolue et universelle, mais un type de beauté
> particulier, raffiné, aristocratique, spiritualisé et individualisé
> auquel on donne le nom de grâce; si raffinée et individualisée
> qu'il n'est pas donné à tous de la percevoir: pour la saisir et la
> goûter, il faut un effort de l'intellect dont seuls quelques-uns
> sont capables.[48]

As we examine the poetry of Tristan L'Hermite for mannerism,
our primary considerations will be rhetorical figures and preciosity

---

larized by John Shearman but formulated earlier, pooh-poohs all the aforementioned emphasis on stress and strain and posits instead a healthy standard of elegant
refinement. For Shearman, there is nothing neurotic or disturbing about mannerism. Descriptively it is 'the stylish style.' A statue by Giambologna and Tasso's
Aminta share an esthetic goal of being nothing other than their beautiful selves.
Mannerism in literature, as in the other arts, is style, for style's sake, feeling perfect-
ly secure in its classical pedigree and in its mission of advancing beyond the great
cinquecento masters in ultimate refinement, without 'a failure of nerve.' Mannered
it will seem to us; beautiful it seemed to them and should seem to us" (13).
[48] "Introduction au maniérisme," in *Du Baroque aux lumières, Pages à la mémoire de Jeanne Carriat* (Paris: Rougerie, 1986), 19.

as they are used in the game of imitation, wherein Tristan demonstrates his *maniera*. For, as will be seen, most of his amatory poetry
is written in imitation of Petrarch and Marino or of their Italian followers. When we find a poem that imitates some aspect of a prior
literary work, is ludic in nature, uses rhetoric in a certain way, is intended for a select audience, and is written between 1550 and 1650,
we have a mannerist work. The *discours maniériste,* as elaborated
upon by Mathieu-Castellani, serves to confirm the assignment of
the term *mannerist* to the style of many of Tristan's poems. The
next step in our study is an examination of the baroque, which will
conclude with its confrontation with mannerism.

CHAPTER IV

BAROQUE

T HE concept of a literary baroque has had a longer and even
more controversial history than that of literary mannerism. In
fact, it has been the eventual acceptance of the term that has paved
the way for mannerism's relatively rapid acceptance into the critical
vocabularies of literature and the arts. Simultaneous with the acceptance of mannerism as a valid critical term has been the birth of a
new dispute over the boundaries that separate the two periods or
styles. Much of what was once called "baroque" is now "mannerism"; but the distinction between the two concepts in literary criticism is still a matter of much discussion and very little agreement.
Today, over forty years after the appearance of Rousset's landmark
study, many questions remain. While a few critics have attempted to
distinguish one style from the other, others have chosen to ignore
the controversy and to examine style in a formalistic manner under
one or the other headings. French critics, who were among the last
to accept the terms, have done much to establish criteria that enable
us both to distinguish between baroque and mannerism and to ana-
lyze the literature of the period as belonging to one or both styles.
This chapter will look first at the baroque in art and literature, from
a historical perspective, with emphasis on French lyric poetry. Next,
the baroque and mannerist styles will be compared and contrasted
and the chapter will conclude with a definition of baroque and mannerism, as the two terms will be used in the final chapters.

The *Oxford English Dictionary* traces the etymology of *baroque*
to the Portuguese *barroco* or Spanish *barrueco* meaning "rough or
imperfect pearl; of unknown origin." [1] Others have seen its source

---

[1] *OED*, 2nd ed., Vol. I. (Oxford: Clarendon Press, 1989), 965.

in the logicians' term *baroko*, "the fourth mode of the second figure
in the scholastic nomenclature of syllogisms." [2] The *OED*, as does
Hatzfeld, speculates that the two became merged, especially in the
later French and English uses. [3] Nevertheless, *baroque* has been, until rather recently, a pejorative term connoting the bizarre, the ex-
travagant, or the grotesque: "styles of ornament characterized by
profusion, oddity of combinations, or abnormal features generally." [4]
Wölfflin, in 1888, began the rehabilitation of the baroque with his
two landmark studies [5] in which he outlined his often-quoted categories of the baroque, wherein he contrasted the Renaissance and
baroque styles. Wölfflin's 1888 study marks the first attempt to
transfer the critical vocabulary of the plastic arts to literature. His
contrast of Ariosto's *Orlando furioso* and Tasso's *Gerusalemme liberata* attempted to differentiate between the Renaissance style of
the former and the baroque style of the latter. In 1915, the sequel to
his groundbreaking first study appeared and contained the five categories or principles within which he contrasted the two styles.
Since Wölfflin's categories are a *sine qua non* in any discussion of
the baroque, they will be summarized briefly here, and the reader
will be referred to other sources for more exhaustive treatment of
them. [6] The linear representation of the Renaissance is contrasted
with the painterly representation of the baroque; the Renaissance
presentation in a series of planes with the baroque creation of
depth; closed forms with open forms; multiplicity or plurality with
unity; and absolute clarity with relative clarity. These traits would
probably describe mannerism better than baroque, but they have
served a useful purpose by showing clearly that there was an anti-

---

[2] René Wellek, *Concepts of Criticism* (New Haven: Yale UP, 1963), 69.

[3] *OED*, 965; Helmut Hatzfeld, "Use and Misuse of *Baroque* as a Critical Term
in Literary History," *University of Toronto Quarterly* 31 (1962): 180-182.

[4] *OED*, 965.

[5] *Renaissance und Barock: Eine Untersuchung über Wesen und Entstehung des
Barockstils in Italien* (Munich: Ackermann, 1888 and *Kunstgeschichtliche Grundbegriffe: Das Problem der Stilentwicklung in der neueren Kunst* (Munich: Ackermann,
1915). The latter was translated into English by M. D. Hottinger (New York:
Dover, 1932) and into French by Marcel and Claire Raymond (Paris: Plon, 1952);
the two translations were used in this study.

[6] For a more detailed treatment of Wölfflin's categories, see B. Chédozeau, *Le
Baroque* (Paris: Nathan, 1989), 10-13; Thomas Barga, "Baroque Imagery and
Themes in the Theater of Tristan L'Hermite," Diss. Rice University, 1970, 10-14;
and especially Marcel Raymond, *Baroque et renaissance poétique*, 3rd ed. (Paris:
Corti, 1985), 24-39.

classical style that followed Renaissance classicism. As has already
been seen in the previous chapter, it is the transferal of these concepts of art criticism to literature that has been central to any discussion of mannerism or baroque in literature. Before this very important question is resolved by means of a survey of baroque
criticism, a brief look at baroque plastic arts is in order.

The name that is synonymous with the baroque in art and architecture is, of course, Bernini.[7] His many fountains and churches in
Rome, such as the *Fountain of the Four Rivers* in the Piazza Navona
and the Church of Sant'Andrea al Quirinale; his striking sculpture,
The Ecstasy of Saint Teresa; the Baldacchino and *Cathedra Petri* in
Saint Peter's; and the massive and overwhelming Tuscan Columns
or Vatican Colonnade are but a few of his masterpieces. In all that
he created, Bernini seeks to dazzle and overwhelm. Central to his
creations is the Church and its mystery, pomp and power. He will
use some of the same techniques as the mannerists but it will be for
serious purposes such as the veneration of a saint or the glorification of a powerful personage such as Louis XIV or Urban VIII. Architecture is his forte because it is that medium, far more than the
painting preferred by mannerists, that best presents baroque *gloire*.
Baroque literature will inherit both this sense of mission and this
preference for bombast and rhetorical display from architecture,
and, to a lesser degree, the other fine arts, just as literary mannerism
inherited most of its mannered elegance from the paintings of
Michelangelo, Rosso et al. In Italy, without question, architecture
was the most important manifestation of the baroque, followed by
sculpture with painting the least important.

This phenomenon, which is the exact reverse order of mannerism,
is explained by Sypher as following the "law of technical primacy in
the arts."[8] According to this law, all of the arts fall under the domination of the technique of the predominant one at a given time. Thus,

---

[7] The discussion of baroque pictorial arts which follows is taken from: Frederick Hartt, *Art, A History of Painting, Sculpture, Architecture* (New York: Abrams,
1976), II, 209-273; Juan-Ramón Triadó, *The Key to Baroque Art* (Minneapolis:
Lerner, 1990); Philippe Minguet, *France Baroque* (Paris: Hazan, 1988); and the very
perceptive and influential interpretations of Jean Rousset, *La Littérature de l'âge
baroque en France: Circé et le paon* (Paris: Corti, 1954). For an excellent study of
baroque versus mannerism in the fine arts, John Rupert Martin, *Baroque* (New
York: Harper and Row, 1977) is highly recommended.

[8] *Four Stages of Renaissance Style* (Garden City, N.Y.: Doubleday, 1955), 30-32.

during the Renaissance and mannerist periods, painting dominated, and the other arts followed its methods and underwent its influence. During the baroque era, the dominant art was architecture, as had been the case in the Gothic and Romanesque periods. This cycle of shifting dominance can be seen in all the arts, including literature, in the period that began with the Renaissance and ended with what Sypher calls the late baroque at the end of the seventeenth century.[9]

As the Gothic style began to disappear, the reintegration of style began in Italy in the fourteenth century and was marked by "classical" values such as harmonious proportion, reason, order, and the other traits mentioned by Wölfflin in his description of Renaissance style.[10] However, since this Renaissance harmony or "classicism" was artificial and forced, it raised more problems than it solved and, in the years 1520-1620, "came a phase of further experiment, or disintegration, in style accompanying a crisis in faith and conscience leading to the Council of Trent (1545-1563) in Romanism and the severities of Protestantism, and marked by disproportion, disturbed balance, ambiguity, and clashing impulses in painting, architecture, and sculpture, as well as 'metaphysical' poetry, Jacobean drama, and all the witticisms of Cultism, Marinism, Gongorism, and emblematic verse. This is the era of mannerism."[11] It is the resolution of these mannerist tensions that is, according to Sypher, the principal aim of the baroque, which is a phase of reintegration in the arts. The final phase of Renaissance style is what Sypher calls the late baroque–a period which began in France and England after 1640. This late baroque style "achieves intense moral and psychological force" in Racine and in Milton's *Paradise Regained*. While Sypher will be supported by Hatzfeld and other *comparatistes* in his contention that French classicism is part of the baroque, this position is not a very common one, especially among French critics. With the excellent background furnished by Sypher's analyses in mind, we may now return to the literary baroque.[12]

---

[9] Sypher 33-34; Helmut Hatzfeld calls this final phase of the baroque "barroquismo," *Estudios sobre el barroco* (Madrid: Gredos, 1966), 72-73. He and Sypher agree on the four stages of Renaissance style in both terminology and order: Renaissance, mannerism, baroque and late-baroque or *barroquismo*.

[10] This discussion follows Sypher (33-34) and is simply a résumé of his observations as I interpret them.

[11] Sypher 33-34.

[12] While French architecture as a whole excelled during the periods under consideration, there is very little in France that is purely baroque–most of the archi-

After Wölfflin, the next important study of the baroque in literature is that of Eugenio d'Ors,[13] who saw the baroque as a recurring phenomenon which alternates with classicism. This is no more
than a simple substitution of new names (the Dionysian and Apol-
lonian) for the old concepts of Asianism and Atticism and seems to
serve no beneficial purpose for the historian of art or literature. The
importance of d'Ors lies in the fact that he attempted to establish
correspondences between the arts; his primary weakness was his
complete failure to understand the periodization of styles as Renaissance, mannerism, and baroque. The same criticisms that were
made in the preceding chapter of recurring mannerism may be applied to the theory of d'Ors–Curtius simply uses mannerism where
d'Ors employs baroque.[14]

In addition to the theory of a recurring baroque (or mannerism)
is the idea of Benedetto Croce[15] and others of a baroque *Zeitgeist*–a
theory very similar to that of the anguished mannerism advanced by
Sypher. Croce, and others who espouse the idea of a baroque *Zeitgeist*, point to the Angst brought about by the religious wars, the
spread of plague and disease, the Council of Trent and the Counter-
Reformation, the constant fighting for supremacy between the nobility and the monarchy, and the ensuing concentration of power in
church and king as causes of the tensions and conflicts that are an
essential part of the baroque mentality. "The same struggle is trans-
posed in the arts and letters depicting man's precarious situation,
his relationship to God, and to death. Stylistically, the baroque
artist, whether he be sculptor, painter or poet, will have recourse to
mass, color, and movement to impress and astonish."[16] The critics
mentioned in the last two paragraphs, although in error as to their

tectural landmarks of the seventeenth century are "classicized"; for example, the
East Front of the Louvre is a much more classical design than Bernini's original
drawing for it. See Germain Bazin, *Baroque and Rococo*, trans. J. Griffin (London:
Thames and Hudson, 1964), 115-125.

[13] Eugenio d'Ors, *Du Baroque*, trans. Rouart-Valéry (Paris: Gallimard, 1935).

[14] Ernst Robert Curtius, *Europäische Literatur und lateinisches Mittelalter* (Bern:
Franke, 1948). Whereas d'Ors used rather absurd Latin terms such as "barochus
pristinus, gothicus or romanticus" to refer to the various incarnations of the
baroque, Curtius represents recurring mannerism and classicism with specific authors such as Xenophon, Cicero, Quintillian, Boileau and Pope for classicism and
Lasus, Sidonius, Calderón, Donne, Mallarmé and James Joyce for mannerism.

[15] *Età barocca in Italia* (Bari: Laterza, 1953) and *Storia della età barocca in Italia:
pensiero–poesia e letteratura–vita morale* (Bari: Laterza, 1929).

[16] Barga 16.

fundamental theses, did much to pave the way for a complete thematic analysis of the baroque, as well as stylistic analyses of baroque
works. Their studies certainly led to the veritable explosion of
baroque literary studies that began in the 1950's and has continued
until the present.

The year 1954 saw the publication of what is still the most influential study of the baroque in French literature–Jean Rousset's *La
Littérature de l'âge baroque en France: Circé et le paon*. The "era" of
Rousset marks, according to Bernard Chédozeau in his 1989 survey
of the baroque in France, the beginning of the third era of French
literary baroque studies. The first was the discovery of the "humanistes dévots" by Bremond in 1915 in his *Histoire littéraire du sentiment religieux en France*[17] and the second was the rediscovery of
baroque theater and lyric poetry by Raymond Lebègue and Antoine
Adam.[18] Bremond did not use the word *baroque* and had very little
appreciation for the style of his "humanistes dévots." Lebègue,
however, was the founder of a "lignée des critiques portés à consi-
dérer le baroque comme un formalisme plus que comme une culture."[19] Without Lebègue, it is difficult to imagine a Rousset or
even his teacher, Marcel Raymond, for so much of their work follows Lebègue's lead. The works of Antoine Adam are cited in virtually all studies of the baroque and have furnished much of the background information on the authors of the period. His study of
Théophile de Viau is a fundamental work for anyone studying the
literature of the early seventeenth century. From the time of Rousset's first work until the present, baroque studies in France have

---

[17] Volume 1 (Paris: Bloud & Gay, 1916).

[18] Among the poets rediscovered by Bremond, all of whom appear in Rousset's
anthology, are: Brébeuf, La Ceppède, Desmarets de Saint-Sorlin, Le Moyne,
Malaval, Martial de Brives (Paul Dumas), Lazare de Selve, Surin, Hopil and Père
Cyprien de la Nativité de la Vierge (André de Compons). Though he rediscovered
these poets, Bremond disdained their style as having "les extravagances d'une préciosité délirante [. . .] des aberrations de goût [. . .] caractère malsain [. . .] sensibili-
té grossière et basse [. . .] (ces auteurs) passent du sublime à l'absurde." The two
most important works by Lebègue are: *La Tragédie française de la Renaissance*
(Brussels: Office de la Publicité, 1944) and *La poésie française de 1560 à 1630*
(Paris: Société d'édition d'enseignement supérieur, 1951). Both of these works,
along with various articles, are Lebègue's contribution to baroque studies, while
Adam's *Histoire* and his *Théophile de Viau et la libre pensée en 1620* (Paris: Droz,
1935), and his article, "Baroque et préciosité," *Revue des Sciences Humaines* 55-56
(1949): 208-224, have been basic to an understanding of the baroque in French literature of the seventeenth century.

[19] Chédozeau 45.

concentrated on thematics and rhetorical analysis rather than on the idea of a baroque *Zeitgeist*. This is probably due as much to Lebègue's influence as to that of Raymond and Rousset, whose own works owe so much to Lebègue.

Rousset may be viewed as the representative of a group of scholars who, in the middle of this century, saw the baroque, following Lebègue, as distinct from and opposite to classicism. Among those who can loosely be grouped with him in this respect are Marcel Raymond, who has already been discussed in regard to mannerism; Gonzague de Reynold; Victor-L. Tapié; R. A. Sayce; A. M. Boase, who was one of the first to label *préciosité* as mannerist, René Wellek, whose history of baroque literary studies is indispensable; Odette de Mourgues; and Imbrie Buffum. [20] The overwhelming majority of French literary baroque students adhere to this position. At the other extreme are such non-French *comparatistes* as Sypher, Hatzfeld, Nicolich, Segel, and Borgerhoff, who will be discussed later in this chapter. A third group, represented by Henri Peyre, is highly skeptical of the existence of a literary baroque in France and is very much opposed to the notion that French classicism is part of a greater European baroque. [21] Because of his impor-

---

[20] See M. Raymond, *Baroque et renaissance poétique* (Paris: Corti, 1955); *La Poésie française et le maniérisme* (Geneva: Droz, 1971); Gonzague de Reynold, *Le XVIIᵉ siècle: le classique et le baroque* (Montreal: Éditions de l'arbre, 1944); Victor-L. Tapié, *Baroque et classicisme* (Paris: Plon, 1957); R. A. Sayce, "The Use of the Term Baroque in French Literary History," *Comparative Literature* 10 (1958): 246-253 and "Boileau and the French Baroque," *French Studies* 2 (1948): 148-152; A. M. Boase, "Poètes anglais et français de l'époque baroque," *Revue des Sciences Humaines* 55-56 (July-Dec. 1949): 155-184; René Wellek, *Concepts of Criticism* (New Haven: Yale UP, 1963): 69-127; Odette de Mourgues, *Metaphysical, baroque and précieux poetry* (Oxford: Clarendon, 1953) and Imbrie Buffum, *Agrippa d'Aubigné's Les Tragiques: A Study of the Baroque Style in Poetry* (New Haven: Yale UP, 1951) and also his *Studies in the Baroque from Montaigne to Rotrou* (New Haven. Yale UP, 1957).

[21] See Henri Peyre, "Common Sense Remarks on the French Baroque," in *Studies in Seventeenth-Century French Literature Presented to Morris Bishop* (Ithaca: Cornell UP, 1962), 1-19. Peyre sees French classicism as a "baroque dompté" (16) in this very reasoned appeal to curb some of the extravagances of critics who were labeling as baroque virtually all literature of the seventeenth century and even giving the appellation to writers in this century. Pierre Charpentrat speaks for the more extreme anti-baroquists when, in 1967, he calls for the abandonment of the term in literary criticism, *Le Mirage baroque* (Paris: Éditions de Minuit), 180. Fernand Baldensperger was one of the first to attack the idea of the baroque in French literature in "Pour une Réévaluation littéraire du XVIIᵉ siècle classique," *Revue d'Histoire Littéraire de la France* 44 (1937): 1-15.

tance and his tremendous influence, Jean Rousset's baroque studies
will be discussed in some detail.

Rousset deals with the baroque in three books and several articles[22] that appeared between 1954 and 1968. His most important
works are his *Anthologie*, which contains an excellent introduction;
La Littérature; and a collection of essays, *L'Intérieur et l'extérieur*,
which appeared in 1968 as interest in the baroque began to wane a
bit and as Rousset himself began to question some of his earlier positions on the subject. The fact remains, however, that it is his first
book that is responsible for the "success" of the baroque as a literary term in French literary criticism and history. Influenced by
Wölfflin, Rousset placed the baroque in France between 1580 and
1665 and attempted to transfer some of Wölfflin's categories to literature. Starting with what is, for him, essential to any study of the
baroque, Rousset establishes the thematics of the baroque: "le
changement, l'inconstance, le trompe-l'oeil et la parure, le spectacle
funèbre, la vie fugitive et le monde en instabilité," and groups them
around the two primary symbols of Circe and the peacock,
"c'est-à-dire la métamorphose et l'ostentation, le mouvement et le
décor" (8). These themes of metamorphosis and ostentation are, he
maintains, contrary to the ideals of classicism, or even pre-classi-
cism, and consequently justify a new appellation, the baroque. He
makes it clear from the beginning that his study in no way infringes
on that sacred notion of French classicism. If the conclusions of his
study be accepted, Rousset says, "le XVIIᵉ siècle 'classique' n'en
serait nullement obscurci ou diminué; mais il apparaîtrait moins ho-
mogène et moins linéaire; au lieu d'un siècle en évolution progres-
sive et monochrome, on verrait se dessiner plusieurs XVIIᵉ siècles
parallèles, alternés ou entremêlés, au sein desquels on reconnaîtrait
au Baroque la valeur d'un ferment actif et d'une composante néces-
saire" (9). This is a very perceptive statement for, as we shall see in
the works of Hallyn and Chédozeau, it is this coexistence of styles
that explains much of the confusion between mannerism and
baroque in France.

He seeks this other seventeenth century, and finds it, in the *ballet de cour*, the pastoral drama, the tragi-comedy, the tragedy (espe-

---

[22] "La Poésie baroque au temps de Malherbe: la métaphore," *Dix-Septième Siècle* 31 (1956): 353-370 and "Le problème du baroque littéraire français," in *Trois
Conférences sur le baroque français, Studi francesi* Supp. to 21 (1963): 49-62 are the
most important.

cially in the use of the play-within-a-play in all dramatic genres, citing especially Corneille's *Illusion comique* and Rotrou's *Saint Genest*), and the poetry of the period 1580-1665 and establishes four major criteria for the baroque: instability, mobility, metamorphosis, and preponderance of decor. From this general picture of the baroque, he determines the principal themes of French baroque literature and illustrates them with abundant examples drawn from the aforementioned genres. Eight years later, he published an anthology of poetry to illustrate even more clearly his concept of baroque thematics. Innovatively following Wölfflin's lead in the fine arts, Rousset guided French literary studies in a new direction as he grouped some 300 poems by over 70 authors around six major themes with various sub-topics:

I. Protée ou l'inconstance.
   1. L'inconstance noire.
   2. L'inconstance blanche.
II. Bulles, Oiseaux, Nuages.
   1. Bulle, balle, neige.
   2. Oiseaux, lucioles, vents.
   3. Nuages et arcs-en-ciel.
III. L'eau et le miroir.
   1. L'eau en mouvement.
   2. Les eaux miroitantes.
IV. De la métamorphose à l'illusion.
   1. Métamorphoses.
   2. Le déguisement.
   3. Le songe et l'illusion.
V. Le Spectacle de la mort.
VI. La Nuit et la lumière.
   1. Le brouillard et la clarté.
   2. La lumière et la permanence.

An important feature of Rousset's book and anthology is that he treats the baroque in a positive manner and divorces it from the always-unfavorable comparison with classicism that pervaded French criticism of the first half of the century. He studies works and authors by means of their own writings rather than comparing them to a Racine or a La Fontaine and finds much that is praiseworthy in the writings of an early, baroque, Malherbe or a Tristan L'Hermite. His chapters that deal with the baroque in the fine arts, especially the architecture of Bernini or Borromini, are the work of one who is genuinely enamored with the baroque esthetic. His study of Malherbe's early, "baroque," poetry; of Corneille's *Illusion comique*; and of the imagery of the poetry of the period is very perceptive and was instrumental in bringing about the subsequent vogue of Théophile, Saint-Amant, Hopil, La Ceppède and many of their contemporaries. The main weakness of the work is Rousset's failure to see that much of what he called "baroque" was in reality mannerism.

His colleague and teacher, Marcel Raymond, published in 1971 his own anthology of mannerist poetry in which he appropriated several poets, such as Sponde, Chassignet, d'Aubigné, Malherbe and Racan, whom Rousset had included among his baroque poets. Rousset comes very close to the idea of a mannerist period that preceded the baroque in a section of *La Littérature*, "Le baroque et la préciosité" (240-242). In his brief discussion of baroque and *préciosité*, Rousset notes that the two currents "ne confondent pas, mais ils se chevauchent par endoits" (240). Both styles love artifice and disguise but use them for different purposes: "L'un et l'autre jouent, le baroque gravement, le précieux sans s'y prendre; le premier voit Dieu et le monde et la vie de l'homme même engagés dans un jeu où il y va parfois de tout; le second ne joue qu'un jeu de société, il aboutit au divertissement; mais la ligne qui sépare le jeu baroque du jeu précieux est souvent si ténue qu'on ne la discerne plus" (241).

He then stresses baroque grandeur over the relatively small scale of *préciosité*, which he likens to a rococo curio. While discussing the lightness of tone and the very mannered (my word not his) style of the *précieux* poets, he provides an excellent analysis of the same metaphor as used by a writer of each style:

> [. . .] l'eau d'un poète baroque est l'image des métamorphoses, du flux et du reflux, du monde en mouvement; l'eau d'un poète précieux est du cristal ou de l'argent potable; la neige est pour Bussières un tourbillon, une danse de papillons et de fantômes volants, elle est pour Tristan le grain d'une peau, la glace d'un coeur, la blancheur d'une main; Le Moyne lance les miroirs dans l'espace, les brise en éclats enflammés qui sont les planètes; le miroir de Cotin est une énigme autour d'un objet de toilette (242).

By stressing the ludic nature of *préciosité* as opposed to the more serious nature of the baroque, Rousset anticipated the later studies of Hallyn and Chédozeau, which will be discussed below. The essential difference between mannerism and baroque is that the former is much less serious than the latter–a truth that Rousset seems to be informing us of, even if, as I believe, he is using the wrong terminology. Much of what he said about *préciosité* becomes even clearer when we apply it to mannerism, for *préciosité* is simply one of the facets of mannerism.

The immense success of *La Littérature* (it is now in its thirteenth printing) and of the *Anthologie* (now in its third edition) did much to establish the baroque as a valid concept in French literary criticism and history. Rousset helped kindle an interest in the baroque that, despite the skepticism of some, resulted in many critical editions, studies, articles and monographs on virtually all aspects of French literature of the Baroque period. Soon, unfortunately, the term began to lose its meaning, as it was applied indiscriminately by many critics who were perhaps carried away in their enthusiasm. It became an object of ridicule in the writings of such authorities as Charpentrat, in *Le Mirage baroque*, and it appeared that the literary world might be witnessing the death of the baroque. Rousset, himself, seems to have undergone a bit of self-doubt that is reflected in the concluding essays of *L'Intérieur et l'extérieur*. Writing in December of 1967, in an essay entitled "Adieu au baroque?" he reaffirms his love for baroque art and architecture and, while admitting some doubt as to the efficacy of the term in literature, he is pleased that his earlier studies have inspired new editions of these forgotten poets as well as monographs which elucidate their works. He concludes the next essay, "Esquisse d'un bilan," with an appeal to his readers: "Revenons en hâte au seul réel, aux oeuvres qui s'offrent à nous dans la plénitude d'une présence, à cette réalité qui transparaît à travers l'oeuvre et nous englobe, parce qu'elle est une pensée, un être saisis dans un langage irréductible à nos catégories critiques" (256). In other words, it is the literature that is important and, if we must, let us talk about the baroque without using the word–which is exactly what he does in the concluding essay.

Rousset's emphasis on the work itself anticipates the more recent studies of Hallyn and others that have emphasized the more formalistic methods of textual criticism. His thematic analyses have been very important despite the fact that they have been either modified or ignored by most recent critics. The great success of Jean Rousset is that he has inspired many students of the baroque to study these works while guiding them with his comprehensive "thématique littéraire" and his very perceptive discussions of the multiple and extended baroque metaphors. [23] It is Rousset, more than anyone else, who must be credited with establishing the concept of a baroque style and period in France that was soon put on an equal footing with other, more established terms, such as Renaissance and Classicism. Since Rousset, the seventeenth century in France is no longer considered as classical and pre-classical and its poets are no longer thought of as *attardés*.

If mannerism was unknown to or ignored by Rousset, it was very well known to two of his contemporaries. Marcel Raymond, as was seen in the previous chapter, did much to distinguish mannerism from the baroque but is also known for his *Baroque et renaissance poétique* (Corti, 1955), his translation of Wölfflin, and various articles on the baroque. [24] His position on the concept falls, generally, within the group who see classicism as a distinctly separate style from the baroque; his four phases of style would be Renaissance, mannerism, baroque, and classicism. Raymond and Rousset both consider the period from the middle of the sixteenth to the middle of the seventeenth centuries as a bridge between Renaissance and classicism—they simply call it by different names. Another, more recent, critic who is very much aware of mannerism is Claude-Gilbert Dubois who, like Rousset, has published a volume of baroque theory, an anthology, and a reappraisal of his earlier works. [25] His 1969 anthology is divided into two volumes: I. *Du Maniérisme au baroque (1560-1600)* and II. *Du Baroque au classicisme (1600-1660)*. He fills the gap between Renaissance and classicism with both styles but is

---

[23] For a very detailed study of the baroque metaphor, see Fernand Hallyn, *Formes métaphoriques dans la poésie lyrique de l'âge baroque en France* (Geneva: Droz, 1975), discussed below, pp. 55-56.

[24] "Le baroque littéraire. État de question," *Studi Francesi* 5 (1961): 23-39, and "Propositions sur le baroque et la littérature française," *Revue des Sciences Humaines* 2 (1949): 133-144.

[25] *Le Baroque, profondeur de l'apparence* (Paris: Hachette, 1973) is his theoretical work on the baroque, while *Le Maniérisme* (Paris: PUF, 1979) is a partial re-thinking of some positions he had taken in *Le Baroque*, such as his repositioning of Montaigne as mannerist from baroque (188-189). Essentially, save for terminology, his positions on the main issues of baroque studies are the same as Rousset, Raymond et al.

much earlier with both periods than most other students of the subject. [26] He remains true to the idea of a distinct classicism and, in that respect, differs from Hatzfeld, Sypher, and others who equate classicism with the baroque. Chronology and the inclusion of classicism under baroque are the fundamental issues that separate the Hatzfeld group from that of Rousset.

Taking their lead from Leo Spitzer and Helmut Hatzfeld, a minority of critics has differed with Rousset on the subject of baroque and classicism in seventeenth-century France. Outstanding among this group are two disciples of Helmut Hatzfeld, Davy A. Carozza and Robert M. Nicolich, and one who disagrees in part with the Hatzfeldian theories, Frank M. Warnke. To them, the baroque is a phenomenon that covers most of the seventeenth century before becoming rococo in the early years of the eighteenth century. Classicism is simply one manifestation of the epoch style of the seventeenth century, which is baroque. This group of scholars has long seen mannerism as the style which, in exact parallel with the visual arts, followed the classical Renaissance style and evolved into the baroque before becoming rococo. Whereas the four styles of the period 1500-1710 were called Renaissance, pre-baroque (mannerism by Raymond and Dubois), baroque, and classicism by Rousset and his adherents; Hatzfeld, Sypher and company would use the terms: Renaissance, mannerism, baroque and baroquismo or high baroque. Frank M. Warnke disagrees with this periodization and rejects a mannerist period but not a mannerist style. Innovatively, Warnke calls the entire period between Renaissance and Neoclassicism *Baroque*–an epoch marked by two *styles,* "mannerist" and "high-baroque." [27] He does not go as far as other *comparatistes* and reserves the term *Neoclassical* for Molière, Racine and La Fontaine. Since many of the poets of the last part of the sixteenth and early seventeenth centuries wrote poetry that is unmistakably baroque (d'Aubigné, du Bartas, Sponde, Chassignet) while also writing mannerist love poetry, and since one can find mannerism and baroque in many poets of the period 1600-1660 (Théophile, Saint-Amant, Tristan), Warnke would seem to be correct that the period 1560-

---

[26] A recent article by Lance Donaldson-Evans supports the idea of an early mannerism, 1520-1580, and assigns the years 1580-1700 to the baroque. "Two Stages of Renaissance Style: Mannerism and Baroque in French Poetry," *French Forum* 7 (1982): 210-223.

[27] *Versions of Baroque* (New Haven: Yale UP, 1972), 9-16.

1660 might be called Baroque with two co-existing styles, Mannerism and High Baroque.[28] The matter of French classicism is treated more thoroughly and in a more controversial manner by Hatzfeld, Carozza and Nicolich.

Helmut Hatzfeld divides the sixteenth and seventeenth centuries in, Italy, Spain, and France as follows:

	Italy	*Spain*	*France*
Renaissance:	1500-1530	1530-1580	1550-1590
	Ariosto	Luis de León	Ronsard
Mannerism:	1530-1570	1570-1600	1590-1640
	Michelangelo	Góngora	Malherbe
Baroque:	1570-1600	1600-1630	1640-1680
	Tasso	Cervantes	Racine
Barroquismo:	1600-1630	1630-1670	1680-1710
	Marino	Calderón	Fénelon[29]

He is seconded in this position by Carozza and Nicolich who have been quick to defend what one of them calls the "Hatzfeldian thesis."[30] For the purposes of this study, which will attempt to differentiate between mannerism and baroque in the poetry of Tristan L'Hermite, the periodization of mannerism as defined by Hatzfeld seems more correct than that of Rousset and Raymond–especially in the field of lyric poetry, and far less logical than that of Warnke in regard to the period *Baroque*. Perhaps too many who have studied the periodization of styles in the years 1500-1710 have sought a dramatic break in literary modes similar to what occurred in the nineteenth century with Romanticism. It seems evident that there were styles which coexisted during this period and that the "baroque" and "mannerist" styles could be found not only in the same time

---

[28] The capitalization of these terms is Warnke's; his use of the term *High Baroque* for what almost everyone else calls *baroque* is probably to distinguish the style from the period.

[29] *Estudios sobre el barroco*, 72-73. Hatzfeld refers to the literature of the eighteenth century as "rococo" in *The Rococo: Eroticism, Wit, and Elegance in European Literature* (New York: Pegasus, 1972).

[30] Davy A. Carozza, "For a Definition of Mannerism: The Hatzfeldian Thesis," *Colloquia Germanica* 1 (1967): 66-77.

frame, but also in the same author. Roy Daniells has shown this to be true of Milton, and I shall show that it is the case with Tristan.[31] It would seem that what we have in reality in this too often raging controversy over mannerism/baroque/classicism is primarily a problem of nomenclature. The importance of Hatzfeld and of those who hold to his chronology lies in their keen analyses of style which have done so much to describe and contrast the styles of the period regardless of what we may call them. After discussing three fairly recent French studies of the baroque, I shall return to Hatzfeld and Rousset, whose writings are still of great value to any student of baroque and mannerism, and rely very much on their insights in an attempt to contrast the two styles.

In 1975, Fernand Hallyn published an exhaustive study of metaphorical forms in French lyric poetry of the baroque era.[32] In a brief but very cogent introduction, Hallyn traces the history of baroque studies and gives his own views on some of the issues involved (1-12). He feels that contemporary criticism has been obsessed by terminology:

> [. . .] la littérature française de l'âge baroque n'a cessé d'apparaître sous des aspects de plus en plus différenciés [. . .] les divisions et les subdivisions se sont multipliées. Dès 1953, Odette de Mourgues proposait de distinguer à côté du baroque proprement dit, une littérature métaphysique [. . .] et une littérature précieuse. Aujourd'hui, le terme de baroque est surtout concurrencé par celui de maniérisme, qui a même reçu la caution d'un des pionniers des études baroques en France: Marcel Raymond. (3)

He calls Hatzfeld's periodization "une substitution de termes" (mannerism for baroque and baroque for classicism) and decries the fact that many critics have lost sight of the literary work in their attempts to categorize it. "A la limite, il faudrait autant de termes qu'il existe d'oeuvres" (5). He will use the term "baroque" in his study to apply to all of the lyric poetry of the years 1580-1660 and eschew all other labels because baroque is the least contested term if it is used in its chronological sense only. He will follow the suggestion of Rousset in *L'Intérieur et l'extérieur* and abandon the anal-

---

[31] Roy Daniells, *Milton, Mannerism and Baroque* (Toronto: Toronto UP, 1963).

[32] *Formes métaphoriques dans la poésie lyrique de l'âge baroque en France* (Geneva: Droz, 1975).

ysis of themes for that of forms. His conclusions are very significant because, although he does not use the word *mannerism*, they do much to help define the style and to delineate the differences between it and baroque. After an intensive study of the use of metaphor in the period under consideration, Hallyn concludes that there are two primary tendencies of its use. First, there is the metaphor, which seeks to express in a spectacular way man's place in the universe and seeks to render tangible the mysteries of the faith. At the other extreme is the metaphor which demonstrates the skill of the poet who has no serious intent but is merely playing with rhetoric in a display of virtuosity: "[. . .] la poésie est avant tout le miroir de l'ingéniosité du poète. La poésie devient ainsi un jeu ingénieux où le spectacle est constitué par le fonctionnement des mots dans le texte, sans référence à ce qui se situe au dehors" (216).

In another fairly recent treatment of the French literary baroque, Bernard Chédozeau calls the two tendencies found by Hallyn the "baroque de déception," which he equates with mannerism, and the "baroque de persuasion" which is the true baroque current. Both styles or currents existed at the same time (1580-1665) and when the ludic predominates we have mannerism, while baroque is the serious side of the same style. The baroque of deception is simply a description of those poets who continued "le jeu ludique et sceptique des maniéristes." Desportes, du Bois-Hus, Saint-Amant, and Théophile are cited by Chédozeau as representatives of this aspect of the baroque. The other is "[. . .] une longue lignée des poètes religieux, protestants puis catholiques, où l'on retrouverait plutôt un baroque de persuasion (de conviction chez M. Raymond) comme d'Aubigné, Chassignet, Drelincourt, La Cep-pède." For the former, the key word is artifice while for the latter it has to be sincerity:

> [. . .] les baroques que l'on appellera de déception qui peut-être ne donnent à leur parole d'autre fin qu'elle-même, sans renvoi à quelque réalité extérieure, jouant d'un langage autarcique, artificiel, qui cherche à troubler pour troubler, au sein d'un univers de fantaisie et de simulacre qui n'en a pas moins, très souvent, un caractère de gravité; les baroques de conviction, ou plutôt de persuasion, pour qui l'écriture n'est pas ludique et de fiction dans la mesure où dire c'est faire, comme à l'oral, pour qui la Pa-

role permet de procéder à un appel à un réel qui n'est pas de ce monde. Pour ces derniers, religion, liturgie, art, esthétique ne font qu'un, et cette vision du monde est aussi politique. (73)

Chédozeau obviously realizes that the two currents are not the same, though he prefers to label them both baroque. He concludes his discussion of the two currents by stating that the libertines, the burlesque and the *précieux* are hardly baroque; even if they are of the baroque period: "L'opposition est assez forte en effet pour que ces héritiers éloignés des maniéristes puissent accepter peut-être les nouvelles valeurs classiques si contraires à la mentalité des baroques de persuasion" (74). Chédozeau seeks and finds these two currents in what he calls the genres destined to be recited or spoken–the theater, sermons, orations, and poetry–and concludes that the baroque does not predominate in genres destined to be immediately printed, such as works in prose (history, philosophy, scientific texts and even the novel). What we see in the baroque and mannerist predilection for certain genres over others is a literary manifestation of the law of technical primacy in the arts that was discussed above. In mannerist literature, the preferred genre was amorous lyric poetry, while that of the baroque was the theater and religious poetry. Rotrou's *Saint Genest* is often cited as the paradigm of the baroque theater in France, while the erotic poetry of Desportes is said to be typical of French mannerist literary activity.[33]

Chédozeau contrasts baroque and mannerist styles by stressing mannerist virtuosity: "Ce maniérisme esthétique repose sur une stylistique des 'excès du langage' faisant surgir la fiction, le feint, en un exercice plutôt ludique et déceptif [. . .]" (72-73). Hence the *effets sonores*, alliteration and assonance, the *vers rapportés*, the *pointes*, antitheses, oxymora, ellipses, inversions and other figures that are used to put emphasis on language over content. When these same figures are used in a more subdued and reasonable manner, and when emphasis is placed on the *sérieux*, we have baroque poetry:

> Bref, cette poésie (maniériste) travaillée et consciente, poésie du langage, serait plutôt une poésie savante et 'sceptique' qui,

---

[33] Rousset, *La Littérature*, 72-73; Buffum, *Studies*, 212-239; Hatzfeld, *Estudios*, 318-332.

> sans s'opposer exagérément à elle, se distinguerait nettement de
> la poésie 'baroque' du début du XVIIe siècle, poésie déjà
> présente chez les poètes du XVIe siècle déclinant, poètes du
> baroque de persuasion récusant le principe même de la fiction
> jugée mensongère et 'païenne', et plus généralement toute 'esthé-
> tique' autonome se donnant librement ses propres règles et
> valeurs. (73)

During the seventeenth century, as Chédozeau correctly states,
there were poets who retained the style of the mannerists or blended
it with the baroque. Those who did so include Tristan, whose theater is largely baroque, as is his religious poetry, while his lyric poetry is primarily mannerist. The distinctions made by Chédozeau and
the excellent analyses of the use of the metaphor in seventeenth-
century French lyric poetry by Hallyn provide an excellent point of
departure for the contrast of baroque and mannerism that will conclude this chapter. They will also provide the basis for the analyses
of the poems that will constitute the final chapters.

Perhaps the best analysis of baroque and mannerism in French
lyric poetry is by Gisèle Mathieu-Castellani in the introduction to her
anthology of baroque and mannerist love poetry.[34] Her thoughts on
mannerism were discussed in the preceding chapter and in the present one her reflections on the baroque will be presented. Her comparison of the two styles will figure prominently in the concluding
confrontation of mannerism with baroque. Since thematic analysis
will not permit one to distinguish between baroque and mannerism,
Mathieu-Castellani seeks to define the *discours baroque*:

> Tentons donc une autre approche, en essayant d'aller vers une ty-
> pologie des discours: on examinera le discours en tant que tel, une
> situation de parole où un locuteur s'adresse à un allocutaire dans
> l'intention de l'influencer de quelque manière; il faudra alors
> étudier la situation de communication et le statut du locuteur, in-
> terroger ce discours dans sa relation à la vérité et à l'autre (22).

She details the five salient characteristics of the baroque in a
very convincing manner: (1) The baroque writer intends to convince or persuade his addressee, as was the case in ancient rhetoric,

---

[34] *Anthologie de la poésie amoureuse de l'âge baroque 1570-1640* (Paris: Livre de
Poche, 1990).

with an appeal to the emotions. To do this, he makes use of the deliberative and judicial branches of rhetoric. (2) The baroque discourse is presented as the expression of a transcendent truth; it is authentic and of divine origin. The didactic nature of the baroque is not to be found in the mannerist discourse. (3) Convinced of the truth and importance of his message, the baroque poet wants to make his hearers believe what he believes. He is a teacher of transcendent truth. (4) The baroque work is marked by frequent aphorisms and *sentences* because it is authoritative. Mimesis is no longer the reproduction of a nature codified by a culture; it is, rather, the representation of a transcendent order. (5) The baroque discourse is very emotional in its use of *pathos*; it seeks to arouse passion in the reader (22-27).

Mathieu-Castellani's formalistic approach to the study of mannerism and baroque is in the same vein as the studies of Hallyn and others who have preferred textual analysis to the thematic, sociological or psychological ones. Her eclectic method emphasizes stylistic analysis, as does that of Hatzfeld and other *comparatistes*; makes some use of rhetorical analysis; and even takes into consideration some sociological insights (see pp. 16-21). The eclectic approach to the problem is similar to that advocated by Mirollo in regard to mannerism and seems to provide the best hope for solving the baroque/mannerism enigma. This procedure will be followed in the concluding portion of this chapter, as mannerism and baroque are contrasted and compared.

If the transferal of terms from art to literature be valid, it would seem that all of them should be utilized in literary history, rather than just baroque, as was the case with many critics of French literature. Therefore, it seems logical that the periodization of Hatzfeld and Sypher is more in keeping with that of the historians and critics of the fine arts. They have advanced the idea that between the Renaissance and the Romantic era, two classifications that virtually all literary historians agree on, there was one epoch style, which was the Baroque. The Baroque epoch lasted from approximately 1550 until the triumph of Romanticism in 1830, as far as France is concerned, and was made up of what Hatzfeld calls generational styles. These are mannerism, baroque, *barroquismo*, rococo, and Neo-classical. I would tend to agree with Frank J. Warnke[35] that perhaps

[35] Frank J. Warnke, "Mannerism in European Literature: Period or Aspect?," *Revue de Littérature Comparée* 54 (1982): 255-260.

what Hatzfeld calls *barroquismo* is, in reality, simply a late manifestation of mannerism and would emphasize, as have Warnke and Nicolich, that the baroque and mannerist styles existed side-by-side in the French literature of the seventeenth century.[36] What has traditionally been called "classicism" in French literature is simply a toned-down baroque, "un baroque dompté" that is peculiar to France. It may be said, then, that the mannerist style distorted and exaggerated the classical style of the Renaissance and provided the stylistic exaggeration which led to the baroque. The mannerism of Scève and Ronsard existed before the baroque of Sponde and d'Aubigné but soon the two styles coexisted at least until the rococo (eighteenth century). In France, at least, the baroque evolved into its subdued version that was for so long called "classicism."

The period of the composition of Tristan's poetry (c1620-1654), is certainly a time when both styles were in wide use. This can be seen in such diverse works as the poetry of Tristan, Théophile, Saint-Amant and most of the lyric poets of their period; *préciosité*; and the pastoral novel and play–all of which reflect seventeenth-century mannerism. The baroque tendency can easily be seen in the "preclassical" works of Malherbe, the religious sonnets of La Ceppède, the theater of Rotrou and in the theater of Tristan L'Hermite.[37] As Denzler has so correctly observed: "[. . .] in France [. . .] the Baroque, Classicism, and Mannerism are intertwined in a three-strand literary braid" (451-452). While Classicism, or *baroque dompté*, has very little relevance to this essay, baroque and mannerism must be contrasted before these elements can be studied in the poetry of Tristan. After considering all of the theories discussed above, I am convinced that the ludic is the essential element of mannerism in the works of Tristan and that *le sérieux* is the dominant characteristic of his baroque efforts. When Tristan writes, he is usually speaking in what Mathieu-Castellani calls the *discours maniériste*, but he is also capable of the *discours baroque* or of a combination of the two. His use of rhetoric is typical of both cur-

---

[36] Robert M. Nicolich, "Mannerism and Baroque: Further notes on problems in the transfer of these concepts from the visual arts to literature," *Papers on French Seventeenth Century Literature* 10 (1983): 441-457.

[37] See the unpublished dissertation of Thomas Barga "Baroque Imagery and Themes in the Theater of Tristan L'Hermite" (Rice, 1970) and the comprehensive study of Daniela dalla Valle, *Il Teatro di Tristan L'Hermite* (Torino: Giappichelli, 1964), 115-224.

rents and a few of his poems show evidence of what was later called "classicism."

Mannerism, in Tristan's poems, will be found in the use of rhetoric for largely playful or non-serious purposes. *Les Plaintes d'Acante, Les Amours,* and *La Lyre* are primarily composed of *précieux* and Marinistic love-poetry that probably reflect real situations only rarely and whose primary purpose was to demonstrate the author's *manière* and virtuosity. Many were written for friends or patrons to send to their objects of conquest. The odes found in *Les Vers héroïques,* as well as the religious poetry composed in Tristan's final years, are generally baroque. As will be seen, Tristan's use of rhetoric is indicative of both the discourses of mannerism and baroque, and it too reflects a toning down of the excesses of both styles, especially in the later, more mature efforts of the poet.

As we look for mannerism and baroque in the poetry of Tristan, style, intent, and purpose will be of primary importance. To facilitate this investigation, a study of baroque and mannerist styles in the period 1560-1660, as they occur in French lyric poetry, is in order. The following remarks are not intended to apply to any other country or to any other genre, because, although there are general baroque and mannerist tendencies in many countries and genres, there are peculiarities that apply only to the poetry written in France during the baroque/mannerist period. These remarks are based on the critical works surveyed above and on other works cited in the Bibliography that concludes this study.

Though there were poets who showed some mannerist or baroque tendencies before 1546,[38] the two styles became evident in the last part of the sixteenth century and the early part of the seventeenth. Mannerism appeared first (Scève) but was soon followed by the Protestant "baroquistes" such as Sponde, du Bartas and d'Aubigné. The next generation of baroque poets (Hopil, Chassignet, and de La Ceppède) took the style to its greatest success as

---

[38] This is the beginning date of mannerism according to Marcel Raymond, others have gone back as far as 1520 for the beginning of mannerism in literature and Rousset's century of baroque has been called a century of mannerism by Hatzfeld in "Mannerism is not Baroque," *L'Esprit Créateur* 6 (1966): 226. The baroque style was a reaction to the early manifestations of mannerism. Sponde, d'Aubigné, and du Bartas are its earliest practitioners. The baroque style was soon assimilated into the doctrines of the Church and became a principal weapon in the Counter-Reformation.

representatives of the Catholic baroque in the seventeenth century.[39] The next generation of mannerists is led by the imposing figure of Desportes, whose followers include Théophile, Tristan, and Saint-Amant, among many others. Religious poetry is the predominant form of baroque poetry but there is also the encomiastic poetry, which deals with matters of state and the praise of eminent personages. Amatory poetry is by far the most important form of mannerist poetry and usually is *pétrarchisant* or *précieux*. Both styles are characterized by rhetorical display, though for different purposes. Since the sometimes excessive use of figures of rhetoric and conceits is common to both styles, it is important that they be identified to increase our awareness of how they are used, for that is the determining factor as to whether they are mannerist or baroque.

The list of figures compiled by Denzler is very comprehensive: She cites the conceit and the following figures, the definitions of which she places in an Appendix: The phrenic figures studied are anacoluthon, antonomasia, apothesis, catachresis, dissimile, hyperbaton, metaphor, metonymy, oxymoron, periphrase, prosopopoeia, solecism, syllepsis, synaesthesia, synecdoche, synoeciosis, and zeugma. She studies two aural figures: annominatio, which she contrasts with paronomasia, and antanaclasis.[40] The most common figure that she found in mannerist poetry is the "far-fetched metaphor" which often takes the form of the catachrestic one (456). Dubois and Raymond list essentially the same figures and stress also the metaphor and the *pointe*. Two sonnets, one baroque and the other mannerist, will illustrate the use of the same figures for entirely different purposes:

> Blanc est le vêtement du grand Père sans âge,
> Blancs sont les courtisans de sa blanche maison,
> Blanc est de son esprit l'étincelant pennage,
> Blanche est de son Agneau la brillante toison.
>
> Blanc est le crêpe saint dont (pour son cher blason)
> Aux noces de l'Agneau l'Épouse s'avantage.
> Blanc est or le manteau, dont par même raison
> Cet innocent Époux se pare en son noçage.

---

[39] Chédozeau, 63.
[40] Denzler, 465-491.

Blanc était l'ornement dont le pontife vieux
S'affublait pour dévot offrir ses voeux aux cieux.
Blanc est le parement de ce nouveau grand prêtre.

Blanche est la robe due au fort victorieux.
Ce vainqueur (bien qu'il aille à la mort se soumettre)
Blanc sur la dure mort triomphe glorieux.

(La Ceppède)

* * *

Douce maîtresse et douces vos façons,
Douce la bouche et douce la parole,
Et doux votre oeil qui doucement affole,
Faisant en moi douces les passions,

Doux vos regards, douces vos actions,
Doux l'entretien et douce la main molle,
Douce la voix qui doucement console
L'âme et le coeur en leurs afflictions,

Douce la grâce et douce la beauté
Qui ont ravi ma douce liberté,
Ô doux le mal qu'il faut pour vous souffrir!

Puisque l'on voit en vous tant de douceurs,
Faites au moins, quand pour vous je me meurs
Je puisse un peu plus doucement mourir!

(Scalion de Virbluneau)

Each of these poems is manifestly rich in rhetorical display and, while both are noteworthy for their abundant use of anaphora, they are obviously of differing styles. Each belongs to the late sixteenth century–a period that many would still call the mannerist era–and yet the poem of La Ceppède is unmistakably baroque while that of Scalion is mannerist. If they use essentially the same figures and use them abundantly, rhetorical analysis alone will not serve to classify either of them as baroque or mannerist. It will be necessary to determine how this rhetorical display is used and for what purpose before we can assign them to either style. An appropriate point of departure for determining the style of a sixteenth- or early seventeenth-century French poem is the intent of its author. If he is writing with much rhetorical display for a serious purpose and seeking to convince his audience that his message is one that it should believe, he is using what Mathieu-Castellani calls the *discours baroque*. La Ceppède, in his preferred genre, the sonnet, is writing to explain the mysteries of the faith and to move his audience both intellectually and emotionally to share his religious convictions. The concluding paradox of the sonnet sums up the essential message of Christianity, Christ's triumph in death, a "triomphe glorieux." The poet is sure of his message and delivers it passionately in order to arouse a similar passion in his reader. Just as the baroque church overwhelms visually with abundant symbols of the faith, La Ceppède overwhelms us with copious sensory images.

The poem of Scalion de Virbluneau is of an entirely different nature. He is writing for no serious transcendent purpose; he is certainly not trying to make us aware of any universal truth and he seeks to convince us of nothing beyond the fact that his *maîtresse* is *douce*. His imitation of Petrarch, and the fact that his poem will be appreciated only by those of his circle, lead us to classify it as mannerist. His use of anaphora is not designed to dazzle us but is, rather, an attempt on the part of the poet to show how cleverly he can play with rhetoric and literary convention. In all probability, his *maîtresse* exists only in language; she is only a very faded Petrarchan conceit with none of the vitality and *vraisemblance* of Laura. It is the skill of the mannerist poet in reworking these commonplaces of amatory literature that is appreciated by his very limited audience, which cares far more about form than substance. When done well, this poetry will please and astonish because it is indeed the stylish style; there is, however, always the danger of triteness and banality which the skillful artist must avoid. As will be seen in subsequent chapters, the mannerist use of rhetoric can result in very pretty descriptions of nature, which, though far from realistic, are pleasing in both sound and image.

The two sonnets quoted above are extreme examples of each style. In the vast majority of cases, the difference is not so clearly delineated and it becomes necessary to look much more closely at the elements of style, intent, purpose, and content. This is especially true when one seeks baroque and mannerism in the poetry of Tristan L'Hermite, because his poetry reflects both styles separately and in combination. There is also the tendency in Tristan toward the *baroque dompté* or classicism that must be considered in a thorough study of the question. Therefore, the eclectic approach enumerated above will be used in this study as Tristan's poetry will be analyzed on a volume by volume basis.

CHAPTER V

MANNERISM AND BAROQUE IN THE *PLAINTES
D'ACANTE ET AUTRES OEUVRES*

B EFORE turning to a study of mannerism and baroque in the
Plaintes d'Acante, a brief survey of prior criticism of Tristanian
poetry is in order. The first significant study of all aspects of the life
and works of Tristan L'Hermite is, of course, that of Bernardin in
1895. [1] Since his thesis involved the theater above all other aspects
of Tristan's life and works, Bernardin devoted very little space to
poetry. He did, however, make several excellent observations that
have served as a starting point for subsequent students of Tristan's
poetic endeavors. After reluctantly admitting that a chronological
study of Tristan's poetry was an impossible task, Bernardin divided
it into four general categories: erotic, religious, burlesque, and
heroic. He found many influences on Tristan; but in the love lyric,
the two important ones were Ovid and Marino (528), while the influence of Malherbe was predominant in the heroic or occasional poetry. [2] Bernardin, reflecting the prejudices of his epoch, tries to excuse Tristan for his *préciosité* by emphasizing his restraint when
compared to Voiture, Gombauld, and Malleville and by attempting
to demonstrate the "sincerity" of his feelings as expressed in his
love poetry. As will be shown in the analysis of the *Plaintes
d'Acante,* sincerity is not easy to identify in seventeenth-century
love poetry and it is rarely important either to poet or to reader.

---

[1] Napoléon M. Bernardin, *Un Précurseur de Racine: Tristan L'Hermite, sieur de
Solier (1601-1655). Sa famille, sa vie, ses oeuvres* (Paris: Picard, 1895). Bernardin
discusses Tristan's poetry in a single twenty-five-page chapter 527-553.
[2] Other sources of Tristan's poetry found by Bernardin include: Virgil, Horace,
Juvenal, Pulex, Villon, Jodelle, Ronsard, Du Bellay, d'Urfé, Théophile, Racan, Annibal Caro, and Tasso.

Nevertheless, he concludes his discussion of the erotic poetry with the statement: "[. . .] ces pièces des *Amours* et de *la Lyre* ont un accent de sincérité indéniable, qui les distingue de presque tous les vers d'amour de la même époque" (534). That very sincerity, he says, is the reason for the success of Tristan's religious poetry:

> [. . .] les autres poètes ont trop souvent rimé en l'honneur de Jésus-Christ, de la Vierge, et des saints, moins par une réelle piété que par une vulgaire spéculation de librairie, ou par une pénitence imposée, ou tout au moins par un simple scrupule de conscience [. . .] tandis que Tristan dans ses poésies religieuses a mis tous les élans de son coeur pieux. (535)

In fact, says Bernardin, the seventeenth century had produced, in the realm of religious lyric poetry, no poet superior to Tristan until Racine's choruses in *Esther* and *Athalie* and his four *Cantiques spirituels*, which are the masterpieces of the genre. Tristan's efforts in the burlesque are also praised, almost apologetically, for: "Naturellement noble et héroïque, Tristan garde ses qualités de grandeur et d'ampleur dans un genre qui réclame ordinairement des qualités plus modestes" (539). This noble and heroic nature of Tristan is best seen, Bernardin says, in the heroic poetry, which is esteemed very highly by the nineteenth-century scholar and reflects the judgment of the era. Bernardin does not mention baroque or mannerism but does speak disparagingly of *préciosité*. He admires Tristan's poetry in spite of its rhetorical excesses and because of its "classical" qualities, such as harmony and clarity. He would rank Tristan's poetry between the odes of Malherbe and the lyric lines of Racine–high praise indeed for an almost forgotten poet. Taking Bernardin's study as a point of departure, many subsequent critics have contributed to our understanding of the many and varied poems composed by Tristan L'Hermite.

The next significant study of Tristan's poetry was made in 1955 by the poet Amédée Carriat,[3] who is most responsible for the renaissance of interest in Tristan. His bibliography and his sponsorship of the *Cahiers Tristan L'Hermite*, have been most valuable to

---

[3] *Tristan ou l'Éloge d'un poète* (Limoges: Rougerie, 1955). Another poet, Jacques Madeleine, edited several of Tristan's plays in addition to the *Plaintes d'Acante.* Though not comprehensive, the earlier studies of Adam, Tortel, and Bray certainly contributed to the "regain de faveur" of Tristan L'Hermite.

subsequent students of Tristan's works. In his *Éloge*, Carriat speaks affectionately and sensitively of Tristan as a fellow poet, who is unfortunately still an unknown. Though the work is more encomium than scholarly, Carriat makes very profound observations on Tristan the poet and on Tristan the man. His comments differ in no significant way from those of Bernardin but are more extensive and sensitive. He speaks of two Tristans:

> [. . .] Tristan se montre à la fois maniéré et spontané, conventionnel et lui-même, dans sa poésie amoureuse. [. . .] Faut-il, parmi ces sonnets situés au confluent de deux influences–les dernières sublimations du pétrarquisme déclinant et l'imagerie plus sensuellement réaliste de Marino et de l'Astrée [. . .] (92-93)

and:

> [. . .] le grand Tristan, le seul Tristan vraiment pathétique, qui laisse loin derrière le Tristan de l'amour et de la nature, des eaux et de la nuit, le Tristan satirique et héroïque. Voici le Tristan humain, en face de la vie et de la mort, ce Tristan quasi méconnu qui se penche sur la condition humaine et médite. Un Tristan grave qui a dépouillé le précieux, le sentimental, le Tristan d'imagerie qu'on nous a fabriqué gratuitement faute d'avoir pris soin de le lire. (120)

These two Tristans are perhaps the baroque and the mannerist Tristans, for most students of the poetry of Tristan L'Hermite have clearly seen the two sides of the artist.

In 1965 two very significant studies of Tristan's poetic output appeared as doctoral dissertations. Professor Charles Mackey submitted his dissertation at Yale;[4] and Catherine M. Grisé, hers at the University of Toronto.[5] While Mackey confined his study to the non-religious poetry of Tristan, Grisé studied virtually all of Tristan's poetic output. Mackey's study is very important to the present one because he devotes entire chapters to baroque and *précieux* elements in Tristan's poetry.[6] He confines his study of *préciosité* to the figures used by Tristan that were considered *précieux* by René Bray

---

[4] "The Poetic Legacy of Tristan L'Hermite."
[5] "The Poetry of Tristan L'Hermite."
[6] See chapters II and III, 97-181.

and Odette de Mourgues: periphrasis, metaphor, antithesis, *pointe*, oxymoron, and hyperbole. He then discusses the complex and the abstract in Tristan's poems as further elements of the *précieux* style. As he admits in his concluding paragraph, these elements can also be baroque:

> Yet, just as we maintain that there is such an evident current in that century, we recognize also that there is a companion esthetic that has been called the Baroque. Moreover the Baroque poet uses to a considerable degree similar themes and stylistic devices which we have labeled précieux. What distinctions can be drawn between Baroque and Précieux? What are their points of contact? In Tristan L'Hermite, a poet who is at the confluence of these two esthetics, we shall hope to provide in the following chapter answers to these questions. (130)

Mackey attempts to answer these questions by defining and studying the baroque according to the thematic categories established by Rousset and Buffum. He concludes that Tristan is a *précieux* poet who is "occasionally a Baroque poet" (181) and that much remains to be done in order to define the baroque. In passing, Mackey suggests that the term *mannerism* might be of use to future scholars.

Catherine M. Grisé, who was later to edit the *Lettres meslées* and the *Vers héroïques,* made the first comprehensive study of all of Tristan's poetry in her excellent dissertation. Adding to the biography of Tristan in Bernardin and completing his study of the poetry, she contributes significant biographical information and a very perceptive analysis of the poetic works of Tristan L'Hermite. Her study of the Italian influences, especially those of Marino, on Tristan's poetry are very valuable in assessing the mannerist and baroque elements contained therein.[7] In her discussions of Tristan's poetry, she discusses many of the mannerist and baroque elements without identifying them as such. It is only in her conclusion that she broaches the subject of the baroque and, perhaps more prudent that the present writer, she refuses to become involved in the controversy which she says is beyond the scope of her thesis (275).

---

[7] She very ably refutes the conclusion of C. W. Cabeen that there was little marinistic influence on the literature of seventeenth-century France. C. W. Cabeen, *L'Influence de G.B. Marino sur la littérature française* (Grenoble: Allier, 1904).

Nevertheless, her studies of Tristan's poetry are a *sine qua non* for any student of Tristan L'Hermite.

In 1971, William H. Bryant submitted his dissertation, "A Thematic and Rhetorical Study of Tristan L'Hermite's *Les Amours*" to the University of Missouri. While this excellent study deals with only one of Tristan's published volumes of poetry, it contains some very perceptive comments on attempts to classify him:

> As to the question of classification, Tristan is probably best considered as an eclectic or transitional poet, his poems reflecting many of the various literary trends and influences at work during his day. From time to time, different critics have tried to pigeonhole Tristan, attaching any of several literary labels to him. This is patently a dangerous procedure to follow in the case of a poet whose work is so diversified. To regard Tristan from only one point of view is to misjudge him completely. Let us admit that Tristan is, according to the particular poem that one adduces, a Marinist poet, a *précieux* poet, a Catholic poet, a Baroque poet, or perhaps even a romantic. It is true that in certain poems he seems to be easily classifiable, while in others the contrary is true. It is also true that, in some instances, several of these literary trends may appear in the same poem. The problem is further complicated by the troublesome fact that no wholly satisfactory definition of certain terms–like *Baroque*, for instance–has yet been devised. In answer to the question, What kind of poet is Tristan?–one can say only that his work reflects several different literary trends or influences. As we have seen, Tristan was too much of an individualist, and his poetic imagination too fertile, to have been restricted to any one particular influence, which he may have undergone. Admitted that he was a continuator of Malherbian pure and simple diction, Tristan was, nonetheless, very inventive in form, subject matter, and treatment. That he was not content to write in just one style is a tribute of one sort to his greatness. (177-178)

This conclusion certainly seems to suggest that a more detailed study of Tristan's styles is in order. If Bryant could find such stylistic variety in just one volume of Tristan's poetry, it is likely that this variety would be even more obvious in a study of his entire poetic production.

Claude K. Abraham has written many articles and books that discuss the poetry of Tristan, but his most comprehensive study is contained in his *Tristan L'Hermite*, which appeared in 1980.[8] He, like virtually everyone who has studied the poetry of Tristan L'Hermite, laments the fact that a chronological analysis is impossible; but he is able to distinguish two aspects of Tristan's poetry:

> Tristan frequently hoarded his poems for later publication: some of the poems published in his last anthology are works of his youth. With the notable exception of certain circumstantial works, a dating of his verses is thus virtually impossible, and a chronological study–however desirable or undesirable it may be–out of the question. Yet those poems that are patently the product of his later years have a decidedly different quality, darker in coloring, more personal in tone, eschewing the *précieux* and marinistic devices he so loved to exhibit in his earlier years. (31)

He therefore divides his study of Tristan's poetry "into broad thematic categories, immense–and admittedly clumsy–tapestries on which circumstantial poems would have to be more or less frequently and artificially grafted" (31). His division of Tristan's poems may be outlined as follows:

I. The individual.
   A. Ego.
   B. The Language of Love.
II. Society.
   A. Court and Servitude.
   B. The Heroic Ethos.
III. Nature.
   A. Images and Impressions.
   B. Habitat and Influence.
IV. The Heavens.
   A. Tristan's Stars.
   B. The Fate of Heroes.
   C. God.

His analyses of Tristan's verses under the preceding headings are especially valuable to the present study because many baroque traits are ably demonstrated by Professor Abraham. Though he does not use the term "mannerism," his division of the poetic output of Tristan L'Hermite into early and late phases is highly sugges-

---

[8] Boston: Twayne. See especially pp. 31-77.

tive of my own division of it into mannerist and baroque. In addition, Abraham's discussions of artifice and sincerity and his very incisive writing on the personal philosophy and religious beliefs of Tristan have been very helpful in understanding the poet.

Though he confined his study to the *Plaintes d'Acante et autres oeuvres,* the insights of Roger Guichemerre, in his 1991 volume *Quatre poètes du XVIIᵉ siècle,*[9] are important to the student of Tristan's poetry. He finds among the forty-one poems in this first collection of Tristan an overwhelming majority of "poèmes galants" of Petrarchan inspiration, but, he notes, there are also a small number of poems of circumstance, which reflect the influence of Malherbe. This study, along with the splendid analyses of the poems in the collection, is valuable in aiding one to delineate the mannerist and the baroque elements that are found in this and the other collections of Tristan's poetry.

The preceding studies of the poetry of Tristan L'Hermite have been supplemented by a vast number of shorter ones, which will be alluded to in the discussions of individual poems. From the very first to the most recent one, there has been an increasing awareness that the poetry of Tristan L'Hermite is not monolithic in nature. The two styles of Tristan have been called by many names, but the fact remains that no one has yet successfully studied this poetry from the point of view of mannerism and baroque. *Précieux,* marinistic, and Petrarchist have been used to describe what is mannerism; while incomplete definitions of baroque have been used to describe the "other Tristan." Relying very heavily on these pioneering studies of Tristan, as well as others which will be discussed later, an analysis of mannerism and baroque in the *Plaintes d'Acante* will now be presented.

The *Plaintes d'Acante et autres oeuvres* were published in Antwerp during the exile of Gaston d'Orléans and his entourage in October 1633.[10] Although this is the first published collection of his poetry, Tristan's two *Vers du Ballet de Monsieur Frere du Roy* and his *La Mer, A Monsieur, Frere du Roy* had previously been printed.[11] There are four editions of the collection that were printed during

[9] (Paris: SEDES), 81-117.

[10] Amédée Carriat, *Bibliographie des oeuvres de Tristan L'Hermite* (Limoges: Rougerie, 1955), 9.

[11] See Carriat's bibliography for this and all references to the editions of the *Plaintes.*

Tristan's lifetime, and he included, with changes, all of the poems in
the *Plaintes d'Acante et autres oeuvres* in his later publication *Les
Amours de Tristan* (1638). The collection includes three Latin poems along with the forty-one French works and also includes the
extensive annotations to the *Plaintes d'Acante*, which reveal many
things about both poet and poem. [12] The title poem and the
"Promenoir des deux amants" are by far the best known of the author's efforts in this collection, but there are many others, typical of
the young Tristan's early works, which are worthy of attention. We
can also see the beginnings of the "other" poetic personality or style
of Tristan L'Hermite in an occasional poem that differs from the
main thrust–the amatory poetry–of the volume.

In 1937, Eugénie Droz discovered the original manuscript of
the "Plaintes d'Acante" and found that the title poem was written
for the duc de Bouillon and was sent to the comtesse de Bergh with
whom the duke had fallen in love. [13] Tristan was nothing more than
the *porte-parole* of the duke, and what had been hailed as sincere
protestations of the poet's true love was found to be simply Tristan's
adroitness in employing the conventions of the seventeenth-century
love lyric. As Philip Wadsworth, Claude Abraham, and many others
have concluded, there is no way to establish the "sincerity" of Tristan, and it is of no real value to do so. [14] He is convincing simply because he has mastered the terminology and the conventions of what
passed for Petrarchism in his day. Whether or not the emotions
portrayed in his amatory poetry are real is of no consequence because he conveys the impression of truth. This very early version of
vraisemblance was sufficient for the poetic demands of the period.
If, however, the emotions are not real and the situations are con-
trived, the poet is playing the game and is playing it well if he per-
suades the reader to believe it. This is of course one of the salient
characteristics of mannerism and it will serve as a starting point for
determining the elements of mannerism and baroque in the poem.

---

[12] All references to the *Plaintes d'Acante et autres oeuvres* are to the critical edition of Jacques Madeleine (Paris: Société des Textes Français Modernes, 1909, 3rd
printing, 1989).

[13] *Le Manuscrit des Plaintes d'Acante de Tristan L'Hermite* (Paris: chez l'auteur,
[1937]).

[14] See Philip A. Wadsworth, "Artifice and Sincerity in the Poetry of Tristan
L'Hermite," *Modern Language Notes* 74 (1959): 422-430. Abraham follows his conclusions in his *Tristan L'Hermite,* 31-33.

To the fact that Tristan wrote "Les Plaintes d'Acante" to assist his wealthy patron in winning the hand of the Countess de Bergh, must be added that Tristan published the poem both in Antwerp and in Paris. His audience, though more broad than a *ruelle,* is nevertheless a very restricted one–the court and the cultivated persons of the nobility who had the leisure and the education necessary to appreciate his poetic skills. This implies, of course, a knowledge of the conventions of the love-lyric and an appreciation of the skills of the poet as he employs the devices of the genre in as clever and original a way as possible. *Far stupir* was certainly one of the means employed to give freshness and wit to the poetic composition. This very restricted audience could appreciate a clever conceit or a dazzling display of rhetoric and Tristan was certainly capable of pleasing these *cognoscenti.* The appeal to an elite audience and the rhetorical skill of the poet are certainly aspects of mannerism as it was defined in the third chapter of this study. Other examples of mannerism in the poem will be discussed in the course of a summary of the work. [15]

The rather long allegorical eclogue, 73 stanzas of 7 lines each (511 lines), begins with a description of the shepherd Acante sitting on a rock and lamenting his unrequited love for the beautiful shepherdess Sylvie. This opening parallels that of Marino's "I Sospiri d'Ergasto" which is a primary source of the poem, [16] though Tristan fails to mention the Italian in his *Annotations.* The opening lines reveal several mannerist traits:

> Un jour que le Printemps rioit entre les fleurs
> Acante qui n'a rien que des soucis dans l'ame,

---

[15] In discussing the "Plaintes d'Acante" of Tristan, I am very indebted to the following: Margaret Belcher, "Tristan's Annotations on *Les Plaintes d'Acante,*" *Papers on French XVII*[th] *Century Literature* 16 (1982): 327-339; Gisèle Mathieu-Castellani, "La Poésie amoureuse et son commentaire: les annotations de Tristan sur les *Plaintes d'Acante,*" *Eros in Francia nel Seicento (Quaderni del Seicento Francese)* 8 (1987): 147-159; Françoise Graziani, "Le Mythe pastoral dans les *Plaintes d'Acante*: Ovide, Virgile et Théocrate," *Cahiers Tristan L'Hermite* 12 (1990): 23-39; Catherine M. Grisé, "The Poetry of Tristan L'Hermite," Diss. U. of Toronto P, 1964, 84-89; and Roger Guichemerre, "Tristan and Marino. Les *Plaintes d'Acante* et *I Sospiri d'Ergasto,*" in *Du Baroque aux lumières, Pages à la mémoire de Jeanne Carriat* (Mortemart: Rougerie, 1986), 40-47.

[16] See the article by Guichemerre already cited for an excellent analysis of the Italian poem's influence of the "Plaintes d'Acante"; see also the chapter in his book *Quatre poètes du XVIIe siècle* (Paris: SEDES, 1991). Guichemerre points out some important differences in the two poems, some of which will be discussed below.

Pour fleschir ses destins, faisoit parler ses pleurs
Humides tesmoins de sa flame;
Et se representant les rigueurs de sa Dame,
Sembloit un morceau du rocher
Sur lequel ses pensers le venoient d'atacher.

Tristan interprets the first line in his annotations: "Un des plus beaux jours du Printemps." Here he is perhaps imitating Muret's commentary on the *Amours* of Ronsard (1553), which he had possibly seen in the library of Scévole; or that of La Ceppède on his *Théorèmes* (1613), but as Belcher and Mathieu-Castellani have pointed out, there is a definite air of burlesque in these annotations. This distortion of a model while imitating it is one of the most frequently observed traits of mannerism.

In the very next line, we see one of Tristan's favorite mannerist devices, the pun, which he most often stretches into a *pointe*. As he tells us in his notes, *souci* "est un equiuoque" based on the word which is either a type of flower or cares or serious and painful thoughts. Tristan builds on this initial cleverness as he continues to dazzle us with rhetorical display. In line 3 he echoes the personification of Spring by making Acante's tears speak (synecdoche and personification), a unique way to express sobbing. The next line is an antithesis (humides/flame) and in lines 5 and 6 the "rigueurs" of Sylvie are subtly reinforced by the fact that Acante seems to be a piece of the rock on which he is sitting. This bit of cleverness is not original with Tristan; it is a direct imitation of Marino's "I Sospiri":

Sovra un sasso posossi e nel sembiante
non men che'l seggio suo, par a di sasso.

(ll. 21-22)

The final line of the strophe contains a third personification, that of his thoughts, which completes the very strong image of Acante as one who is tortured by being bound to the boulder. Two other *jeux des mots* are found in these lines as Tristan exploits the double meanings of *flame* (flame and love) and *tesmoins* (witness and testimony). This abundant use of rhetoric is found throughout the poem and is not in itself evidence of mannerism. It is Tristan's use of it that determines whether it is mannerist or baroque, and that discussion will conclude this analysis of the poem. Continuing with the summary of the poem, the second through the fifth stanzas are Acante's very Petrarchan laments about the cruelty of his Lady, for neither he nor she convinces us of their pastoral origin. Marino's shepherds are believable; Tristan's are persons of the nobility, who are playing shepherds. Sylvie is very much the traditional cruel Lady of the Provençal love lyric, the Petrarchan *Canzoniere,* and the *Pléiade*'s sonnets, and Tristan's mastery of this tradition can be seen in these four stanzas.

Ariosto, Michelangelo, Garcilaso, Góngora, and Ronsard may be counted among the great poets who subscribed to the poetic tradition of Petrarch. These renaissance poets took the imitation of the Italian master about as far as possible without severely distorting his manner and style. In the late XVIth century, when mannerism first appeared on the scene in France, the imitation of Petrarch had been replaced by imitations of his followers, further distorting the tradition.[17] By the time of Desportes, only a few Petrarchan themes and conceits were imitated, and these were blended with the French courtly tradition, which had never become completely extinct. Those who followed Desportes, such as Tristan, were imitating simply a very pale and limited form of the tradition and demonstrated their poetic prowess in the same way as mannerist painters. They took a part of the masterwork and exaggerated, distorted, and intellectualized it. This is why Tristan cannot be called a Petrarchist poet–he is, at least in his love poetry, a mannerist who seeks to emulate a part rather than the whole. When this aspect of Tristanian style is combined with that of the poet most imitated by Tristan, Marino, we have a pale form of Petrarchism combined with *acutezza* and the will to dazzle and stupefy his audience. An examination of these four strophes will demonstrate this very clearly.

As mannerism replaced the "classical" imitation of the *Pléiade* in the late XVIth and early XVIIth centuries, the themes that were imitated from Petrarch became progressively fewer and a great deal less serious. Where Petrarch had celebrated a Laura who was human and had conceived of a most serious love with religious overtones, the poets who followed him began to intellectualize the ama-

---

[17] For a more complete discussion of Petrarchism, see Lu Emily Pearson, *Elizabethan Love Conventions* (Berkeley: UP of California, 1931) and Stephen Minta, *Petrarch and Petrarchism, The English and French Traditions* (Manchester: UP of Manchester, 1980).

tory genre and "[. . .] they developed a type of mind, clever rather than deep, witty rather than profound." [18] This *Petrarchismo* "[. . .] is the art of treating cleverly and wittily matters of the heart, of composing love-poems without the emotion in the soul, of feigning passion for an imaginary mistress, and of singing a fiction of amorous intrigue, whose phases and whose stages are fixed, and, as it were, established by an immovable tradition." [19] This is simply the "art for art's sake" of the mannerist poets from the *Cinquecento* through Desportes, and it is in this tradition that is found the *petrarchismo* of Tristan L'Hermite. The subject matter and the language of this type of poetry became rigidly fixed by convention as can be seen in the "Plaintes d'Acante." Sylvie's eyes are the envy of the sun, Acante is "mal traité," and under her "amoureuse loy" (ll. 15-21). Acante describes his suffering:

> Depuis que je la sers, les Cieux m'en sont tesmoins,
> Les soupirs et les pleurs sont mes seuls exercices:
> Mais l'ingrate qu'elle est, rebute tous mes soins
> Et se rit de tous mes supplices,
> Et le ressentiment de tant de longs services
> Ne sçauroit porter son orgueil
> A tourner seulement les yeux vers mon Cercueil.
>
> (ll. 22-28)

Tristan uses the old courtly terms appropriated by the followers of Petrarch of feudal loyalty to the Lady who is "ingrate" and only laughs at his service which is marked by loyalty mixed with tears and sighs. The concluding hyperbole is a common-place that Tristan uses quite often in his poetry and it is impossible to determine whether he is being ironic, sarcastic, or imitative in the passage which seems to be written tongue-in-cheek. Whatever the case, he is not being very serious and it seems obvious that his intentions are ludic in nature. The next strophe echoes this one but is more a display of Tristan's virtuosity as is evidenced by his use of paradox, that most mannerist of figures, and oxymoron. In the two strophes, Tristan uses *Petrarchismo* as defined by Berdan and his appropriation of the Italian's conceits and themes is very limited and very much determined by convention.

---

[18] John M. Berdan, "A Definition of *Petrarchismo*," *PMLA* 23 (1913), 699-710.
[19] Berdan, 704.

The mannerism of the poem continues in the next several stanzas as Acante explains his worthiness to Sylvie and invites her to his *locus amoenus* to share his love. As Tristan tells us in the annotations, most of this long section of the poem is inspired by Ovid's *Metamorphoses,* though he fails to mention the strong influence of Marino. Acante tells Sylvie that he is noble (l. 92), brave in battle (l. 51) and faithful–a virtue he illustrates by telling of his rescue of a "Beauté d'vne rare excellence" from a Centaur[20] who had tied her to a tree and had stripped her of her clothing:

> Se voyant exposée à nud deuant mes yeux;
> Son corps possible estoit d'yuoire,
> Mais soit qu'elle fut blanche, ou bien qu'elle fut noire,
> La belle se peut asseurer
> Que je la destachay sans la considerer.
>
> (ll. 80-84)

The eroticism here is very subdued but nevertheless present here as well as in two other places in the poem (ll. 290-294 and 407-413). These three examples are far more restrained than that found in other poets of the day and the very refined beauty of Tristan's descriptions is reminiscent of a mannerist painting such as Clouet's *Lady in the Bath.*

In the description of the private garden of Acante, which is based on the royal gardens in Brussels, we see much that is mannerist. Tristan describes a nature that is peopled by mythological beings, and uses the garden to relate both in poem and in notes his knowledge of the *Metamorphoses*:

> Je vous pourrois monstrer si vous veniez un jour
> En un parc qu'ici prez depuis peu j'ay fait clore,
> Mille Amans transformez, qui des lois de l'Amour,
> Sont passez sous celles de Flore :
>
> (ll. 106-109)

This theme of metamorphosis was called baroque by Rousset, but Raymond and others have considered it mannerist. An interesting aspect of Tristan's description of the garden is his dissertation, in

---

[20] Catherine M. Grisé has pointed out a similar incident in "I Sospiri d'Ergasto," ll. 361-368.

the poem and especially in his notes, on the properties of flowers and their medicinal uses (ll. 120-126 and *Annotations*, 41-42). This seems to be a serious attempt of Tristan to show his erudition, as is his discussion of melancholia in the notes (45-46). Rather than a stylistic effort, this show of erudition seems to be a natural desire of the young poet to show off his knowledge and, as such, cannot be classed as mannerism or baroque.

Lines 155-168 present us with a typical mannerist landscape–a mythological setting with mannerist distortion in the form of a "petite Mer" where:

> On void tousjours mouuoir de *petits personnages*;
> Icy des charpentiers, et là des forgerons,
> Qui travaillent à leurs ouvrages.
> Et force *moulinets,* faicts à diuers usages,
>
> (ll. 162-166, italics mine)

The small-scale picturesque nature of this description is reminiscent of the *putti* and other small personages in mannerist painting, such as the prophet in the *Madonna with the Long Neck.* In a mannerist *tour de force,* Tristan describes "Un grand bassin de Cedre" on which is engraved the story of Vertumnus and Pomona (ll. 190-210); thus Tristan, in his commentary, "s'enchante [. . .] d'un discours *décrivant* un bel objet *décrivant* une fable *décrivant* la ruse de Vertumne. [. . .] Dans ce jeu de miroirs, où s'affiche le maniérisme, la représentation d'une représentation."[21]

The remainder of the scene of the *locus amoenus* serves primarily as a source of metaphor and analogy, as Catherine M. Grisé has pointed out:

> The flowers draw this exclamation from Acante: "Dieux! que ne suis-je entre ces fleurs/ Si vous devez un jour m'arroser de vos pleurs!" (l. 112) (sic); the breeze incites his jealousy: "Car aimant en un plus haut point,/ Je vois que mes soupirs ne vous emeuvent point" (ll. 132-133); in the shady grove one gets lost: "Comme entre mille aimables noeux/ Mon Ame se perdit parmi vos beaux cheveux" (ll. 146-147). Acante tells Sylvie that if she picks up birds they will, like human beings, "perdre leur franchise entre vos belles mains" (l. 231); and the bees will teach her

---

[21] G. Mathieu-Castellani, "La Poésie et son commentaire," 158.

THE *PLAINTES D'ACANTE ET AUTRES OEUVRES* 79

a lesson: "Leur petit Roi volant qui n'a point d'aigûillon,/ Vous enseigneroit la clemence" (ll. 248-249). The descriptive ends are completely subordinate to the ends of love poetry.[22]

Each of these themes cited by Grisé shows the ingenuity of the poet and is thus firmly rooted in the mannerist tradition. Tristan is playing with rhetoric and we can imagine the smile on his face as he wrote these lines, as well as that of his knowing audience as it read them. This part of the poem ends with an exhilarated Acante imagining a boat ride with Sylvie who, as she approaches the water, "[. . .] par un miracle nouveau/ Faire voir à la fois deux Soleils dessus l'eau" (ll. 258-259). Is there a more common mannerist conceit than this? He imagines Sylvie in the boat with him as they pass through that "Christal liquide" peopled by sea nymphs who swim nude to the waist around the craft:

> Et je vous ferois rire apres cette avanture
> Voyant de quelle agilité
> Je ferois le Forçat en ma captivité.
>
> (ll. 292-294)

The final section of this rather lengthy poem (ll. 295-511) begins with Acante's realization that this is an impossible dream and that he will never win the love of Sylvie–it is not in the stars. Tristan was an ardent believer in astrology and here we see a rare glimpse of the poet who blamed his own misfortunes on the stars. Acante, who can only rarely sleep because of his anguish, relates two dreams that are rather bizarre. In the first, when Sylvie tells him "Va t'en loing de mes yeux & ne retourne plus" (l. 343), Acante runs toward a steep precipice to end his pain only to wake up with a start. This is fairly conventional–in the love-lyric many a lover has threatened suicide because of his Lady's cruelty. The next dream is, however, a rather strange one. Acante dreams that Sylvie will marry a rival; an act that will cause his death:

> Embrasé de cholere en cette extremité
> Il m'est avis qu'à l'heure au combat je l'invite;
> Pour l'empescher d'ataindre à la felicité

---

[22] "The Poetry of Tristan L'Hermite," 87-88. The spelling is more modernized than that in Madeleine's edition.

> Qui sembloit deüe à mon merite.
> Mon bras du premier coup heureusement s'aquite
> Du soin de m'en rendre veinqueur,
> Et l'ayant terrassé, je luy mange le coeur.
>
> (ll. 358-364)

This rare instance of the morbid in Tristan's love poetry is probably not an instance of baroque realism but is, rather, as Tristan says in the notes: "N'estoit qu'il recite un songe; & que l'irassible n'est guere moderé par la raison, en une personne qui dort : durant qu'il est en cet estat, les passions reignent confusement en son esprit."[23]

Acante concludes his plaints with a description of a portrait of Sylvie drawn by a skilled *berger* and we get a portrayal of Sylvie through the painting, rather than a real description. The likeness could be of any beautiful lady because there are no real concrete details of her physiognomy given, only the usual mannerist or *précieux* vagaries. The poem concludes when Cloris, a lady experienced in the ways of the world, advises Acante to give up his love. Reason is pitted against love in a lively conversation between the two but Acante will stay the course and continue his sufferings. We are told, as the poem ends, that all of Acante's lamentations have been faithfully taken down by Daphnis who:

> [. . .] de cette amour si fidelle et si tendre
> Marqua les mouvemens diuers,
> Qu'avec peu d'artifice il a mis dans ces vers.
>
> (ll. 509-511)

Tristan is again playing the game, for the poem abounds with artifice.

As we have seen in the preceding discussion, Tristan, in the "Plaintes d'Acante," is very much the mannerist poet. Rhetorical display,[24] imitation, and a ludic spirit are but a few of the mannerist

---

[23] *Annotations* 46; it is also possible that Tristan is simply imitating a fable from the *Metamorphoses* or from Celtic legend. See Gertrude Jobes, *Dictionary of Mythology, Folklore, and Symbols* (New York: Scarecrow, 1961), Part 1, 488, "Eating the Heart."

[24] There are over 20 *pointes* in the poem as well as many examples of paradox, periphrasis, metonymy, synecdoche, personification, antithesis, antonomasia, oxymoron, hypallage, apostrophe, litote, and metaphor, which is usually in the form of a conceit.

traits in these verses. We have what Mathieu-Castellani called a "discours maniériste," nature is mythified, there is no didactic intent in the poem, and Tristan certainly is not trying to convince us of anything. There is no realism in the poem; only an attempt to *faire semblant*, and the objects in the poem exist only in language. Though Acante and Sylvie represent real people, the duc de Bouillon and the comtesse de Bergh, they could be anyone of that class. We have a poem that entertains without moving us, that is pretty, and that is accessible only to an elite audience. I can find no baroque elements in this very early effort of Tristan L'Hermite.

The next poem in the collection, "Contre l'Absance," is echoed by poems XX ("Le Depart de Philis") and XXII ("Aprehension d'un despart") and treats the theme of absence and separation of the lover from his "objet"–a theme that we will see much more of in *Les Amours*. [25] Once again, we see poems in which Tristan follows very closely the Petrarchan tradition that he enhances with rhetorical display reminiscent of his Italian master, Marino. Though others, including Bernardin, have seen these poems as evidence of a great passion in the life of our poet, a more formalistic approach will reveal them as nothing more than mannerist *tours de force*. The theme of the pains of absence from the beloved is as old as the Provençal lyric and it was used extensively by Petrarch and his followers. [26] It is simply a manifestation of the primary theme of the suffering of the lover. Tristan's treatment of this very common motif contains much that can be termed "mannerist."

At first glance the poem opens in a very grandiose manner that recalls the more serious baroque style of d'Aubigné or Sponde:

> La Terre dans ses tremblemens,
> La Mer en ses desbordemens,
> Mars, en sa plus grande licence;

---

[25] Other poems by Tristan on the subject of the absence of the loved one are: in *Les Amours*: "L'Absence ennuyeuse" (23), "Le Despart forcé" (24-25), "L'Amant en langueur" (30), and "L'Absence de Philis" (57-62); *La Lyre*: "Pour une absence" (28-29), "Le Depart" (93-94), and "Les Avantages d'une longue absence" (199); *Les Vers héroïques*: "O Beauté qu'un depart afflige" (209), "Consolation sur un depart" (213), and "Sur une facheuse absence" (322). Page numbers refer to the editions of Camo, Chauveau, and Grisé.

[26] Grisé, in "The Poetry of Tristan L'Hermite," gives examples of this theme in the poetry of Petrarch, Ronsard, Desportes, d'Urfé, Georges de Scudéry, Théophile, Saint-Amant, and Malherbe (96, note 26).

Toutes les matieres de pleurs,
Et tous les plus cruels malheurs
Qui font soupirer l'Innocence;
Auprix des maux qui fait l'absance
Ne sont rien que jeux & que fleurs.

(ll. 1-8)

The hyperbolic opening of the strophe is soon reduced to the familiar use of a *pointe* in the chute, by which the grand is reduced to the trivial. This procedure effectively introduces the theme of the poem, which will be a conventional rendering of the topic of the pains of separation. Mackey praises the first three stanzas but refuses even to discuss the remainder of the poem which "[. . .] degenerates into the disappointing verbosity and lack of unity that is not unusual in Tristan's longer efforts" (57). This seems to be a rather harsh judgment because Tristan shows great skill in his manipulation of the Petrarchan theme. He links the pains of absence to the old *topos* of the *lausenghier* who has slandered both him and her during this period of separation:

Les Rivaux, de devoirs pressans
Corrompans les meilleurs courages,
Font sur mille faux temoignages
Condemner les pauvres absans.

(ll. 37-40)

The poem concludes with the very Petrarchan statement that Philis is not like other women for she is divine:

Ce seroit fort mal raisonner
Que de la vouloir soupsonner
Des deffauts d'un sexe infidelle:
Si l'on en croit mille bontez
Et mille rares qualitez
Qui sont d'une marque immortelle,
Les sentimens de cette Belle
Sont divins comme ses beautez.

(ll. 81-88)

Once more, as is so often the case with Tristan's love poetry, we have an *objet* that is devoid of any authenticity. She is no more than an abstraction who lacks any physical reality and serves only as a means for the poet to demonstrate his mastery of the conventions of the genre. The other two poems in the collection are shorter variations on the same theme. The playful nature of "Le Despart de Philis" may be seen in Tristan's choice of the madrigal as the form of the poem. Though the madrigal was a serious form of poetry in the sixteenth century, it had become far less so in the seventeenth and was primarily used to show the wit of its author. Tristan uses it in this instance as a vehicle to demonstrate his cleverness in the composition of a *pointe*. After the usual hyperbolic description of his suffering at the thought of separation from his beloved, Tristan delivers his very mannerist paradox/conceit:

> Je n'ay plus qu'un moment à vivre
> Et plus de mille ans à mourir.
>
> (ll. 9-10)

He says the very same thing in the "Aprehension d'un despart" but says it better and more cleverly. After lamenting his prospective separation from Iris in the same hyperbolic manner as is his wont, Tristan concludes the sonnet with an ingenious conceit:

> Quoy, tu ne me dis rien dans ces extremitez?
> Ah! par cette froideur mes jours sont limitez,
> Adieu donc, o Beauté d'insensible courage.
>
> Puis que ma passion ne t'en peut divertir,
> Nous ferons, à mesme heure, un different voyage,
> Mon Ame est comme toy toute preste à partir.
>
> (ll. 9-14)

These three poems all conform to the definition that has been established for mannerism: elite audience, imitation (petrarchismo), rhetorical display, ludic nature, and use of the *discours maniériste*.

Placed after "Contre l'absence" and just before the "Promenoir des deux amans" is a "Consolation à Idalie, Sur la mort d'un Parant" (56-57). In a volume of *poésie galante* this poem and the other consolatory poem, "Consolation à Antoine de Villeneuve, seigneur de Monts" (83-85), seem badly out of place. A closer examination of the former, however, reveals an ingenious combination of a Malherbian consolation with one of the favorite motifs of the mannerist poets, the *carpe diem*. The poem abounds with Horatian commonplaces: Death comes to all no matter how noble, brave, or beautiful, as is demonstrated by examples from mythology and history (ll. 1-16). Though the poem is written to a specific individual, Idalie, it may be assumed that she does not necessarily exist beyond the imagination of the poet. The name Idalie is a common one in the amorous poetry of the period and can refer to a fictitious person or be used to hide the name of a real one. If the poem did not suddenly turn to gallantry in line 17, the latter might be the case. It is hard to believe that Tristan would use a real tragedy to seduce the grieving relative. Therefore, despite the baroque and Malherbian beginning, the poem ends as a mannerist love poem replete with rhetorical display and *Petrarchismo*. Rhetoric in the first half of the poem is used seriously to reflect on death; in the second half, it is a tool of seduction:

> On ne vous verra plus avant qu'il soit cent ans,
> Si ce n'est dans mes vers qui vivront d'auantage.
>
> (ll. 19-20)
>
> [. . . . .]
>
> Dés que nous commençons à raisonner un peu,
> En l'Avril de nos ans, en l'age le plus tendre,
> Nous rencontrons l'Amour qui met nos coeurs en feu,
> Puis nous treuvons la Mort qui met nos corps en cendre.
>
> Le Temps qui sans repos, va d'un pas si leger,
> Emporte avecque luy toutes les belles choses :
> C'est pour nous avertir de le bien mesnager
> Et faire des bouquets en la saison des roses.
>
> (ll. 25-32)

The poem is a clever manipulation of convention, which surely was well received by the courtiers at Brussels and, later, in France. It is interesting to note, as Guichemerre has pointed out,[27] that Malherbe used the same device in his "Consolation à Caritée." A reading of the two poems reveals Tristan to be the more skillful at combining the two elements. Indeed, this poem is a complete success according to the standards of mannerist poetry that had be-

---

[27] *Quatre poètes*, 115.

come enamoured with the Marinistic aim of *fare stupir.* The reader is dazzled by the sudden shift of the poem's tone, delighted at the plays on words, and amused by the subtle introduction of the *carpe diem* motif.

The other consolation is different and cannot by any means be considered ludic or lacking in seriousness. In the seventeenth century, the poem and letter of consolation followed the dictates of the Demonstrative genre of rhetoric, which was based heavily on classical models. In this poem, there is very little of the dazzling rhetorical display that we associate with mannerism or baroque. This is probably because of the example of Malherbe, who was considered the model to follow in this genre. Malherbe was highly esteemed by Tristan, who follows him in most of his occasional poetry. The poem is logical in content, universal in its didacticism, and its stanzas of five alexandrines followed by an octosyllabic line are clear and harmonious. In stanzas 1 and 2, he tells de Monts that his grief for his deceased brother has lasted too long and that he, like nature, must put aside adversity in order to thrive once more: "Et les mesmes Vergers se couronnent de roses/ Qui se herissoient de glaçons" (ll. 29-30). He then appeals to the example of de Monts' ancestors and, next, to that of Hector:

> L'invincible Troyen que la gloire animoit
> Fut privé comme toy d'un Frere qu'il aymoit,
> Ainsi qu'ils s'acharnoient sur une Grecque bande :
> Mais bien qu'il fut touché d'un sentiment humain,
> S'il pleura tout un jour d'une perte si grande,
> Il s'arma dès le lendemain.
>
> (ll. 49-54)

The very last lines of the poem provide an excellent summation of Tristan's advice to de Monts on one hand and to all who read the poem on the other: "Lors qu'on ne peut gauchir la mauuaise auanture,/ On la braue en la suportant" (ll. 65-66). This poem, with its restrained, clear verses is very clearly not a mannerist creation. It is, rather, an excellent example of the *baroque dompté.*

Due to the economic situation of the poet in the seventeenth century, Tristan, like almost all of his fellow writers, was forced to be a *poète à gages* dependent on a patron. Because his patrons, most notably Gaston d'Orléans, were not always reliable sources of in-

come, Tristan, like many of his colleagues, often wrote poetry for
wealthy noblemen at court who enlisted his aid in their amorous
pursuits. We have already seen this in our discussion of the
"Plaintes d'Acante" and we will see much more evidence of this in
his other love lyrics. In the very restricted coterie for whom Tristan
wrote, certain conventions were expected to be observed and that
restricted the freedom of the artist to innovate. The basis of these
conventions was Petrarchism, but it soon became so routine and
predictable that even the most dull-witted courtier grew weary of it.
The innovations of Giambattista Marino gave this very sterile poetry a new set of themes and a new poetics without breaking completely with the Petrarchan tradition. [28] When he composed poetry
for friends or patrons, Tristan often wrote in the old manner but
soon began to imitate Marino and his most successful efforts en-
sued. As we examine the many love poems in the *Plaintes d'Acante*,
we will see poems of both types.

There are twenty sonnets in the *Plaintes d'Acante et autres oeuvres*, seventeen of which can be classified as *poésie galante* and are
mannerist. They reflect imitation, are for an élite audience, and use
many figures of rhetoric; they all end with a conceit in the final tercet. Since these poems are so similar, I will undertake a study of the
most outstanding ones, most of which use Petrarchan vocabulary
and images but are spiced by the influence of Marino. An excellent
summary of the Petrarchan vocabulary of love may be found in
Grisé's study:

> Throughout the love poetry, Tristan's vocabulary is largely Pe-
> trarchan in provenance. Love is alluded to as a *poison* ("Plainte à
> l'Amour," *Amours*, p. 14), as a *flamme* or *feu* ("Les Tourmens
> agréables," *Plaintes*, p. 65), as *chaînes* ("Le Bracelet," *Amours*, p.
> 81). The lover spends his nights and days in *pleurs* and *soupirs*
> ("L'Humeur ingrate," *Plaintes*, p. 87). He undergoes *tourments*
> ("Chanson," *Plaintes*, p. 89), *supplices* ("La Fatalité d'amour,"
> *Amours*, p. 23), a *martyre* ("Le Depit salutaire," *Amours*, p. 20),
> and cannot sleep ("Les Travaux inutiles," *Amours*, p. 33). The
> lady, his *vainqueur* ("L'Avis considérable," *Plaintes*, p. 66), his

---

[28] I am indebted to Catherine M. Grisé for many of these observations; for a
much more detailed account of Petrarchism and Marinism in the poetry of Tristan
L'Hermite, see her "The Poetry of Tristan L'Hermite," 47-101. See also Abraham,
Tristan L'Hermite, 31-77.

soleil "Pour la belle esclairée," *Amours*, p. 29), is full of *orgueil* ("Le Depit corrigé," *Plaintes*, p. 66) and *cruauté* ("La Pitié cruelle," *Amours*, p. 31). She is as unfeeling as a *roc* ("Le depit corrigé," *Plaintes,* p. 66), and her heart is as cold as *glace* ("Résolution d'aimer," *Plaintes*, p. 69).[29]

The following examples from the love sonnets will demonstrate further the Petrarchan vocabulary of Tristan, as well as the combination of Marinistic and Petrarchan themes, images, and conceits.

Poem IX, "L'Excusable erreur," is typical of the love sonnets; it is very Petrarchan in vocabulary and ends with *acutezza* in imitation of Marino. After having described his *maîtresse* in hyperbolic terms (she is his "veinqueur," and he even loves her cruelty and "rigueur,"), he closes the sonnet with a witty message to the gods:

> Si je l'adore aussi, pardonnez moy grands Dieux ;
> En un pareil sujet on se peut bien mesprendre,
> Il n'est rien icy bas qui vous ressemble mieux.
>
> (ll. 12-14)

This pattern is seen in the other sonnets, but on occasions he will take a metaphor and "spin" it throughout the poem. "Les Cheveux blonds" is an excellent example of this device, which was much used by mannerist writers. The extended metaphor is the idea of the lady's hair as spun gold that forms the web in which the poet is trapped. The lady takes the freedom of the hair away as she holds it with her hand, just as it has taken Tristan's freedom away. As she binds her golden tresses: "On oste la franchise à qui me l'a ravie" (l. 14). Since he is a very gifted poet, Tristan succeeded in giving his love sonnets enough variety to avoid the sameness that is found in those of some of his contemporaries.

Marino and his Italian followers had sought variety by placing their ladies in unusual circumstances where the pure Petrarchan would never find beauty. As a result, new themes were developed which became very popular throughout Europe in the seventeenth century: *la bella malata, la bella nera, la bella mendica, la bella cieca, la bella vedova, la bella zoppa*, etc. In the *Plaintes d'Acante* is found one of Tristan's masterpieces in which he deals with "La Belle en

---

[29] "The Poetry of Tristan L'Hermite," 55-56.

dueil." The poem is a superb imitation of a poem by Marino, "La bella vedova" (*La Lira,* III, 4).[30] The poem uses the device of *chiaroscuro,* which was very popular with baroque and mannerist poets, as a means of making the antithesis between this "belle nuit animée" and the brightness of day, which is envious of her. The theme continues with a very effective simile:

> La flamme esclate moins à trauers la fumée
> Que ne font vos beaux yeux sous un si sombre atour,
>
> (ll. 5-6)

Her divinity is established in the following lines (7-8) and it is made clear that she, unlike those divinities who are no longer worshipped, has been personified as Love through the intercession of Venus:

> Car vous voyant si belle, on pense à votre abord
> Que par quelque gageure où Venus s'interesse,
> L'Amour s'est desguisé sous l'habit de la Mort.
>
> (ll. 12-14)

Another poem of this type is "La Belle malade" in which the poet, seeing his beloved Philis on her deathbed, invokes Cupid to change the dart of Death into an arrow of love and, in doing so, Death "Pensant perdre vne vie, elle en conserve deux" (l. 14). Though one might see this poem as reflecting a true situation in which Tristan is sincerely grieving, it seems far more likely that he is only showing his virtuosity in playing the game that was the mannerist love lyric.

Two of these sonnets contain more eroticism than is usual for Tristan and are interesting examples of his ludic temperament. Though he starts "La Negligence avantageuse" in a very erotic manner, he ends with a simple play on words and a conceit about her uncoiffed hair pressing his heart. The other amatory sonnet is far more erotic and clever than the preceding one. "Jalousie" is a well played game in which Tristan playfully complains that a god of

---

[30] For a more detailed study of the imitation of Marino, see Grisé, "The Poetry of Tristan L'Hermite," 81-82. The poem is also discussed by Guichemerre, *Quatre poètes,* 103-104.

the water in which Clorinde was bathing nude has seen "tous les apas dont la Belle est pourveue" (l. 6) and worse:

> Le traistre, l'insolent, n'estant qu'une eau versée,
> L'a baisée en tous lieux, l'a toujours embrassée ;
>
> (ll. 9-10)

To make matters even worse, this water divinity has been only very lightly punished by Clorinde who:

> Après tous ces excez n'a fait pour le punir
> Que donner à son Onde une couleur d'albastre.
>
> (ll. 13-14)

If one of the demands of poetry in Tristan's day was the use of wit within the conventions of the love lyric, he was fully capable of meeting them, as the preceding sonnets abundantly demonstrate.

These openly mannerist *tours de force* are accompanied by a poem which I believe to have been inspired by a well-known painting by Rosso, which was on display at Fontainebleau at the time Tristan lived there. "Le Ravissement d'Europe" was obviously the source of Tristan's description of Europa's being carried off by Zeus who was disguised as a white bull. The painting clearly shows Europa with one hand on the croup and the other on one of the bull's horns.[31] His graphic description in the first quatrain soon turns to mannerist word play as Neptune appears and says to Zeus, reflecting the seventeenth-century French obsession with *cocuage*:

> Puisque malgré Junon tu veux avoir des cornes,
> Que ne s'en resoust elle à t'en faire porter.
>
> (ll. 13-14)

Another very mannerist trait is a fondness for the *blason* in which the beauty of the lady is described in very conventional terms. Such a poem is the last sonnet in the collection, "Portrait d'vne rare beavté," in which Tristan attempts to paint a portrait of Iris in his verses. Working with the aid of Amour, the poet starts the portrait:

---

[31] Marino had also written about this subject, so perhaps the inspiration is twofold.

> Son visage de lys & sa bouche de roses
> Ou dans un double rang, des perles sont encloses
> Qui n'ont jamais paré les Nimphes de la Mer.
> Faisons ce teint de neige & composons de flame
> L'esclat de ces beaux yeux, de ces Rois de mon Ame,
> Par qui l'Astre du jour se verroit effacer.
>
> (ll. 6-11)

This description which in no way refers to any specific person is simply another mannerist game that Tristan is enjoying. By his mastery of these Petrarchan commonplaces, he is demonstrating that he can play it well.

Because of their titles, two of the sonnets might be considered baroque: "A des cimetières" and "Sur un tombeau." The former begins on a very "baroque" note as Tristan describes this "Seiour melancholique" with "tombes relantes," "ossemens entassez," and "pierres parlantes." He then addresses the Tombeaux:

> Vous donnez de la crainte et de l'horreur à tous ;
> Mais le plus doux object qui s'ofre à ma pensée
> Est beaucoup plus funeste et plus triste que vous.
>
> (ll. 12-14)

Once more, despite a very serious beginning, we have a witty love poem with no serious intent on the part of its creator. "Sur un tombeau" is considered, at first glance, as the reflection of a real situation in the life of our author and, hence, is a baroque poem because of its "sincerity." While I do not dispute this notion, I would suggest an alternate reading of the poem and another interpretation of it. Because of the poetry of Ronsard and others,[32] the theme of the death of the loved one had become a commonplace and was treated seriously in some cases and with levity in others. In the case of this sonnet, it is possible that Tristan, in his search for variety in theme and discourse, used the theme of death as a vehicle for the very clever conceit that ends the poem:

---

[32] See, for example, Ronsard's "Sur la mort de Marie," a series of poems on the death of Marie de Clèves; Desportes ended his sequence, *Les Amours d'Hypolyte*, with the death of the loved one and Théophile treated the subject with levity in "Maintenant que Philis est morte" and in "Je songeois que Philis des enfers revenüe."

La Parque n'a coupé nostre fil qu'à moitié,
Car je meurs en ta cendre & tu vis dans ma flame.

(ll. 13-14)

Whether or not the poem is "real," it is *vraisemblable,* and that is all that is required of a mannerist poem that seeks to please its elite audience. There is no didacticism nor is there any attempt to convey universal truth–it is simply an excellent sonnet that appealed to its select audience.[33]

There is one sonnet in the volume that is apparently baroque, "L'Amour divin," wherein Tristan rejects profane love in favor of divine. In this sonnet, the issue of sincerity is relevant to our interpretation and classification of the poem. Both Carriat and Abraham[34] are of the opinion that the young Tristan was rather a free thinker in matters of religion and that he became sincerely religious in his last years. We will examine this question in the chapter that studies Tristan's religious verse, but, for the present, let us accept the first proposition that Tristan was a libertine in the sense that he was not orthodox in matters of the Faith. If this is true, two questions immediately come to mind: Was he sincere? and if not, Why did he write such a poem and include it in his first volume of poetry?

Though it cannot be established beyond any doubt that Tristan is either sincere or disingenuous in this poem, it is likely that he wrote it without the passion of such baroque writers as Chassignet or Sponde and that he has no intention to bring anyone to belief by means of it. The most likely reason for Tristan's including this poem in his first volume of poetry is simply survival. One of the most traumatic experiences in his youth was the imprisonment and persecution of Théophile de Viau, whom Tristan both admired and imitated. When the volume was published, Tristan was in exile with Gaston d'Orléans, who was accused of treason. It is likely, then, that the young poet inserted this poem into the volume for his own safety–he did not wish to be accused of free thinking, which cer-

---

[33] It should be noted that Tristan, in the "Advertissement à qvi lit," states very clearly that he intends the volume for the *élite*: "Au reste ie t'auertis que cet Ouurage n'est point fait à l'vsage de tout le monde, Et que s'il y a icy de mauuais vers, ils ne sont pas toute-fois de la Iuridiction des esprits vulgaires, encore qu'il m'importe peu s'ils sont condemnez mal à propos, par des juges qui ne seroient pas capables de les fauoriser de bonne grace" (p. 4).

[34] See *Tristan L'Hermite*, 69-77 for a very logical presentation of Tristan's religious thinking.

tainly would increase his problems with Richelieu. Therefore, he probably feigned piety to save himself from the kind of treatment that Théophile received. Tristan, himself, admitted, in one of his *Lettres meslées*: "Vous sçavez que j'ay le bruit d'estre plutost libertin que bigot." [35] It is not difficult to doubt Tristan's sincerity while admiring his skill at self-preservation. The *pointe* in the last two lines, based on the two meanings of *trais*, and the theme of the ingratitude of the lady are perhaps further evidence of the insincerity of a poem which, on the surface, is a sincere statement of the superiority of divine love to profane.

There are six *stances* in the collection that have not been discussed (XV, XVI, XVIII, XIX, XXV, and LXXIX). The first four are simply Petrarchan lyrics treating the theme of the power of love over reason and lack the witty conceits of the sonnets. They are mannerist in the same way that the sonnets are but are very conventional and lack the *ingegno* that characterizes his shorter efforts. The fifth *stance*, "Louanges du vert," is a poem written for Puylaurens during the exile in Brussels. Puylaurens had worn blue, the color of Henriette de Lorraine, but had recently fallen in love with Anne de Beaumont and had changed the color that he wore to green, the preferred color of Anne. [36] It is a clever encomium of the color, presented in a mock-serious manner that shows more *esprit* than do the others. The last of the *stances* is an occasional piece that celebrates the arrival of Madame, Marguerite de Lorraine, in Brussels after she had escaped the authorities by dressing as a man. This is a very baroque encomium, for Tristan, along with all of Gaston's retinue, was genuinely impressed with Madame's bravery and delighted to see her in the Belgian capitol. He follows Malherbe's example and uses hyperbole to praise Marguerite's bravery, parentage, and beauty. [37] The baroque nature of Tristan's occasional pieces will be discussed in more detail in the chapters on *La Lyre* and the *Vers héroïques*.

Tristan's madrigals, poems XXVI, XXXIII, and XL are nothing more than hyperbolic encomia of the poet's "maistresses." His poem, "Pour une excellente beauté qui se miroit," could serve as a

---

[35] *Lettres meslées*, ed. Grisé, 192.

[36] This information was found in the memoirs of Gaston d'Orléans by Grisé, see "The Poetry of Tristan L'Hermite," 50-51.

[37] For more on the influence of Malherbe on this poem, see Guichemerre, *Quatre poètes*, 114-115.

textbook on *préciosité,* for he uses many of the favorite devices of the *habituées* of the *ruelles.* The first four lines gave birth to a favorite conceit of the salons:

> Amarillis en se regardant
> Pour se conseiller de sa grace
> Met aujourdhuy des feux dans cette glace
> Et d'un christal commun fait un Miroir ardant.

The poem continues with praise of her charms and spins the metaphor delightfully:

> O Dieux! que de charmans apas
> Que d'oeillets, de lys & de roses,
> Que de clartez & que d'aymables choses,
> Amarille destruit en s'escartant d'un pas!

(ll. 21-24)

This poem is clearly of the *précieux* style of mannerism.

The last poem to be considered in this chapter, "Le Promenoir des deux amants," is the one by which Tristan is best known, thanks probably to the fact that Debussy put it to music. From a strictly literary perspective, it is certainly one of his masterpieces and it is Tristan's finest effort in the style of mannerism. The poem is built around the central motif of the *locus amoenus* and is an invitation to Climène to join the poet in this secluded paradise and receive his protestations of love. If there is one adjective that describes a mannerist work of art, it is "pretty." Tristan provides us with a description of nature that is idyllic, restful, calming, and conducive to seduction. This is an idealized landscape that is peopled by mythological beings who serve to reinforce the pastoral ambience of the poem. It is the happy combination of idealized nature and love that Tristan blends in verses of exquisite harmony that is the explanation for the charm of the work. This, combined with a dazzling rhetorical display, gives us a mannerist work *par excellence.* A look at the rhetorical devices employed by Tristan in this poem will aid in our appreciation of his effort.

Among the many figures of speech used by Tristan in the poem are: personification (ll. 3, 13-16, 25-28, 49-50), antithesis (ll. 111-112, 4), oxymoron (l. 100 and oxymoron based on antithesis, ll. 111-112), periphrasis (ll. 105-106, 107-108, 91, 17-20), hyperbole (ll. 71-72), paradox (l. 76), and metonymy (l. 51). He uses *pointes* (ll. 95-96 and 91-92) and *pointes doubles* (ll. 79-80) and sensory appeals such as olfactory (ll. 2 and 63), visual (ll. 4, 66 and throughout the poem), and auditory (ll. 3 and 57-58). Mythological images abound in the poem and all but one (strophe 25, an allusion to *L'Astrée*) are to classical sources, most notably the *Metamorphoses* and the *Aeneid*. In many mannerist paintings, there are always present one or more *putti* and Tristan adds them to his landscape in lines 43, where he has two *putti* attending the meetings of Venus and Anchises, and 77-80, where he has:

> Voy mille Amours qui se vont prendre
> Dans les filets de tes cheueux ;
> Et d'Autres qui cachent leur feux
> Dessous vne si belle cendre.

This rich display of rhetoric, for no purpose other than the amusement of his aristocratic audience, is clearly the mannerist Tristan at his best.

With the very few exceptions noted above, this first volume of the poetry of Tristan L'Hermite is clearly mannerist, as will be *Les Amours*, and most of *La Lyre*. In examining these two volumes, I shall try to avoid the poems that are exactly like those of this volume and concentrate on the ones that offer something different to discuss, while not omitting his better efforts. In addition, an attempt will be made to show the evolution of Tristan from his youthful endeavors to his more mature works. Increasing attention will be paid to Malherbian influences as representative of the baroque in Tristan–a subdued and "classical" *baroque dompté*.

CHAPTER VI

MANNERISM AND BAROQUE IN *LES AMOURS DE TRISTAN*

I N 1638, Tristan, who was now something of a celebrity because
of the success of *La Mariane* in 1636, decided to capitalize on his
renown by issuing a second volume of poetry. He decided to issue
an augmented version of the *Plaintes d'Acante,* which had been
published five years before. He left all the poems of the *Plaintes* in
the volume but omitted the *Annotations* and included, in addition
to the forty-one previously published compositions, eighty-one
"new" poems, most of which deal with love. He dedicated the work
to Edme de La Châtre, Comte de Nançay, and, in the *Avertissement,* he made a very important distinction between this, his early
work, and that which was to follow. Tristan seems to be dividing his
works into mannerism and baroque:

> Voicy des premieres productions de mon esprit, & des effets de
> ma jeunesse : Il faut que le Printemps pousse des fleurs, auant
> que l'Automne produise des fruits. C'est un ordre de la Nature
> qui se rencontre dans le cours de nôtre vie, comme dans celuy de
> l'année. Aussi ie vous donne ces ouurages qui sont faits seule-
> ment pour plaire, attendant que i'en mette d'autres au jour, qui
> puissent plaire et profiter tout ensemble. Cela fera voir, que pour
> reparer la perte du temps que i'ay mis au moins quelques loisirs
> en des travaux plus vtiles & et plus serieux. [1]

---

[1] Tristan L'Hermite, *Les Amours de Tristan,* ed. Pierre Camo (Paris: Garnier,
1925), 5. All quotations from *Les Amours* will be from this edition. Madelaine's edition of the *Plaintes d'Acante* also contains the complete text of the *Amours.*

The initial sonnet in the volume, appropriately entitled "Le Prélude," sets the tone for the entire volume as Chauveau[2] has demonstrated:

> Ie n'escry point icy l'embrazement de Troye,
> Ses larmes, ses soupirs, & ses cris éclatans,
> Ny l'effroy qui saisit ses tristes habitans
> Lors que des Grecs vainqueurs ils se virent la proye.
>
> I'y dépeins seulement les pleurs dont ie me noye,
> Le feu qui me consume, & les deuoirs constans
> Qu'auecque tant de soing i'ay rendus si long temps
> A celle dont l'orgueil au sepulcre m'enuoye.
>
> Aussi ie n'atten pas que le bruit de mes vers,
> Portant ma renommée au bout de l'Vniuers,
> Estande ma memoire au delà de ma vie :
>
> I'en veux moins acquerir d'honneur que d'amitié;
> Les autres ont dessein de donner de l' enuie,
> Et le point où i'aspire est de faire pitié.

As he tells us, the work will consist primarily of variations on the neo-Petrarchist theme of unhappy or impossible love. The tone of the volume is still overwhelmingly mannerist, but it is not only the witty, picturesque mannerism of the *Plaintes d'Acante*; it is the beginning of what Abraham has called the other, darker Tristan–a Tristan who is beginning to show evidence of his baroque side.

The volume contains much that is like that of the *Plaintes d'Acante* and some of these poems are excellent demonstrations of Tristan's mastery of the genre. Indeed, they excel in the use of the Petrarchan language and the Marinistic *acutezza* that were the trademarks of his earlier publication. Among the many sonnets added to those of the *Plaintes d'Acante* are several that are worthy of note because they embody new mannerist variations on the Pe-

---

[2] Jean-Pierre Chauveau, "Le Prélude, Stances A l'honneur de Sylvie, Ode A Monsieur de Montauron," *Cahiers Tristan L'Hermite* 14 (1992): 7-15. Professor Chauveau ably demonstrates that each of these poems serves as a sort of overture to the volumes they head. He likens them to an operatic overture where parts of the arias and choruses are played to give the audience a taste of what is to come. This is certainly true of the *Amours* and the *Plaintes d'Acante* and is true to a lesser degree of *La Lyre*.

trarchan themes of which Tristan was so fond. There are nine of these sonnets that are typical of the group and each reflects an interesting variation on the theme of love in its many aspects. All, however, reflect the general traits of mannerism as outlined by the Spanish critic Emilio Carilla, who contrasted mannerism with baroque as follows:

Manierismo

Anticlasicismo.
Subjetividad, intelectualismo.
Aristocracia, refinamiento.
Ornamentación (excesiva).
Dinamismo (movimiento y torsión).
Medievalismo (o goticismo).

Barroco

Límite borroso entre Clasicismo y Anticlasicismo.
Predominio de valores religiosos, contrarreformistas.
Contención (determinada particularmente por vallas políticas y religiosas).
Dinamismo (menos forzado que en el Manierismo).
Monumentalidad y pomposidad.
Realismo (con inclinación a lo feo y lo grotesco).
Popularismo (mayor captación popular que en el Manierismo).
En fin, continuidad y aprovechamiento de ciertos caracteres manieristas. [3]

To these general characteristics of mannerism should be added some remarks about the mannerist (and Tristanian) treatment of the lady and the poet's relation to her.

Where Petrarch had described a definite person in Laura and where Ronsard and his followers had written whole volumes to the same lady, Tristan writes to many different ladies who are simply abstractions. He uses as many themes as Ronsard but his poems are not sequential and his addressees are impossible to identify because they either did not exist, except in the poet's mind, or they were the *maistresses* of courtiers, for whom Tristan served as a *poète à gages*.

---

[3] *Manierismo y barroco en las literaturas hispánicas* (Madrid: Gredos, 1983), 153-154.

As Yvonne Bellenger has demonstrated, while Tristan observed strictly the lexicon of Petrarchism, he rejects completely its Grammar:

> L'attitude de l'amant devant sa maîtresse est codifiée dans la poésie depuis quelques siècles. Les avatars du pétrarquisme occupent toute la Renaissance et Tristan est contemporain de la période qui en voit la fin. Il serait donc possible [. . .] d'énumérer point par point les motifs et les composantes de l'attitude pétrarquiste, puis de montrer dans quelle mesure Tristan (c'est à dire, par convention, celui qui dit « je » dans les poèmes de Tristan) les respecte, les enfreint ou les oublie. Tristan aime, souffre, gémit; il proteste, il regimbe. [. . .] dans ces poèmes lyriques, l'attitude de l'amant se caractérise par le respect de plusieurs données traditionnelles héritées du pétrarquisme : la posture plus ou moins morfondue de l'homme, sa soumission aux cruautés d'une belle indifférente ou capricieuse, ses sursauts sporadiques de révolte, sa réaction quelquefois irritée ou blessée. [. . .] Tristan est bel et bien un amant pétrarquiste qui « fait l'amoureux transi » . . . R. Melançon observe que « par pétrarquisme, il ne faut pas entendre tellement l'imitation de Pétrarque ou des poètes italiens qui s'inscrivent dans son sillage, que le recours à un code–à des thèmes et à un langage particuliers–pour parler d'amour », code qui n'est pas seulement un lexique, c'est-à-dire un répertoire de thèmes, de situations-types–en somme, ce qu'on trouve abondamment chez Tristan–mais une grammaire, c'est-à-dire des structures-types organisant ces thèmes, ces motifs, ces topoi : schémas oxymorontiques, assemblages de poèmes en séquences ordonnées, etc. L'analyse de R. Melançon aide à montrer comment Tristan, qui respecte le « lexique » pétrarquiste dans sa poésie lyrique (*l'inventio*), en rejette complètement la « grammaire » (la *dispositio*).[4]

She describes Tristan's rejection of the "grammar" of Petrarchism as: (1) His collections of poetry are not *canzonieri*; they contain poems to several different women. (2) His women have no real existence; they are "purs personnages de papier" (p. 9). (3) Even in his dedicatory letters to real women, the praise is determined by mannerist tradition. (4) In Tristan's amorous poetry, décor, such as the

---

[4] "L' « Objet » amoureux dans la poésie de Tristan," *Cahiers Tristan L'Hermite* 5 (1983): 8.

locus in the "Promenoir des deux amants," predominates over the person loved. (5) Only those women who fail to conform to the Petrarchist norm are described in any detail ("La Gouvernante importune," "La Belle esclave Maure"). With the input of the studies of Bellenger and Carilla, added to the previous discussions of mannerism and baroque, we may turn to specific poems in the *Amours* to consider Tristan's utilization of the two styles.

As was the case with the *Plaintes d'Acante et autres oeuvres*, *Les Amours* consists primarily of sonnets and *stances*, plus some odes and, unlike the first volume, a large number of epigrams. The sonnets reflect very well the above-mentioned characteristics and will be discussed first, followed by the *stances*; the odes and the epigrams in the volume are of no real significance to this study and will not be discussed. This chapter will conclude with a discussion of the very small baroque part of the collection. As will be demonstrated, the *Amours*, like the *Plaintes d'Acante*, are overwhelmingly mannerist, but one can perceive the beginning of a change in tone that will presage the increasingly baroque tendencies of Tristan L'Hermite.

"Les Agréables pensées" (34-35) [5] is a sonnet used as an example of Tristan's mannerism by Helmut Hatzfeld in a very discerning article published in 1966. [6] He points out a characteristic of mannerist poetry that he calls "riddle-metaphors" and cites the first line of the sonnet as the riddle and the second as its solution. This build-up occurs in a much lighter form than does the same phenomenon in baroque poetry. The fact that both mannerism and baroque have many common motifs and devices has caused many critics to confuse the two: "But indecisive Mannerism lacks seriousness when using for instance *sham paradoxes*. In Mannerism there never will be found *necessary* paradoxes of Pascal's symbolic type: *un roseau pensant,* but only playful ones like 'ces mains *celestement blanches* avec leurs bras *mortellement divins*' (M. Scève, *Dizain* 367)..." (228). The variation on the theme of *souffrances amoureuses* in the sonnet is the very traditional one of the lover in prison, this time he is the prisoner of Ysabelle the sight of whom is his "souverain bien."

---

[5] All page numbers refer to the Camo edition.
[6] "Mannerism is not baroque," *L'Esprit Créateur* 6 (1966): 225-233. Hatzfeld points out the interesting fact that Valéry Larbaud took the opening words of this sonnet as the title of one of his *Monologues intérieurs*, "Mon Plus secret conseil."

An interesting treatment of the theme occurs in the very clever piece, "Les Remèdes inutiles," which he addressed to the noted physician, Charles de Lorme, "premier médecin de Gaston d'Orléans," who had treated Tristan for his recurring fever on at least two occasions.[7] Unlike his letters to Dr. de Lorme, this poem is nothing more than another form of the suffering lover motif and its mock-seriousness provides an interesting vehicle for one of the poet's favorite metaphors and themes. Tristan tells the physician that he has been cruelly wounded and that he has been unable to recover. The sestet of the poem is a very Petrarchan description of the pains of love and the final line provides a humorous *pointe* to conclude this excellent *tour de force*:

> Je sens dans mes humeurs un grand feu s'embraser :
> Travaillé de douleurs je ne puis reposer,
> Et n'espère plus rien qu'en ton sçavoir extresme.
>
> Mais que peux-tu fournir qui serve à ma langueur?
> Las! j'ay le coeur atteint, et tu m'as dit toy-mesme
> Qu'il n'est point de remède aux blessures du coeur.
>
> (ll. 9-14 ; p. 17)

"Le Despit salutaire" (p. 20) is worthy of note because it contains one of Tristan's favorite metaphors to describe the cruelty of his "objets." He uses with great frequency the image of the lady as a rose with either thorns or a snake waiting to harm the hapless lover. He finishes the second quatrain with the lines:

> Les Roses qu'on y void dont i'estois amoureux,
> Couurent de leur esclat vne noire vipere.

He then concludes the poem with a reprise of the metaphor and ends with a witty turn of phrase:

> Quand ie voy qu'vn serpent souz des fleurs se retire,
> l'abhorre à mesme temps le serpent & les fleurs.

---

[7] See in the *Lettres meslées*, Letters LXXIV and LXXV, in which Tristan thanks the doctor for his skill and for the care that he gave him during his illnesses (Grisé edition 165-168).

The familiar concept of the lady's miniature portrait worn by the lover next to his heart as a talisman in war is the *leitmotif* of the little gem entitled appropriately "Le Talisman" (33-34). The first quatrain praises the artist who painted this portrait, for nothing could depict Angelique's beauty any better, except for "[. . .] les traits dont Amour l'a peinte en ma memoire" (l. 4). A very mannerist blason is contained in verses 5-8:

> Voila l'aimable tour de son beau sein d'yuoire,
> Voila son poil, son teint, sa bouche & ses beaux yeux,
> Ces yeux dont les regards sans dessein m'ont fait boire
> Vn poison preferable au doux nectar des Dieux.

This stanza contains much rhetorical flourish in describing with the vocabulary of Petrarchism the Beauté, but there is not one concrete description that would identify her or that would distinguish her from any other addressee of Tristan's amatory lyrics. One must admire the force of the oxymoron in the last line that makes poison of her regard preferable to the nectar of the gods! The first tercet describes the powerful effect of the amulet and the last one is an apostrophe to the painting that is notable for its erroneous allusion:

> Beau portraict...
> Vous m'est auiourd'huy ce que fut autre-fois
> L'image de Minerue à la ville de Troye.

Minerva, of course, sided with the Greeks in the Trojan War.

Most of the sonnets in *Les Amours* are like those discussed above. There are two, however, that are significantly different; they will be discussed now. "Les Médecins téméraires" (32) is an example of the rare eroticism in Tristan's poetry that he placed within a very witty context. The setting is the bedroom of Clorinde, who is being examined by a group of doctors. There are no concrete details either of the room or of Clorinde and the only setting is the presence of the ever-present mannerist *putti* who are weeping at the prospect of her death. They, in a very mannerist conceit, are telling each other that the same "rigueur" that is altering her beauty will destroy their own empire. The second quatrain addresses the physicians and asks them to examine her pulse and heart to determine the exact nature of her illness. The concluding sestet is a witty and not at all serious admonition to the medical men:

Mais quoy? vous abusez de vostre priuilege;
C'est trop vous arrester dessus ces monts de neige,
De qui le feu secret brusle tous les humains.

Il vous est bien permis d'approcher de sa couche,
Mais non pas de tenir plus d'vn instant vos mains
En des lieux où des Rois voudroient mettre la bouche.

(ll. 9-14, p. 32)

All of the sonnets discussed thus far have conformed to the
same general model of theme, variation, rhetorical virtuosity, and
ingenious conceit. They have no serious intent and are simply dis-
plays of Tristan's wit and mastery of the genre. They reflect no real
situation and the women in the poems fit the description provided
above by Bellenger–they are mere abstractions; they exist only on
paper. Other than their form, the sonnets display no traits of
baroque or classicism; they contain no didacticism and are for an
aristocratic elite, which was capable of appreciating their refinement. The fact that much of what Tristan uses as *topoi* are traceable
to the medieval *troubadours* and to Petrarch betray much more of a
medievalism than a classicism in his sources of imitation. These
poems were intended to *plaire*, not to *instruire*.

One sonnet that does not quite fit the mold is "La Plainte es-
crite de sang" (21). Though the theme is certainly that of the other
sonnets, there is a noticeable change in tone in the poem and its imagery is more baroque than mannerist. There is no way to tell when
the sonnet was written; but it is likely that it was written between
1633 and 1638, the same time that the other new sonnets in the volume were composed. If it had been written earlier, Tristan would
probably have included it in the *Plaintes d'Acante*. The graphic descriptions of blood as "traits de pourpre" recall La Ceppède's sonnet where pourpre is used to describe the blood of Christ:

O pourpre, emplis mon test de ton jus précieux
Et luy fay distiller mille pourprines larmes,[8]

Lines 4-11 contain many harsh terms that seem out of place in a Petrarchan sonnet:

_____

[8] Jean de La Ceppède, "J'ensanglante ces carmes," in Rousset, *Anthologie de la
poésie baroque française, T. 2* (Paris: Armand Colin, 1968), 121.

Par les vifs argumens d'vne raison *sanglante.*
Ces vers sont de ma flame vne preuue euident,
Et tous ces *traits de pourpre* en font voir la grandeur :
Cruelle, touche les pour en sentir l'*ardeur,*
Ceste escriture *fume,* elle est encore *ardante.*
Voy nâger dans *le sang* mes esprits desolez ;
Pour apaiser *ta haine* ils se sont *immolez*

(italics mine)

This combination of blood and hate is not found in any other poem in the *Amours* and it seems very out of place when compared to the other poems in the collection. Perhaps it is the influence of the baroque Marino that Tristan is undergoing rather than that of the earlier, mannerist Marino. Lest we be tempted to call this a baroque poem, an examination of the conclusion of the poem will return us quickly to reality. His "esprits desolez," he tells her, have formed for her such a devotion that, if it has dwelled so near to his heart,

C'est afin seulement de conseruer le Temple
Où ton diuin Portrait est tousiours adoré.

(ll. 13-14)

This very mannerist conceit dispels any temptation to call this a baroque sonnet, but it may certainly be used to show that Warnke was right when he stated that mannerism and baroque existed side by side in the same epoch, the same author, and even the same work.[9]

The volume contains many poems that Tristan calls "stances"; these, like many of his longer efforts, tend to become very banal and do not offer the sustained conceits or imagery of the sonnets. Some are quite good and offer original variations on the basic themes of the work. We will examine three of these that are mannerist in the same way as are the sonnets. Their greater length allows the poet more room to develop his themes and ideas and each of the three introduces an important topic in the lexicon of mannerism/Petrarchism/préciosité. The first, "Les Vains plaisirs," introduces a theme that Tristan excelled in treating–that of the dream; the second, "L'Enchantement rompu," treats the theme of the lover

---

[9] See *Versions of the baroque,* 1-12.

taking leave of his lady (palinode); and the third, "La Belle mal-
heureuse," is concerned with the triple theme of the jealous husband, the evils of contemporary marriage customs, and the idea
that wealth does not mean happiness. As will be shown in the following discussion, the first two are mannerist *par excellence* and the
third, despite its apparent didacticism and its strong images, is not
baroque because of its ending and overall tone.

"Les Vains plaisirs" begins with an apostrophe to sleep and describes very well its functions with imagery that is certainly not original, but is beautifully stated:

> Fils de la nuict & du silence
> Qui d'vn aimable violence
> Charmes les soucis des Humains,
> Quand sur le crespe de tes ailes
> Tu viens de tes humides mains
> Clore doucement nos prunelles :
> Sommeil, entre les Immortels
> Tu merites bien des Autels.
>
> (ll. 1-8, p. 69)

The mythologizing and personification of sleep, along with the
beautiful picture of the winged being gently closing a human's eyes,
place the poem in a dreamlike setting that is the background of this
very mannerist idyll. The description of the magic powers of sleep
continues with an antithetical description of the body at rest while
the mind, which never sleeps, wanders about and sees many places
and things. The third stanza personifies the sun and has it dream-
ing:

> Il court soudain toute la Terre,
> Et trouue mille objets d'Amour,
> [. . . . .]
> Ressentant selon tes desirs
> Des maux feints, ou de faux plaisirs.
>
> (ll. 20-21, 23-24)

After having established the dreamy, mythological and very unreal-
istic setting of the poem, he turns to its main subject, his dream of
Climène. In this dream, Tristan finds that Climène has no duenna
watching her every step; she has only Love, Youth, and Grace along
with "mille autres divins appas" (l. 31).

After Climène has expressed her love for Tristan, he replies in very Petrarchan and hyperbolic terms:

> Que i'aime à soupirer pour vous,
> Et que ie tiens à plus de gloire
> De mourir deuant vos beaux yeux,
> Que de viure avecque les Dieux.
>
> (ll. 43-46)

In the next stanza Tristan admonishes Climène for fearing the remarks of the "vulgaire," the jealous person, who might disparage her beauty and he tells her that one look from her would charm "ce monstre à cent testes." As he speaks these words to her, she modestly lowers her eyes, "[ses] deux cheres idoles," and boldly tells him:

> Qu'il est temps de bannir nos craintes
> Et de rappeller nos desirs
> A la recolte des plaisirs.
>
> (ll. 52-54)

A rather vivid description for Tristan, of their impassioned embrace follows and concludes with the two lovers "tous deux pasmez" on the poet's bed. At this moment of supreme happiness "le grand bruict du jour" arrives, awakens him, and "traist mon amour." The poem ends as the personified Sun comes through the window, lights up the room:

> Et rid de voir qu'auec les bras
> Ie la cherche en vain dans mes draps.
>
> (ll. 85-86)

Realizing that it was all a dream, the frustrated lover reflects on life:

> Que le sort de l'homme est volage,
> Il ne luy monstre bon visage
> Que pour le tromper à l'instant :
> S'il souffre ce n'est point mensonge,
> Mais s'il aduient qu'il soit contant
> Il trouue que ce n'est qu'vn songe
> Dont la vaine felicité
> Dis-paroist deuant la clarté.
>
> (ll. 87-94)

Though one might be tempted to classify this poem as baroque because of its rather graphic eroticism and because of the "philosophical" nature of its final stanzas, I believe that this poem has very little to do with the pessimistic and cynical Tristan of later efforts.
While those poems were very probably written when Tristan was
penniless and ill in his last years, this one was composed obviously
before 1638 when Tristan was a celebrity and enjoying his fame as
both a dramatist and poet. Despite the unreliability of Gaston,
there were many noblemen to whom Tristan could turn for support, as is evidenced by the numerous letters and poems addressed
to those personages. It seems logical that, given the very pretty
mannerist background of the poem, and given the fact that this is a
love poem, the philosophical reflections are only the traditional poetic commonplaces concerning reality and happiness. The eroticism
is evidence of the influences of Théophile and Marino on Tristan
L'Hermite and is far less graphic than that of his models. At the
most, one could conclude that there are a very few baroque elements in a very mannerist poem.

"L'Enchantement rompu" is nothing more than a well-written
palinode wherein Tristan retracts his previous declarations of love
to Climène. Whether or not this is the same Climène of the
"Promenoir" or the "Vains plaisirs" is impossible to tell, but it is of
very little importance to our appreciation and understanding of the
poem. The poem is a humorous variation on the theme of the
"amant transi" because, having seen Climène in the light of day, he
no longer finds her beautiful and says that he was probably attract-
ed to her because of her too vigilant husband. He is now free of any
feelings for her and can even laugh at his previous captivity. This
openly humorous poem seems to reflect the tendency that will be
seen in the *Lyre* and the *Vers héroïques*–a decided strain of *précieux*
or *poésie mondaine*. [10] It is not at all burlesque but is simply a light,
jocose work that was probably intended to be read in courtly or salon society for the amusement of the group.

A favorite device of the followers of Marino was to put the
Belle in a situation that offered the poet a subject for his paradoxes,
antitheses, oxymora, and *pointes*. Tristan, in "La Belle mal-

---

[10] For a detailed discussion of Tristan's *poésie mondaine*, see Chauveau's introduction to *La Lyre*, LIV-LXII.

heureuse," created such a situation–the beautiful young lady is contrasted with her jealous, ugly and decrepit husband:

> Auprès d'vne ieune Beauté
> C'est vn mort infecté.
>
> (ll. 23-24, p. 72)

He then turns to the cause of Climène's problems, the society that
demands that one marry for money:

> Voyez vn peu quel mauuais choix
> On vous a conseillé de faire.
> [. . . .]
> L'or plus faict pour nous esblouir
> Que pour nous resioüir.
>
> (ll. 27-28, 35-36)

The poem ends on a witty note as Tristan tells Climène what she
must do to solve the problem:

> Vous ne sçauriez vous consoler
> De sa fascheuse compagnie,
> Qu'en prenant vn Amant discret,
> Qui soit sage & secret.
>
> (ll. 45-48, p. 73)

The predominant theme of this poem is the seduction of Climène
by means of a description of her unhappy marriage, with a concluding invitation to become his mistress, because the poet-lover is always wise and discreet. The poem, as were the other two *stances*, is
clearly in the mannerist tradition as are almost all of the lyrics in the
collection. There are two longer poems and a sonnet that are very
different from the ones we have seen thus far and they will be considered next.

"La Gouvernante importune" is a very rare example of the burlesque in the poetry of Tristan L'Hermite. It is very much in the tradition of the pastoral to condemn the old who interfere with young
love, [11] and it is very interesting to note that Tristan uses the vehicle

---

[11] Francis L. Lawrence studied this poem at length in an article in *French Forum,* "Tristan L'Hermite's 'La Gouvernante Importune': The Structure of a Pasto-

of the old, cruel duenna as the framework for a travesty of the Petrarchan *topoi*. The poem is amusing because of Tristan's willing-
ness to parody the vast majority of his poetry, which was, of course,
very much in the Petrarchan tradition. The horror images–death, a
skeleton, a serpent, crows, Charon, witches' Sabbaths, old abandoned houses, and owls–are treated in a mock-horror manner that
lacks the realism of baroque horror. All of these images are used
only to make the duenna look more ridiculous; they are not intended to frighten us into believing anything, as were the graphic descriptions of death and the rotting corpses in real baroque poetry. [12]
We have an excellent parody in this poem but it is still in the playful mode that characterizes mannerism.

The long "Plainte à la belle banquière" is certainly atypical of the
vast majority of the *Amours*. Though it begins in the very usual manner of many of Tristan's love poems, it certainly contains elements
that have not been seen in his previous efforts. The poem opens with
the usual Petrarchan lament of the cruelty of the lady, Philis in this
instance, and follows with an extended nautical metaphor likening
Philis to the sea and its many changes that cause shipwrecks. This is a
favorite metaphor of Tristan and he spins it over two stanzas. We
then learn that a well-meaning friend of Tristan who was praising him
to her let it slip that Tristan was far from wealthy. [13] He then blames
her wealthy father for her change in attitude toward him:

> Quoy, cet auare auiourd'huy
> N'acceptera pas vn gendre
> S'il n'est riche comme luy.
>
> (ll. 40-42)

---

ral Satire," 4 (1979): 239-248. He found the poem to be in the same tradition as
Pyrame's verbal assault on Thisbé's old nurse, Bersiana in the play by Théophile.
Additionally, he found much the same imagery as used by both Tristan and
Théophile in a pastoral drama by La Barre, *Clénide* (1634). Lawrence's study is
highly recommended for a complete analysis of the poem.

[12] See for example the very baroque sonnet by Chassignet, "Un Cors mangé de
vers":

> Mortel, pense quel est dessous la couverture
> D'un charnier mortuaire un cors mangé de vers,
> Descharné, desnervé, où les os descouvers,
> Depoulpez, desnouez, delaissant leur jointure;
> Icy l'une des mains tombe de pourriture, . . .
>
> (ll. 1-5)

[13] It is interesting to note that Tristan wrote a letter on this same subject, "A
R.R. Philargire, Reproches d'infidelité et d'avarice," *Lettres meslées,* 89-90.

Perhaps remembering the poems of Théophile and Saint-Amant [14] on the virtues of the simple life, Tristan turns to a diatribe against greed and an encomium of the simple pleasures that life offers. The fierceness of his statements regarding the desire for wealth at all costs ring sincere because of the other statements that he made on the same subject. [15] The commonplaces regarding the evils of greed are related in a clear, precise manner that is evidence of a desire on the part of Tristan to lecture his readers on the subject. His audience included many courtiers who sought advancement at all costs and many ladies who, either because of the contemporary marriage customs or because of their own greed, sought marriage only with those who were wealthy. He, who will never be a slave to money, then turns to his very strong personal views on the subject:

> Et ie ne me rends esclaue
> Des hommes, ny d'argent.
>
> (ll. 65-66)

He then makes the transition to a description of what he considers important in life:

> Abhorrant l'émotion
> Et la sale passion
> Des Ames interessées,
> Ie laisse courir mes sens
> Et promener mes pensées
> Sur des objets innocens.
>
> (ll. 67-72)

In verses of great harmonious beauty, Tristan describes the joy that he receives from nature:

> Le bien de sentir les fleurs
> De qui l'ame & les couleurs
> Charment mes esprits malades,
> Et l'eau qui d'vn haut rocher

---

[14] See Saint-Amant, "La Solitude," and Théophile, "La Maison de Sylvie."
[15] See in the *Lettres meslées*, Letter LXXVI, "A Monsieur le C. de M.," 65-69. See also the "Ode à Monsieur de Chaudebonne" in the *Lyre*, ed. Chauveau, 133-143.

> Se va jettant par cascades
> Sont mon tresor le plus cher.
>
> Le doux concert des oyseaux,
> Le mouuant christal des eaux
> Vn bois, des prez agreables;
> Echo qui se plaint d'Amour,
> Sont des matieres capables
> De m'arrester tout vn iour.
>
> (ll. 73-84)

In this quiet contemplation of the beauties of nature, he seeks the lines of poetry, which will please him as well as the "honnestes gens." The final stanza admonishes Philis for not paying attention to what he has just written. "You would consider what I have just told you," he says:

> Si i'auois tout plein mes coffres
> Des Dieux que vous adorez.
>
> (ll. 95-96)

The mixture of conventional love *topoi* with those of the pleasures of the simple life to provide a framework for sincerely felt social criticism makes this poem a unique mixture of baroque didacticism and mannerist love and nature poetry. As we move into the study of the *Lyre* and the *Vers héroïques,* we will see more of this, especially in his later efforts.

The sonnet that concludes the *Amours* finds no pleasure in life and is a very pessimistic and cynical look at life and love. After we are born, we suffer the rigors of life to learn and to grow in strength only to serve an ungrateful *maistresse*:

> Qu'on ne peut acquerir, qu'on ne peut obliger ;
> Ou qui d'vn naturel inconstant & leger,
> Donne fort peu de ioye & beaucoup de tristesse.
>
> (ll. 6-8)

The dark tone of the poem continues with the observation that, after having plotted and schemed at court, man retires from the hubbub there to await, in his own residence, "Ce qu'ont nos derniers ans de maux inevitables" (l. 11). The conclusion of the sonnet is an ironic observation followed by a rhetorical question:

C'est l'heureux sort de l'homme. O miserable sort!
Tous ces atachemens sont-ils considerables,
Pour aimer tant la vie, & craindre tant la mort?

(ll. 12-14)

In the *Amours*, this concluding sonnet followed "L'Amour divin," which was discussed in the preceding chapter as a seemingly baroque profession of faith. The name was changed to "La Sage consideration," immediately preceded by "Sur un Tombeau" (whose title became "L'Amour durable") while lines 5-7 were changed to include an indirect reference to God. It can only be assumed that Tristan wanted to end his volume on a more serious note because, as he said in the *Avertissement*, this volume was to please and other efforts would be made to please and instruct. Perhaps this is Tristan's method of showing that he can be serious as well as frivolous –this fact will be seen in the *Lyre* to some extent and in the *Vers héroïques* to a much greater one. Nevertheless, we have here a very definite example of the *discours baroque* in its realism and in its classical universality.

Les Amours de Tristan is a volume of essentially mannerist love lyrics that demonstrate that Tristan can play the game and write of love within the rather limited conventions of his day. Most of these poems are subjective, aristocratic, highly refined, and intellectualized. They are not for anyone except those at court or in the salons who are capable of appreciating them. Most reveal no classical traits except for versification, which is almost always consistent with the doctrine of Malherbe.[16] Despite the considerable number of poems that are addressed to various ladies, none is a real creation and there is no concrete description of any of them. They are simply abstractions who exist only on paper and they are almost always presented as cruel and distant, while the poet/lover is mainly presented as the Petrarchan "amant transi." The volume never varies from the theme of love but includes two poems, "Plainte à la belle banquière" and "Misère de l'homme du monde," that use love as a vehicle for personal lyricism and didacticism–both traits that are

---

[16] For a thorough treatment of Tristan's Malherbian characteristics, see the introduction to Jean-Pierre Chauveau's edition of *La Lyre*. The influence of Malherbe on Tristan will be discussed in some detail in the chapters on the *Lyre* and the *Vers héroïques*.

hardly mannerist. The "Gouvernante importune" shows that Tristan is fully capable of writing satire and parody, and it is regrettable that he did not write more of it. Three years after the publication of the *Amours*, Tristan gathered more of his poetry together for publication, including a much greater variety of genres and themes. This volume, to be considered in the following chapter, was called *La Lyre*.

CHAPTER VII

MANNERISM AND BAROQUE IN *LA LYRE* *DU SIEUR TRISTAN*

THREE years after the publication of *Les Amours*, Tristan collected some more of his poetry and included it in the collection which he called *La Lyre*. The volume, while still primarily one of amatory poetry, contains other poems which make it the most varied collection published thus far. The superb critical edition of *La Lyre* by Professor Jean-Pierre Chauveau, published in 1977,[1] goes far beyond the usual critical edition; it contains abundant, informative footnotes about allusions and sources; it includes a very perceptive introduction that discusses the types, sources and characteristics of Tristan's poetry; and it analyzes the poet's use of various strophic forms in the volume. In short, it makes the poems far more accessible to the reader because Chauveau has done the research necessary for an understanding of the volume. Anyone studying these poems surely owes a considerable debt to him, as does the present author.

There are 104 poems of various types and lengths in the collection and it contains the "pièce maîtresse" of the group and Tristan's longest poem, "L'Orphée," which he dedicated to the musician, Berthod, "Ordinaire de la Musique du Roy." Following the classification of Chauveau, the poems in the volume may be classed as heroic and official poetry, poems of praise, gratitude or request; *poésie galante et mondaine*, salon poetry and ballets; epigrams, inspired by works of art or by poems in the *Anthologie grecque*; *vers funèbres*, consolations and eulogies; and poems of philosophical or moral inspiration. In selecting the poems to be published, Tristan

---

[1] Geneva: Droz. All references to the poems in *La Lyre* refer to this edition.

chose works written between 1625 and 1641 and seems to be fulfill-
ing his promise made three years earlier in the *Avertissement* to the
Amours: "Je vous donne ces ouvrages qui sont faits seulement pour
plaire, attendant que j'en mette d'autres au jour qui puissent plaire
et profiter ensemble."

The large number of heroic poems, epigrams, eulogies and consolations, some with evident didacticism, seem to denote a sincere
effort on Tristan's part to show that he was capable of writing to
please and instruct. The dominance of the theater in 1641 and the
fall from favor of the heroic (Malherbian) style of poetry made it
difficult for Tristan to sell his poems,[2] so he made a determined effort to write in the manner favored by the salons. These two facts
account for the fact that this volume is very different from his first
two poetic collections. In examining the poems of *La Lyre* for mannerism and baroque, I shall follow the preceding classification with
one exception. Because of its importance as the main work of the
volume and because, despite its imperfections, it is one of Tristan's
masterpieces, "L'Orphée" will be considered first.

Late in 1639, Tristan wrote his poem on the Orpheus legend in
imitation of an *idillo favoloso* that had been written by Marino and
had been published in Paris in 1620 during his sojourn in France. The
"Orfeo" of Marino was part of a volume entitled *La Sampogna* which
also contained "I sospiri d'Ergasto," the source of Tristan's "Plaintes
d'Acante." While the primary source for the "Orphée" is Marino,
there is also strong evidence of the influences of Ovid's *Metamorphoses*, Virgil's *Aeneid*, and Tasso's *Gerusalemme Liberata*.[3] A comparison of Tristan's work with that of his Italian forerunner reveals the
French work to be much shorter, much more dramatic and better organized, and far more restrained in its rhetorical excesses than its
model. In fact, one can easily see that Tristan the dramatist is at work
because of the organization of the poem and, especially, because of
Tristan's selections of episodes from the legend. "Tristan resserre, mal-
gré tout, son action, concentrant l'attention sur la tragédie intérieure

---

[2] The fact that *La Lyre* had only one printing is evidence of this fact; lyric poetry was fast becoming *passé* except for religious poetry, which will be Tristan's next
poetic endeavor.

[3] For a detailed analysis of the influences on Tristan's poem, see the notes and
introduction of Chauveau's edition of *La Lyre*. Marino's influence on the poem is
treated in detail in Cecilia Rizza, "*L'Orphée* di Tristan e *L'Orfeo* di Marino," *Convivium* (N.S., 1954): 429-439.

que vit Orphée le musicien, victime d'une fatalité cruelle, et dévelop-
pant avec bonheur les données psychologiques de la situation." [4] I believe that Tristan's adaptation of the legend to meet his own standards
is a significant step toward the type of poetry that was to dominate
the literature of the rest of the century. While there are certainly many
examples of a lack of classical restraint in the poem, there are enough
examples of Tristan's control of his subject and style to enable us to
label it as an early example of *baroque dompté.*

This can be seen in the organization of the poem to enhance its
dramatic impact–an organization that resembles that of the Cornelian
or Tristanian tragedy and perhaps even justifies Bernardin's appellation of Tristan as a precursor of Racine. The Malherbian beginning of
the poem (ll. 1-34) is a paean to Berthod, in which the French musician's traits are blended with those of the legendary protagonist of
the story. The action begins *in medias res* as we first see Orpheus after the death of Euridice as he sings his lament over her grave. As in
the classical tragedy, we are spared the portrayal of Eurydice's death
which we learn about in a sort of *récit* that recalls those found in the
theater of the time (ll. 35-54). The baroque element enters forcefully
in the following scenes in which we are dazzled by the long enumeration of trees (ll. 55-92), birds (ll. 93-130), and animals (ll. 131-180)
who come to hear the lament of the grieving widower. Though this
enumeration lacks any monumental purpose, it is baroque in the long
listing of the animals and trees, which are catalogued in an obvious
attempt to overwhelm and dazzle the reader. If there is any purpose
other than entertainment of the audience, it is probably a sincere attempt by Tristan to convey his respect for the art of music–an art that
was traditionally allied to poetry.

A curious episode follows (ll. 181-304) in which a Bacchante is
smitten with love for Orpheus and, after being rejected by him, reacts in the manner of a Racinian or Tristanian heroine. Indeed the
entire scene, with its description of the effects of love on the Bacchante is reminiscent of that of Phèdre:

> Son effrené desir souffre un mors importun,
> Elle avance deux pas, puis elle en recule un ;
> Sa flame à s'affranchir treuve de la contrainte,
> Elle en rougist de honte, elle en paslit de crainte,
>
> (ll. 243-246)

---

[4] Chauveau, LIII-LIV.

As Chauveau has remarked, these lines certainly recall Phèdre's famous line:

> Je le vis, je rougis, je pâlis à sa vue
>
> (l. 273)

When Orpheus rejects her by pushing her hand away from his lyre after her profession of love for him, she reacts in the manner of many a classical heroine (Hermione, for example):

> Le despit est si grand dont son coeur est attaint
> Qu'il enflame à la fois & ses yeux & son teint ;
> Elle s'en mord la lèvre avecque violence
> Gravant dans ce rubis son desir de vengeance.
> Rien ne peut moderer ce furieux transport,
> Desjà de ce qu'elle aime, elle a conclu la mort ;
>
> (ll. 283-288)

Despite the lapse into Petrarchism in line 286, the overall impression of the scene is one of horror—we soon fear for Orpheus' life because in her fury, the rejected lover tries to kill him. He is saved, however, by the magic powers of his lyre and voice. This is a long episode (223 lines) and it is used by Tristan to make a liaison between the first half of the poem and the second. In addition, to those familiar with the legend, it provides dramatic preparation for the death of Orpheus as described in Ovid (*Metamorphoses*, XI, 1-84) and in Marino but not described by Tristan. Perhaps Tristan wished to spare his readers the grotesqueness of the event and thus be true to both the *bienséances* and the idea of *vraisemblance*. Marino's treatment of the event is true to neither doctrine as he vividly describes the death of Orpheus at the hands of the Bacchantes[5] and ends his poem in an almost ridiculous manner:

> Vassene giù per l'acque
> Dal miserabil tronco
> Scema l'orrida testa: e mentre esala
> L'anima fuggitiva,
> Con la lingua già fredda

---

[5] This episode which was elaborated on by Marino may be found in the *Georgics*, IV, ll. 521-527.

A la lira s'accorda, e fievolmente
Seco mormora e geme e seco molce
Con moribondo e tremula armonia
L'onde e l'arena, e 'n su la voce estrema
Pur gorgogliando e singhiozzando dice:
Euridice, Euridice!

(ll. 1115-1125)

The fact that Tristan eschewed the temptation to follow either
Marino or Ovid probably was well received by the French elite,
who knew the legend well and were becoming increasingly "classical" in their tastes. It must also be remembered that Tristan was
writing at a time when the influence of the *ruelles* was becoming
dominant and he obviously wished to please this segment of society
by making his poetry conform whenever possible to their refined
and somewhat prudish tastes.

The next act of the poem takes place as the distraught lover trav-
els to the underworld in order to seek Eurydice's release from Pluto.
The horrors of hell are only obliquely alluded to as Tristan, the narrator, puts them in the form of questions addressed to the Muses:

Combien de cris sifflans & de clameurs funebres
Perçoient l'espaisse horreur de ces moites tenebres?
Combien de noirs Serpens & d'Hydres furieux
De Dragons & de Sphinx erroient devant ses yeux,
De Chimeres en feu, de Scylles aboyantes
De Fantosmes glacez, & de Larves sanglantes?

(ll. 349-354)

The action of the narrative resumes as Orpheus crosses the Styx by
charming Charon with his music and enters Hades. The underworld
is described as a "vaste Amphitheastre au centre de la Terre," where
the eternal torments take place and in the centre of which is the
throne of Pluto, who is vaguely described in three lines:

Le poil tout en desordre & le front renfrongné,
Ce front dont la fierté pleine de vehemence
Montre assez de son coeur la barbare inclemence.

(ll. 395-397)

The next hundred or so lines consist of descriptions of Orpheus' virtuosity at playing the lyre and of his lament and plea be-

fore the lord of the underworld. The description of Orpheus' technique is quite different from that of Marino, who devotes ninety lines to a discussion of technique. Tristan's description is restrained and very vivid. In a passage describing the serpentine harmony of his song, Tristan uses a snake-like movement with the alliteration of *s* sounds:

> Cette aymable armonie imite le serpent,
> Ondoye à longs replys, se retire, & s'estend,
> Et dans ces roulements, d'un artifice extresme,
> Se quitte, se reprend, sort & r'entre en soy-mesme ;
> Tandis que par l'oreille elle espand un poison
> Qui se glisse dans l'ame & trouble la raison.
> Tantost elle languist, & tantost elle esclate,
> Repousse, tance, & fuit ; r'apelle, appaise & flate ;
>
> (ll. 419-426)

After his music has caused a deep silence in the underworld, Orpheus begins to sing of his troubles and beg Pluto for Eurydice's return to the world. As the song begins, the verse shifts from the alexandrine couplets of the rest of the poem to *stances* of three alexandrines followed by a line of six syllables, with the rime: *aabb*; the first rime is always feminine and the last masculine. In the theater of the first half of the seventeenth century, the *stance* was employed for soliloquies of great lyrical content such as those of Dom Diègue and Rodrigue in *Le Cid* or those of Mariane in Tristan's play of the same name (IV, 2). [6] The shift in strophic form lends itself to the portrayal of emotions and it is also designed to arouse the compassion of the audience. The song of Orpheus is intended to move, and Tristan uses the classical rhetorical method to convince Pluto to release Eurydice. As Grisé has demonstrated, [7] the entire plea is based on the rhetorical pattern of the judicial oration as elaborated upon in the pseudo-Ciceronian *Rhetorica ad Herennium* (III, iii):

> In the *exordium* (ll. 441-452) Orpheus briefly states his cause in a deferential attempt to make Pluto a receptive listener [. . .] The

---

[6] He had also used them in *Panthée* (II, 1) and would use them again in what may be his best play, *La Mort de Sénèque* (V, 1). See Jacques Scherer, *La Dramaturgie classique en France* (Paris: Nizet, 1964), 285-297, for a detailed description of the use of *stances* in the classical tragedy.

[7] "The Poetry of Tristan L'Hermite," 193-194.

story of his wife's death and of his own sorrow are told in the *narratio,* or statement of facts (ll. 453-476). The *divisio,* Orpheus' summary of what is to follow in the body of the speech, is extremely simple: "Amour . . . m'a fait venir ici / Te conter mon souci" (ll. 477-480). The fourth part of a classical speech, the *confirmatio,* was supposed to contain arguments addressed to the listeners' minds and hearts. In his *confirmatio* (ll. 481-508), Orpheus appeals to Pluto first in the name of love whose power Pluto, himself, had experienced. . . . Anticipating a possible objection, in the *confutatio* (ll. 509-524) Orpheus makes it clear that he is not asking that his wife be given immortality . . . The *conclusio* (ll. 525-532) is, just as classical rhetoric prescribed, *artificiosus orationis terminus*: "Laisse moi donc là haut ramener cette belle, / Ou permets qu'ici bas je demeure avec elle" (ll. 525-526).

The logical, well-reasoned, yet emotional style is an element of the baroque[8] in the poetry of Tristan L'Hermite–a baroque that was far more restrained than that of his Italian source. These *stances* would not be out of place in the tragedy before Racine, and they are an excellent example of the blending of baroque and classical traits that was to characterize the literature of the remainder of the century in France.

The *dénouement* of the story follows immediately as Pluto, moved by Orpheus' lament, releases Eurydice, and the two embrace and set out on their return to the world of the living. There is no mention of the conditions of her release until after the fact and Tristan seems to be far more interested in characterization and in describing love than in the actual narration of events. In a monologue on the "theme that heedlessness cannot be condemned if motivated by love"[9] that is reminiscent of Corneille's characters, Eurydice accepts her fate and exculpates her spouse. Her speech consists of three parts:

1. Eurydice cannot understand Orpheus' actions and she blames him for their separation:

> Pourquoy du vieux Minos n'as tu gardé les loix,
> Et temperé tes yeux aussi bien que ta voix?

---

[8] Mathieu-Castellani, in the introduction to her anthology, lists this as a primary characteristic of the *discours baroque* (23).

[9] John C. Lapp, *The Brazen Tower: Essays on Mythological Imagery in the French Renaissance and Baroque* (Saratoga, California: Anma Libri, 1977), 103.

O faute sans remede ! ô dommageable veuë !
Avec trop de travaux tu m'avois obtenuë :
Mais je pren tes regards & ma fuite à tesmoin,
Que tu m'as conservée avec trop peu de soin.

(ll. 583-588)

2. She uses her reason to understand that it was because of his love
for her:

Tu craignois de me perdre en cette sombre horreur,
Et cette seule crainte a produit ton erreur :
De ton affection ma disgrace est éclose,
Et si j'en hay l'effet, j'en dois aymer la cause.
Encore que tes yeux me donnent le trespas,
Cette attainte me tuë & ne me blesse pas :
Ta foy, charmant Espoux, n'en peut estre blâmée ;
Tu n'aurois point failly si j'estois moins aymée :

(ll. 591-598)

3. She assures him that they will be reunited:

Tu te verras encore avec ton Euridice :
Si l'Enfer ne me rend, la Parque te prendra,
L'Amour nous des-unist, la Mort nous rejoindra ;
Il faudra que le Sort à la fin nous r'assemble
Et nous aurons le bien d'estre à jamais ensemble.

(ll. 606-610)

The monologue is in every way reminiscent of those of the
baroque/classical theater and it is a superb climax to the drama that
is unfolding from the pen of Tristan L'Hermite, poet and dramatist.

The poem ends quickly after the words of Eurydice because
Tristan has succeeded in portraying the two themes of the poem—
the power of love and that of music. Rather than repeat the morbid
scene of Orpheus' death at the hands of a frenzied mob of Bacchantes, a scene that would shock and offend the sensibilities of his audience, Tristan ended the poem in a manner that has been criticized
and ridiculed by many critics:[10]

---

[10] See for example Lapp, p. 103: "[. . .] Tristan once again veers toward the
burlesque, for the gravest outcome of Orpheus' sorrow is that he catches cold."

Il a beau s'affliger, conjurer, & prier,
Il ne gaigne qu'un reume à force de crier ;
Et n'ayant plus de voix pour forcer le passage,
Il perd en mesme temps l'espoir & le courage.

As Chauveau has shown, the seventeenth-century meaning of *rhume* was not simply "a cold." It was an illness that affected the throat to the extent that it "altère la parole." [11] Since this is the case, I take Tristan at his word when he describes Orpheus as having lost hope and heart—he has now lost both things that mattered most to him, Eurydice and his ability to sing. This ironic ending seems most appropriate for a tragic song written in praise of love and music.

Tristan's "L'Orphée" is an important development in the evolution of his poetry from the Petrarchist efforts of the first two volumes to a poetry that was more in keeping with the tastes of the day. His early mannerist works are certainly among his most beautiful poems; he is showing that in mid-career (1639) he is capable of writing those more serious works that he had promised in the *avertissement* to the *Amours*, while certainly not abandoning the subject of love. He is adding to the simple and beautiful style of the "Plaintes d'Acante" and the "Promenoir" and beginning, with his baroque and pre-classical (*baroque dompté*) efforts, an odyssey into other realms of poetic endeavor. He has taken many different elements of the styles of Ovid, Virgil, Marino, and Malherbe and incorporated them into one that is uniquely his own. He will continue to employ the mannerist and baroque styles when necessary, but he will also show that he can write for the salons, the Church, and the Academy. It must be recalled, however, that Tristan's fondness for two of his early styles—the Petrarchan love lyric (mannerist) and the Malherbian heroic ode (baroque)—are never completely absent from his poetry. An examination of the rest of the volume, starting with his heroic poetry, will reveal the diversity of Tristan's poetic output.

At this point, it should be recalled that heroic or occasional poetry includes poems written to great and famous personages in order to celebrate important events in their lives or to console them in times of loss. They are usually written in what is called the Malher-

---

[11] See Chauveau's note to l. 636, p. 80.

bian or the "grand style héroïque." [12] The avatars of this style were established by Malherbe who was imitated by many seventeenth-century poets, including Tristan, who employed this style as early as 1625 in his oft-quoted "Ode à Monsieur de Chaudebonne," which he included in *La Lyre*. In 1648, he called a volume of his poetry that was published the *Vers héroïques,* and stressed the heroic aspect of his poetic endeavors. Certainly, Tristan's poetry contains a strong heroic strain that is evident both in his earliest and in his last published works. [13] In *La Lyre,* there are some works of this type but a better classification would be "occasional poetry."

Among the occasional poems in *La Lyre* there are some that are pure encomia, others that request a favor of some notable personage, and others that express the poet's gratitude for some service rendered. These last two are primarily requests for help in Tristan's quest for reinstatement in the entourage of Gaston d'Orléans, and thanks to those who helped him in this matter. The first group is the most "heroic" and reflects Tristan's mastery of the "grand style héroïque." [14] The introductory poem in the volume, "Ode à Monsieur de Montauron" (4-7), is a very Malherbian encomium which has as its primary theme *exegi monumentum*–all things disappear except those celebrated in poetry. Chauveau lists its Malherbian traits as: (1) its solemn tone, (2) its brief but striking allusions to mythology, (3) its theme of the immortality of the hero and the poet who celebrates him, and (4) its form of stanzas of ten lines, seven syllables. To this might be added Tristan's restraint in the use of metaphor and the clarity and harmony of his lines. He avoids baroque excesses and follows the lead of Malherbe is his use of commonplaces derived primarily from Horace but also from other Latin and Greek sources. The ode is baroque, as are most of Tristan's serious works, if one accepts the idea that classicism is *baroque dompté*; it is certainly not baroque in the manner of Sponde or Chassignet, for it lacks the verbosity and rhetorical excesses of the

---

[12] See the introduction to Chauveau's edition of *La Lyre* (XXXVII-XLV) for a detailed discussion of the heroic style of Tristan and also the third chapter of Grisé's "The Poetry of Tristan L'Hermite," 102-163.

[13] The ode to Chaudebonne is, of course, one of his earliest works, while his "La Renommée," dedicated to his last and most generous patron, the duc de Guise, was published in 1654, a year before his death.

[14] For a discussion of the various poems of this type in *La Lyre* see Chauveau's introduction, XXXVII ff.

style. The third dizain of the poem will serve to illustrate Tristan's use of mythology, within a strophe of clear and regular lines, to illustrate a commonplace of heroic poetry, the vicissitudes of fortune and the immortality of poesy:

> Le Temps a détruit de Rhodes
> Le grand Colosse d'airain :
> Mais non pas gasté les Odes
> De l'agreable Thebain.
> Et quoy que Mars ait pû faire
> Pour se rendre tributaire
> Ce Lieu qui fut sans pareil ;
> Une chançon plus qu'humaine
> Nous apprend que le Soleil
> En fit son premier Domaine.
>
> (ll. 21-30)

The poetry of Pindar is still with us while the Colossus of Rhodes has disappeared, a very effective blending of commonplace, mythology, and clear lines of poetry that would certainly please Malherbe.[15]

Also in the vein of *baroque dompté* is the final poem in the volume, the ode to Monseigneur le Grand (286-292). This poem was written in 1641, as was the preceding one,[16] and its style and content are the same. Tristan had written a similar ode in 1625 which is less classical in some respects than his later efforts, but it is the harbinger of what was to become his more personal poetry. It is a masterpiece that combines many baroque and mannerist elements to create one of Tristan's most often-quoted poems. The analysis that follows will attempt to isolate those elements through a study of the entire poem.

The "Ode à Monsieur de Chaudebonne" (133-143) is an eclectic poem of one hundred forty octosyllabic lines divided into stanzas of ten lines with the rime: *abbaccdede*. It is ostensibly a poem of request since Tristan had apparently fallen from Gaston's favor and

---

[15] It should be pointed out that while Chauveau and others see considerable Malherbian influence in the poetry of Tristan, Claude K. Abraham concludes that the influence is slight. See his *Enfin Malherbe. The Influence of Malherbe on French Lyric Prosody, 1605-1674* (Lexington, Kentucky: UP of Kentucky, 1971), 165-170, 210-218.

[16] Chauveau was able to date with reasonable certainty sixty-nine of the hundred and four poems in *La Lyre*; see "Annexe III," page 302.

was seeking reinstatement in Monsieur's entourage, but it is much more than that. The poem opens with a request to Chaudebonne that he "laisse faire à la destinée" because it is useless to oppose the stars. If the stars continue to oppose his happiness, he has a solution to the problem:

> J'iray perdre dans ma maison
> Les ressentiments d'une injure
> Dont je ne sçay pas la raison.
>
> (ll. 28-30)

He then picks up the very common mannerist theme of solitude as he describes the beauties of the countryside around Solier. The description consists of an idealized nature, peopled by mythological beings, and of praise for the rustic life. Here the influence of Théophile is very evident as the twenty-four year old poet imitates his friend and mentor who had expressed similar sentiments in his "Lettre à son Frère." [17] Like the Romantic poets of the nineteenth century, Tristan will find solace amidst the beauties of nature. He expresses the very common theme of disdain for the riches of the world and consolation in nature:

> Jamais le desir des richesses
> Ne troublera mes sentimens ;
> La Nature & les Elemens
> Me feront assez de largesses,
> L'Or éclatant dont le Soleil
> Vient couronner à son réveil
> Le front orgueilleux des Montagnes ;
> Et l'argent pur qui va coulant
> Sur l'émail fleury des Campagnes
> Me rendront assez opulent.
>
> (ll. 51-60)

This idyllic description of Nature continues in the same vein as Tristan uses colors to heighten the sensory appeal of his description culminating in the vivid rainbow into which Iris has metamorphosized. He then goes to the auditory images such as the singing of a thousand birds and the sound of water:

---

[17] Théophile de Viau, *Oeuvres poétiques,* ed. Streicher (Paris: Minard, 1951-1958), T. II, 185-197.

> La Musique de mille Oyseaux,
> Le bruit & la cheute des eaux
> Qui se précipitent des roches,
>
> (ll. 75-77)

This very mannerist description of nature is very typical of the young Tristan L'Hermite as has already been seen in the discussions of the "Plaintes d'Acante" and the "Promenoir des deux amants." [18] Tristan's very mannerist treatment of the *topoi* of solitude and the pleasures of the simple, rustic life soon takes an unexpected turn toward a very stoic discussion of the joys of the cultivated mind.

If he were to lose Solier, Tristan states, he would still have "Des Biens qui ne sçauroient perir" (l. 90). [19] He then, in a very personal outburst, extols his own sincerity and fidelity while indirectly noting the lack of those traits at court and stating the *topos* that he, the poet, can confer immortality on even the least deserving prince. This is, of course, a reference to Gaston, and it leads into the request of the ode:

> Mais toy qui gouvernes les Anges [Gaston's courtiers]
> Qui peuvent tout pour mon bonheur,
> Fay qu'ils m'acordent cét honneur
> Pour le prix de mille loüanges.
>
> (ll. 121-124)

The poem ends with a very clever request to Chaudebonne to send him the good news; but if the news is not good:

> Trahy moy le plus doucement
> Que peut faire un Amy fidelle ;
> Ne me fais faire le rapport
> D'une si funeste nouvelle,
> Qu'une semaine apres ma mort.
>
> (ll. 136-140)

Tristan's use of oxymoron and antithesis is typical of a young poet who wanted to show that he could write with wit in the manner of

---

[18] See chapter V, above, 71-81 and 93-94.

[19] Ironically, he did lose Solier due to the ruinous financial conditions of the provincial nobility and, perhaps, to the financial ineptitude of his mother.

Marino. The poem is certainly different from the two odes mentioned above–they are Malherbian; this is an eclectic blend of mannerism and personal lyricism that is of indisputable beauty.

Another example of heroic poetry in *La Lyre* is the celebration of the great deeds of notable personages such as Gaston d'Orléans in "Pour Monseigneur le duc d'Orléans" (123-128). The poem was written as the subtitle states "Lors que son Altesse commandoit les Armes du Roy en la Province de Picardie." It is an encomium in the true Malherbian sense but ends with a muted request for Gaston's favor. The other type of encomium in the volume is the light and witty poem such as the one addressed to Mlle de Soucarière, the mistress of Montauron, the dedicatee of the volume. In it, Tristan combines praise of her beauty with a final *pointe* that recalls Tristan's earlier Petrarchan verses. The other occasional poems are those that he had previously published in two different volumes and are *ballets de cour.* Rousset[20] considers the ballets of that era as baroque, but their frivolity and lack of any serious purpose would seem to indicate mannerism.

Closely related to the heroic or occasional poems are those which Chauveau calls "vers funèbres"; that is to say poems written to lament a death and poems which seek to console the loved-ones of someone recently deceased. The poems dealing with the death of the Infanta, who was hostess to Gaston, Maria de' Medici, and their entourages in Brussels, Isabella Clara Eugenia (Poems LXXXVI-XCI) are noteworthy for Tristan's obvious feeling of personal loss. In poem LXXXVII, he uses the familiar Horatian commonplaces that death comes to all and that even her most noble lineage will not spare her. The stanzas that describe those mourning her take on an immense proportion and are typical of baroque exaggeration. He concludes with a well-reasoned rationalization that in death the princess is free from all earthly cares and concerns.

One of the best examples of a poem of consolation is the one addressed "A Madame de Gournay sur la mort de Mademoiselle sa fille" (Poem XCVII, 269-270). In this sonnet, a curious mixture of baroque consolation and Petrarchan vocabulary, Tristan calls Mlle de Gournay by the poetic name of Amarillis and describes her in Petrarchan terms. He continues by calling her a flower that is des-

---

[20] See *La Littérature*, 11-31.

tined to adorn the altars of heaven. The consolation is Christian, for it is Christ who will pick this flower and take it with Him to heaven. He closes the sonnet with one of his favorite metaphors in his love poetry, the flower/thorn conceit, used to describe Christ's suffering and to justify the death of the young woman:

> C'est mal vous souvenir de ses bontez divines,
> Faut-il avoir regret s'il emporte nos fleurs,
> Il a bien pris le soin de porter nos espines?
>
> (ll. 12-14)

As has already been mentioned, Tristan sought to expand his audience by demonstrating his mastery of salon or *précieux* poetry and he devotes a large portion of the volume to precisely that type of lyric. Inspired by the *Galeria* of Marino, he includes a series of poems inspired by real or imagined works of art (Poems LXV-LXXXI) with the exception of LXXIII, "A Monsieur de Saintot," which is very different from the others. There are eight pieces before the poem to Saintot and eight after it. This has led one critic to conclude that Tristan placed these poems in this manner for a definite purpose. The first eight celebrate love as an invincible power, the second eight show the deceit of love, and the poem to Saintot, dealing with the "Misères Humaines," serves as a bridge between the two.[21] While this is a possible interpretation of the poems, the fact remains that this is essentially an imitation of Marino's *Galeria* and is an attempt on the part of Tristan to show that he, too, can write the witty epigramatic poetry that was "furieusement aimée" in the *chambre bleue*.

One of his better efforts, "La Fortune de l'hermaphrodite" (LXXVII, 220-221), will serve as an example of these short, witty works. The poem is clearly an imitation of a fourteenth-century Latin poem by Polci or Pulex. Tristan used a device, also used by his source, which was much esteemed by mannerist and baroque writers of the late sixteenth and early seventeenth centuries, the *vers rapportés*. Perhaps the most outstanding example of which occurs in a sonnet by Sponde:

---

[21] Richard Crescenzo, "Une Poétique de la Galerie? Sur quelques pièces de « La Lyre »," *Cahiers Tristan L'Hermite* 14 (1992): 46-61.

> Tout s'enfle contre moi, tout m'assaut, tout me tente,
> Et le Monde, et la Chair, et l'Ange révolté,
> Dont l'onde, dont l'effort, dont le charme inventé
> Et m'abisme, Seigneur, et m'esbranle, et m'enchante. [22]

In this case the device is obviously used for serious purposes and can be called a baroque device. In Tristan's case, the *vers rapportés* are simply a device to demonstrate his *acutezza* and is mannerist. The mock-serious sonnet begins as the hermaphrodite tells of the dispute over his sex among the deities: Jupiter wanted a son, Venus a daughter, and Mercury "l'un et l'autre"; he was both: "je fus tous les deux" (l. 4). He then tells us that other divinities chose the means of his death: Saturn by means of a snare, Mars by means of a blade, and Diana by means of murky water. In the sestet of the sonnet we learn of his fate:

> Je suis tombé d'un saule à costé d'un estang,
> Mon poignard desgainé, m'a traversé le flanc,
> J'ay le pied pris dans l'arbre, & la teste dans l'onde.
> O sort dont mon esprit est encore effroyé !
> Un poignard, une branche, une eau noire & profonde
> M'ont en un mesme temps meurtry, pendu, noyé.

The poem is exactly what Tristan intended it to be–a witty *tour de force*. Even the unusual rime scheme (*abbacdcd*) in the octet suggests the abnormal subject of the poem. Tristan has simply shared a moment of humor with his readers in this excellent mannerist sonnet.

Many of the love lyrics in *La Lyre* are exactly like those discussed in previous chapters and will not be studied here for fear of redundancy. There are two sonnets, however, that deserve mention. In 1635, Voiture included in a letter to Mlle de Blois a sonnet that renewed the "Belle Matineuse" theme in French poetry. It had been treated by both Ronsard and Du Bellay in the previous century and was a popular motif among Italian poets such as Caro and Rinieri. Malleville composed three sonnets on the theme and Tristan two, his "Imitation d'Annibal Caro" in *La Lyre* (XXXIX, 150-151) and poem XXXIX, 197 in the *Vers héroïques*. The theme was the source of an intense competition between the *dévoués* of Voiture and of

---

[22] Quoted in Rousset's anthology, 197.

Malleville, as well as of other poets, who championed the efforts of their favorite. Is it a deliberate act on the part of Tristan that both poems have the same number in their respective volumes or is it sheer coincidence? Nevertheless, Tristan's entry into the contest is another example of his desire to be accepted by the *précieuses* and it is a successful one. Allen Wood, who has studied the poem, insists that it is baroque, but an examination of the poem reveals the contrary.[23] As Wood himself says:

> Evening and winter, death, apocalyptic destruction, or eternal salvation are frequently the concepts which motivate, and finally terminate the baroque poems. [. . .] Against the dark background of baroque poetics, obsessed with the terror of night and death, a group of poems appears which emphasizes light, beginnings, and love. (64)

The first sentence quoted does, indeed, describe some of the baroque but the second description is of mannerism. Tristan's poem is a *tour de force* in which he shows his ability to write amatory poetry for the salons, just as he had previously written it for the court. Both types lack the seriousness of baroque poetry since they are simply intellectual games designed for an elite audience that sought amusement rather than persuasion.

The same may be said of another of his best-known sonnets, "La Belle esclave more," in which Tristan shows himself as a master of rhetorical expression. The use of oxymora, antitheses, and extended metaphors provides extensive rhetorical decoration for the poem that dazzles with its images. The last line with its antithesis of night/day describing the face and eyes of the Moor provide a vivid picture of her striking beauty: "La nuit sur son visage et le jour dans ses yeux." The use of periphrasis in lines three, four, and thirteen and fourteen is especially effective:

> Et l'Ebene poly qui te sert d'ornament
> Sur le plus blanc yvoire emporte l'avantage.
> [. . . . .]
> D'où cét Astre est venu, qui porte pour ta honte
> La nuict sur son visage & le jour dans ses yeux.

---

[23] Allen G. Wood, "The End of Dawn: Poetic Closure in the 'Belle Matineuse'," *L'Esprit Créateur* 20 (1980): 64-74.

Tristan uses oxymoron in the first words of the poem, "Beau Monstre de Nature" and continues it in line eleven: ". . . une Esclave me dompte." The rhetorical richness of the poem is considerable and yet the lines are clear and the images succinct. The theme and the purpose of the poem are consistent with those of mannerism and there is only one element that could possibly be called baroque. The situation of the poem in which someone not normally considered beautiful is so described is certainly not Petrarchist. It is a theme that Marino popularized to insert some variety into the love poetry of the seventeenth century, which was growing weary of the same Petrarchan themes and language. While it is certainly not mannerist in the way that much of Tristan's earlier amatory poetry was, it in no way varies from what we have established as the parameters of mannerism.

There is one major love lyric in the collection, the "Plainte de l'Illustre Pasteur" (VII, 18-27), which is an excellent pastoral. As Chauveau has pointed out, the poem contains all the conventions of the genre but certainly: "peut compter parmi les chefs-d'oeuvre de son lyrisme amoureux." [24] This beautiful eclogue is of the same type as the "Plaintes d'Acante" and is mannerist in the same way. There are three poems in the *Lyre* that are vastly different from the others and are unmistakably baroque. A discussion of these three compositions will conclude this chapter.

Poem XXXVIII, 146-149 is entitled "Les soins superflus, à monsieur de . . ." and is didactic in the sense that it urges its dedicatee to live a virtuous life because nobility founded on blood alone, without virtue, is nothing:

> L'esclat de ta naissance est le moindre ornement
> Qui puisse mettre en prix un merite si rare.
>
> (ll. 29-30)

"L'Ambition tancée" (XXV, 104-106) is an emblem sonnet with the didactic theme of the futility of ambition. The poem opens with an image of the peacock in all its glory, another rainbow, but as soon as it folds its plumage, its pride and glory disappear. The sestet calls upon man to forget earthly glory and remember the lesson of Nebuchadnezzar's dream as interpreted by Daniel (2, 31-35): those who

---

[24] Introduction to his edition of *La Lyre*, XLIV.

seek to possess the world are but the idol with clay feet. This poem is certainly moral, didactic, and in line with the teachings of the Church. It is very effective in its use of tropes and images and fits the description of a baroque poem. It is, however, a rather close imitation of a poem in Marino's *Lira* entitled *Memento homo quia cinis*.[25] The fact that it is such a close imitation of Marino might lead some to question the sincerity of Tristan's teachings in the poem; but given what we know about his disdain for courtly aspiration, it is probably a sincere attempt on his part to warn his readers of the folly of excessive ambition.

The final poem to be discussed is the long and rather clumsy poem which Tristan placed in the middle of his gallery (LXXIII, 200-211) "Les Misères humaines. A Monsieur de Saintot." Lines 1-40 deal with the theme that man's lot in life is sad when compared to fish, the lion, and the eagle because he is born without wisdom, strength, or virtue. To make his lot even worse, man is born helpless to oppose the dictates of the stars or the elements. When he finally reaches the age of reason, Love enters his life and makes him miserable. The next part of the poem tells of the miseries of life at court where one encounters envy, jealousy, and slander. The only way to deal with this is to seek solitude away from court, among friends, but death takes them away from us. The last part of the poem is a long litany in which the theme of universal death is expounded upon and a tribute is paid to such deceased persons as Richelieu's brother and other nobles of the court, poets such as Homer, Pindar, Virgil, Horace, Ovid and Malherbe "qui fut sans pareil," and two of the ladies to whom he had written poems, Philis and Idalie. After this very long listing, he concludes with a very moral lesson:

> Puisque ce n'est rien qu'un passage
> L'insensé suit la vanité,
> Mais il faut que l'esprit du Sage
> Butte droit à l'ETERNITE.
>
> (ll. 130-133)

---

[25] For a comparison of the two poems see Catherine M. Grisé, "La Vraie source de « L'Ambition tancée » de Tristan L'Hermite," *Revue de Littérature Comparée* octobre-décembre 1967, 585-588.

Because of its didacticism and its seemingly sincere sentiments, this poem is certainly not mannerist; its Malherbian lines and its lofty teachings make it an example of the *discours baroque*.

The great variety of themes and genres used by Tristan in *La Lyre* demonstrate his maturation as a poet and his desire to excel at all types of poetry. While the poems in this volume are still predominantly mannerist, we are beginning to see the serious side of Tristan and we shall see even more of it in the next two chapters. In 1647 he presented his *Office de la Sainte Vierge* to the Queen and soon followed it with the *Vers héroïques*, the ensuing year. Since the latter volume reflects a greater variety of poems, it will be studied in the next chapter and the religious poetry of Tristan will be studied in the final chapter.

CHAPTER VIII

MANNERISM AND BAROQUE IN THE *VERS HÉROÏQUES*

IN 1648, Tristan gathered together a large number of poems of various dates and published them in a volume that he called the *Vers héroïques*. He had recently left the service of the Duchesse de Chaulnes and had found great satisfaction in the retinue of Henri de Lorraine, Duc de Guise, who was a generous benefactor for the aging and infirm poet. He had left the service of the Duchesse in the fall of 1645 and immediately entered that of the Duc de Guise. In 1646 his new master left for Rome to seek an annulment of his first marriage so that he could marry his mistress, Suzanne de Pons. While there, he accepted a proposal from the Milanese who beseeched him to free their city from Spanish domination. He was successful, acquiring considerable fame as a warrior in Italy, and Tristan strongly desired to accompany him there. The volume was intended to raise enough money for that purpose but, after initial triumphs, the Duke was taken prisoner and Tristan's plans were foiled. Fortunately for Tristan, the duke was finally freed and Tristan was able to spend his last years with him in the Hôtel de Guise.

The volume, as its title suggests, is primarily composed of occasional poetry, most of it "heroic." There are four primary "cycles" of heroic poetry – the poems dedicated to Gaston d'Orléans, to Saint-Aignan, to the Duchesse de Chaulnes, and to the Duc de Guise. These illustrate very well the situation of the *poète à gages* in seventeenth-century France – the complete dependence of the artist on the patron.[1] There are also the numerous *poésies galantes,* the

---

[1] For an excellent discussion of the social and economic status of seventeenth-century artists, especially writers, see: John Lough, *An Introduction to Seventeenth Century France* (London: Longmans, Green and Co., 1954), 173-214 and Georges Montgrédien, *La Vie littéraire au XVIIe siècle* (Paris: Tallander, 1947), 253-309.

series of epigramatic poems, the personal poems, and some that cannot be easily classified, such as "Les Terreurs nocturnes" and "La Maison d'Astrée." [2] The volume contains several long poems and two of Tristan's best sonnets, [3] plus some of his "personal" poetry. [4] The styles of the poems range from mannerist to baroque to "classical." As Odette de Mourgues has remarked, Tristan, "when he is neither baroque nor *précieux*, is already a classicist poet." [5] As was the case to a lesser degree in *La Lyre,* Tristan has selected poems in all styles but with a tendency toward the classical in his heroic verse and toward mannerism in his love lyrics. His personal poems are closer to the baroque than the others, but are not completely so, as will be seen in the following analyses.

In 1634, Maria de' Medici sought asylum in England and sent Tristan on a secret mission to negotiate with the King and Queen for her exile there. Tristan wrote one of his longest poems as a result of this visit, "Pour les serenissimes majestez. Eglogue maritime" (I, 37-55). The poem consists of two sea nymphs, Leucothea and Circene, who are having a contest, judged by Proteus, to see who can write the "vers les plus doux" in praise of Charles I and Henrietta Maria, the sovereigns of England. The contest takes place and each of the nymphs tries to outhyperbolize the other in her extensive encomium of the royal couple. As might be expected, Proteus declares the contest a draw and ends the poem with extensive praise of Charles and Maria, followed by a prophecy of great things to come. The narrative style of the composition is clear and the lines have considerable beauty and harmony. Circene speaks of the couple:

> Deslors que Thetis aperceut
> Ce couple d'amans adorables,
> En sa faveur elle conceut
> Mille prodiges agreables ;

---

[2] All quotations and references to the *Vers héroïques* refer to the edition of Grisé (Geneva: Droz, 1967).

[3] "La Mer," "Eglogue maritime," "La Maison d'Astrée," and "Terreurs nocturnes" are among the longest in the volume. "La Belle Gueuse" and "L'Extase d'un baiser" are among Tristan's finest sonnets.

[4] "La Servitude," "Prosopopée de FTL," and the sonnet number CXXIX.

[5] *Metaphysical, Baroque and Précieux Poetry* (Oxford: Clarendon, 1953). Cited in Geoffrey Brereton, *An Introduction to the French Poets* (Fair Lawn, NJ: Essential Books, 1957), 48.

De là vient, que vers ces confins
On a veu de nouveaux dauphins
Portans des couronnes dorées,
Et qui sur les miroirs polis
De leurs écailles azurées
Avoient des roses et des lys.

(ll. 221-230)

This stanza, typical of the poem as a whole, contains hyperbole, conventional in encomia, and it ends with a very Petrarchan conceit. The "prettiness" of mannerism is evident in the above lines as well as in many others, such as:

Les flots qui viennent assaillir
Le flanc de ces rochers
Font jusques aux cieux rejaillir
Mille et mille perles liquides ;

(ll. 81-84)

and in the description of the golden age which has come to England because of the royal couple:

Aussi comme en cet age d'or
Où les coeurs se treuvoient sans vice,
La gloire et le bon-heur encor
Y regnent avec la justice.
Il n'y croit jamais de poisons,
Le soleil y fait des saisons
Qui ne sont ny froides ny chaudes ;
Les champs de fruits s'y vont chargeant,
Les herbes y sont d'esmeraudes,
Et les ruisseaux y sont d'argent.

(ll. 281-290)

The abundant use of mythological[6] allusions would only be appreciated by those of the *cour et la ville*, and, indeed, the poem was

---

[6] In the poem, Tristan alludes to the following mythological personages: the Fates, Neptune, the Nereids, Ino (Leucothea), Vulcan, Mars, Venus, Minerva, Achilles, Pallas, Proteus, the Amazons, Aurora, Zephyrus, Jupiter, Europa, Thetis, Hymen, Cupid, Themis, the Tritons, the Nymphs, the Dryads, and Diana. In addition, Arthur (l. 88) and Merlin (l. 125) are mentioned, the former as an ancestor of Charles and the latter as one who rose from the grave to prophesy the king's illustrious future.

written expressly for the English monarchs. It contains all of the usual elements of the heroic ode but has an entirely different tone. Instead of the high-sounding encomia found in the Malherbian ode, Tristan uses comparisons with divinities and mythological personnages who are always inferior to Charles and Henrietta. Comparing Minerva to Henrietta, Cupid says to the goddess:

> Superbe, dit-il, penses-tu
> Pour l'esprit et pour la vertu
> Gagner le premier avantage ?
> Cette isle fleurit sous un roy
> Dont l'espouse est cent fois plus sage
> Et plus genereuse que toy.
>
> (ll. 115-120)

The cuckolded god, Vulcan, compares Charles to Mars, his wife's lover:

> Vulcain dans son antre voûté
> Fait pour Charles une cuirasse
> [...................................]
> Venus y portant ses regars
> Est en peine si c'est pour Mars
> Que ce beau chef-d'oeuvre se grave ;
> Mais le vieillard plein de couroux
> Dit que c'est pour un Mars plus brave
> Que celui qui le rend jaloux.
>
> (ll. 101-102; 105-110)

The poem lacks the pomposity of much of the heroic poetry in Tristan's time. It contains many tropes favored by mannerist poets; its lines are clear, harmonious, and regular; and its tone is a mixture of the baroque and mannerist *discours*. Tristan's use of Petrarchan sensory images to accomplish the purposes of the heroic ode is an excellent example of the originality and creativity of the artist. The poem is a superb illustration of the eclecticism of Tristan L'Hermite, who was proficient in all of the styles that were available to him.

One of Tristan's oldest poems was written during a military campaign of Gaston d'Orléans against the Protestants of La Rochelle in 1627. Louis XIII had reluctantly sent his brother to deal

with the insurrection but soon realized his mistake and ordered
Gaston to cease operations until Louis could arrive and take over
the command. During the lull in the action, Tristan wrote "La Mer"
(II, 57-69) as an elegy on the death of his friend Maricour, who had
died in the ill-fated assault on La Rochelle.[7] Meanwhile, Gaston decided to disobey Louis' orders and delivered supplies to the island
of Ré, which had been besieged for two months by the English. The
successful outcome of this operation gave Tristan cause to celebrate
his master in the ode, "La Mer," a tribute to Maricour that also glo-
rifies Gaston. "La Mer" is perhaps Tristan's most beautiful poem.
Since Maricour's death, Tristan tells us that he seeks escape from
the court and solace in the beauties of Nature:

> Depuis la mort de Maricour
> J'ay l'esprit plein d'inquietude ;
> J'abhorre le bruit de la cour
> Et n'aime que la solitude.
> Nul plaisir ne me peut toucher
> Fors celuy de m'aller coucher
> Sur le gazon d'une falaise,
> Où mon dueil se laissant charmer
> Me laisse rêver à mon aise
> Sur la majesté de la mer.
>
> (ll. 1-10)

Following this brief introduction, the poet turns to a description of
the sea in all its aspects. He laces this long description of the sea
with mythological allusions and images of striking beauty such as:

> Le soleil à longs traits ardans
> Y donne encore de la grace,
> Et tasche à se mirer dedans
> Comme on feroit dans une glace ;
> Mais les flots de vert émaillez
> Qui semblent des jaspes taillez,

---

[7] For a more detailed and comprehensive study of "La Mer," see Jan Miernowski, "Sur La Mer de Tristan: Espace et vision," *Cahiers Tristan L'Hermite* 5 (1983):
30-35. Volume V of the *Cahiers* is devoted entirely to Tristan's lyric poetry. Robert
Corum has also written an excellent study of the poem: "A Reading of Tristan
L'Hermite's 'La Mer'," *Papers on French Seventeenth-Century Literature* 9 (1978):
11-28.

S'entredérobent son visage,
Et par de petits tremblements
Font voir au lieu de son image
Mille pointes de diamants.

(ll. 41-50)

He shows himself adept at visual imagery as he describes the sun-
rise in a pretty, mannerist strophe that is rich in color and ornamentation; excessive decoration is, of course, very mannerist:

Quand cet astre ne vient encor
Que de commencer sa carriere
Dans des cercles d'argent et d'or,
D'azur, de pourpre et de lumiere,
Quand l'Aurore en sortant du lit,
Elle que la honte embellit,
Rend la couleur à toutes choses,
Et montre d'un doigt endormy
Sur un chemin semé de roses
La clarté qui sort à demy ;

(ll. 51-60)

This very beautiful description of dawn is typical of those used by
Tristan to depict the calm sea. These scenes are reminiscent of the
pastoral and the "Promenoir des deux amants," and were intended
for the elite at court to enjoy. The imitation of Homer and Virgil is
obvious and the dazzling display of rhetoric throughout the ode is
typical of a mannerist description – there is no real attempt to describe Nature accurately; it is intellectualized, idealized, and refined
in order to present Nature in an artificial manner that would be appreciated by Tristan's audience.

This mannerist prettiness and the calm world of myth and illusion in the first part of the poem soon give way to a long description of a storm at sea and the reaction of the crew of a ship caught
in the storm. The waves are personified and their attack on the hapless ship is described:

Le vaisseau poussé dans les airs
[. . . . .]
Tantost il est haut élancé,
Tantost il se treuve enfoncé

Jusques sur les sablons humides,
Et se void toujours investir
D'un gros[8] de montagnes liquides
Qui s'avance pour l'engloutir.

(l. 121; ll. 125-130)

In this poem, we have an excellent example of Tristan's very effective use of stasis and kinesis as calm mannerist description is replaced by the dynamism of the storm. The reactions of the captain and crew of the ship are related in nine stanzas in the original published poem, but six of these were deleted when the poem was placed in the *Vers héroïques*. These six stanzas are definitely not what a 1648 audience would appreciate; they describe death and suffering:

Les poissons d'abord effroyez,
Voyant des corps demy noyez,
Devorent tous ces miserables[9]

Tristan was well advised to shorten the poem in this manner while suppressing some stanzas which were either in bad taste or were simply too long and tedious to be of interest to the sophisticated coterie that was his readership.

The poem ends with a rather long tribute to Gaston d'Orléans whom Tristan praises in the usual hyperbolic manner of the Malherbian heroic ode. He celebrates Gaston's victory at Ré, which was due solely to Monsieur's generosity, courage, and foresight. The soldiers who took part in breaking the blockade owe everything to Gaston, as Tristan states with a curious use of metonymy:

Ils devoient leur bonne fortune
A ton oeil qui les conduisoit.

(ll. 219 220)

The final note of the poem is the obligatory prophesy wherein Tristan predicts many great victories for Gaston because of his virtue. The very last lines of the poem are the poet's boast of the immortality of his verses:

---

[8] Gros: n. m. Troupe nombreuse (Dubois et Lagane, *Dictionnaire de la langue française classique*), Grisé's note.

[9] Quoted in Grisé's edition, p. 65.

Ce sera lors qu'avec des vers
Qui naistront d'une belle veine,
Je feray voir à l'univers
Que ta valeur est plus qu'humaine.
Mes trais auront tant de clartez,
De pompe, d'art et de beautez,
Que l'Envie en deviendra blesme,
Et baissant ses honteux regars,
Pensera qu'Apollon luy mesme
Ait écrit les gestes de Mars.
(ll. 241-250)

This very early poem of Tristan L'Hermite is a blend of the dominant styles in France in the early seventeenth century. It is mannerist in its conception, baroque in the scenes of horror during the
storm, and is Malherbian/classical in its praise of Gaston d'Orléans.
The poem certainly is an example of a writer using different styles
in the same work.

Another example of Tristan's occasional poetry is the very moving poem (CVIII, "A Madame la duchesse de . . .," 290-292) in
which he leaves the service of the Duchesse de Chaulnes, saying
that he is too ill to leave Paris and join her in Auvergne. [10] On the
surface, it is the sad lament of a sick and dying poet, who is too infirm to make the short trip from Paris to Auvergne. The poem was
written in 1645, well before Tristan sought to join the Duc de Guise
in Italy. Either he had a remarkable recovery or he simply exaggerated his condition because he could not bear to leave Paris. What is
remarkable about the poem is its verisimilitude; Tristan makes us
believe that it is true and he uses many rhetorical devices for that
purpose. The poem is a combination of Tristan's heroic poetry with
his personal, it is very effective, and *vraisemblable*, and it certainly
conveys a personal lyricism that seems genuine. Even if, as I sus-
pect, Tristan was exaggerating his illness to avoid leaving Paris, the
poem is moving and gives the impression of sincerity.

The poem relates Tristan's excuses for not going to Auvergne,
through the use of pathos, obviously designed to move the Duchess
and make her accept his departure from her service. He cites his illness, his depressed state of mind, and the cruelty of his Fate and

---

[10] Her husband had recently been made governor of Auvergne.

does so by the very skillful technique of a refrain that is both haunt-
ing and pathetic: "Belle Duchesse, je me meurs." [11] The first eight
lines reveal the subject of the poem and, in rhymed couplets, Tristan establishes the poignancy of the lyric:

> C'est en vain qu'Amour romp ses armes,
> Esteint son flambeau de ses larmes,
> Et fait de plaintives clameurs,
> Belle Duchesse, je me meurs.
> Il faut que par d'autres Orphées
> Il face chanter ses trophées,
> Puis que pressé de m'en aler
> Je ne puis chanter, ni parler.
>
> (ll. 1-8)

Coupled with his litany of his illness and his sad situation as a vic-
tim of Fortune, is a rather extensive adulation of the beauty and
character of the Belle Duchesse. This laudation in very serious
terms is marred by some bad rimes and a Petrarchan description of
the power of her eyes:

> Le devoir enfin vous engage
> A faire un plus heureux voyage
> En des lieux de neige couvers,
> Et que vous alez rendre vers,
> Car vos yeux ont le privilege
> De fondre la glace et la neige
>
> (ll. 29-34)

He concludes the poem with a description of his miserable state:

> Quand à moy je ne verray rien,
> Et ne sentiray point de bien,
> Car, ô dame tres-honorable,
> Je le dis, et suis veritable
> Plus que tous les autres rimeurs,
> Belle Duchesse, je me meurs.
>
> (ll. 71-76)

---

[11] He uses this refrain six times in a poem of seventy-six lines and at times when
it is most effective.

Perhaps Tristan doth protest too much in line 74; he had possibly already secured entrance into the service of the Duc de Guise. Whatever the situation, the poem conveys an impression of sincerity and pathos and is thus a very successful poem. One of the aims of baroque literature is to move its readers to a certain point of view. Here Tristan presents both a picture of his turbulent emotions and an extensive glorification of a patron whom he truly seems to admire. Both are accomplished; the poem moves us to pity for him and admiration for her and is thus an example of the *discours baroque.*

Tristan wrote many poems for the Duc de Guise, both to praise him and to assist him in his courtship of Suzanne de Pons.[12] He celebrates the Duc's nobility and divinity in several poems found in the *Vers héroïques.*[13] The series deals primarily with the voyage of his patron into Italy and the effect of that expedition on both his mistress and his *poète à gages.* There is much uniformity in this series of poems, which celebrate de Guise's prowess as lover and soldier, but some are worthy of consideration because they illustrate the versatility of Tristan's poetic style. Following in the Malherbian tradition, Tristan wrote sonnets, odes, and *stances* to celebrate the virtues of the Duc de Guise and of his beloved Suzanne de Pons. The central themes of these poems are the beauty, courage, and military prowess of the Duke and his subservience in love to Suzanne. When Tristan deals with love or beauty, he speaks of them in Petrarchan terms and uses the same images that he used in his earliest efforts. When he celebrates a victory or praises his patron, he is less inclined to use Petrarchan figures and seems to prefer the clear hyperbolic style of Malherbe. It is not at all unusual to see both styles within the same poem, as will be seen in the following discussion. As Catherine M. Grisé has so ably demonstrated, Tristan's occasional and heroic poetry utilizes the categories of the epideictic branch of rhetoric.[14] It is very conventional in its praise of the dedicatee, celebrating his or her ancestry, education, wealth, power, beauty, wisdom, and courage. There is very little room for originality in the genre, but Tristan does show some innovation

---

[12] Poems in the *Vers héroïques* written for de Guise and his mistress are: XX-XIV-LV, LXXIX-LXXXI, and CXXIV). The encomiastic poetry will be discussed here; the love poetry on pages 149-151.

[13] His long tribute to the Duke, *La Renommée,* will be discussed in the next chapter.

[14] "The Poetry of Tristan L'Hermite," 146-149.

that is worthy of note, as is shown in the following discussion of several of these poems.

Sonnet XXXIV (188) is a typical example of Tristan's encomiastic poetry in an abridged form which he would expand in his odes and stances. The sonnet is written around the motif of the attractiveness and courage of the Duc de Guise. He begins his laudatory remarks, which are directed to the Duke:

> Prince qu'on peut nomer la gloire de nostre age,
> J'observe ton merite avec étonnement,
> C'est l'oeuvre en qui le Ciel joint le plus hautement
> La grandeur de l'esprit à celle du courage.

> (ll. 1-4)

The words: *Prince, gloire, merite, hautement, grandeur,* and *courage* intensify Tristan's purpose in the first quatrain – to praise the nobility and bravery of his patron. He observes the merit of the Duke with "étonnement," hyperbolically referring to him as the *oeuvre* of heaven that is the zenith of intelligence and courage. In the second quatrain, Tristan praises the Duke for his personal attributes such as charm, physical beauty, and the ability to inspire love in all who see or hear him:

> Par tout, ta grace éclate avec tant d'avantage,
> Et d'un charme subtil ravit si doucement,
> Qu'on ne peut sans amour observer un moment
> Le son de ta parole et l'air de ton visage.

His grace, charm, voice, and appearance are accented by the verbs *éclater* and *ravir*, while his attractiveness inspires everyone to love him. The two tercets praise first his soldierly prowess and then his loveableness, and conclude with an antithetical statement that his "force" can make him either feared or loved. Tristan compresses many images and ideas in a few lines and is very successful in this short encomium of the Duc de Guise. The sonnet is free of Petrarchan metaphors and is a fine example both of an excellent encomium and of the skill of its author. It is very reminiscent of Malherbe's occasional poetry, without the mythological allusions, and it shows the classicism or *baroque dompté* that Tristan reveals in most of his laudatory or heroic poems.

In 1646, on entering the service of de Guise, Tristan composed some stances (XXXVI, 190-192) that are an interesting example of the Malherbian encomium mixed with the mannerist commonplaces of love. He describes his joy in servitude to the Duke and expresses it in a combination of Malherbian and Petrarchan terms. The invocation to the "Souverains directeurs des affaires humaines" (l. 3) is followed by a description of his servitude to the Duke, utilizing the same terms that he employs in his amatory lyrics:

> En me donnant des chaînes
> Vous m'avez octroyé ce que j'aime le mieux.
>
> (ll. 5-6)

The hyperbole continues:

> Et les plus libertins que la contrainte étonne
> Fuiroient une couronne
> Pour embrasser les fers où je suis engagé.
>
> (ll. 10-12)

In the third and fourth stanzas, Tristan celebrates the *gloire* of the Duc de Guise and praises his noble birth, his intelligence, and his courage. The fifth stanza serves as a climax to the praise of de Guise and sums up his virtues in very euphonious lines:

> Jamais une celeste flame
> N'infusa dans une ame
> Tant de lumiere et de chaleur ;
> Jamais des qualitez dignes d'estre adorées
> Ne sont rencontrées
> Avec tant de bonté, de grace, et de valeur.
>
> (ll. 25-30)

Tristan then praises Suzanne de Pons (Elize) in a rather novel way. She is the only thing in the world that can vanquish him and she has already done so, much to the credit of both:

> C'est qu'il s'est laissé prendre à la beauté d'Elize,
> Et qu'Amour le maistrise,
> Amour qui bien souvent a maistrisé les dieux.
>
> (ll. 34-36)

In a typically mannerist conceit, Tristan says that whoever might see this beauty can easily excuse the Duke's *défaut*:

> Et ne s'étonne point qu'un si charmante visage
>   Prenne tant d'avantage
> Sur l'ame la plus grande et le coeur le plus haut.
>
> (ll. 40-42)

To emphasize this exceptional beauty, Tristan shows her to be superior both to Helen of Troy and to Omphale, whom Hercules served as a slave. This "nouvel Alcyde" is then praised for his devotion to honor in a stanza that blends the heroic style with the amatory language of the Petrarchan tradition:

> Et quand Mars le demande on void bien que cette ame
>   Qu'Elize met en flame,
> Brûle aussi du desir de l'immortalité.
>
> (ll. 52-54)

The poem closes with a witty prognostication of the Duke's future as a soldier:

> Et tout couvert de sang, de fumée, et de poudre,
>   Il va lancer la foudre
> A l'honneur des beaux yeux dont il est foudroyé.
>
> (ll. 58-60)

In a brilliant mixture of the baroque encomium and the mannerist love lyric, Tristan has shown, once again, his versatility and his mastery of both styles.

A very different approach is taken to the heroic poem in "A la Ville de Rome, En Faveur de Monseigneur le duc de Guise" (LI, 210-212). The poem is addressed to the city of Rome and is completely free of the Petrarchan traits that abound in his mannerist works. The stances are written in the heroic style of Malherbe and his followers, and are thus baroque, but a baroque that is restrained and clear and very powerful. The eloquent alexandrines suggest the power and glory of Rome and the virtues of Henri:

> Maistresse des citez et le chef de la terre,
> Solide fondement du siege de Saint Pierre

> Dont le nom glorieux vole de toutes pars,
> Tu dois réjouir, superbe et sainte Rome,
> En recevant un homme
> Que nous tenons égal au premier des Cesars.
>
> (ll. 1-6)

He continues with praise of the Duke's ancestry, his birth under a favorable star, his physical attractiveness, and his deserving of respect and love. The highest value of de Guise, Tristan tells Rome, is his military capability. In an eloquent, impressive stanza of six lines, Tristan's use of tropes and suggestive vocabulary dazzles the reader and drives home the idea of the greatness of the Duke:

> Mais sa haute *valeur* est un nouveau *prodige*
> Qui *brille* avec *éclat* où la *Gloire* l'oblige
> *D'agir avec le fer* pour *l'immortalité*,
> Et s'il avoit en teste *un des plus vaillans* hommes
> De ceux que *tu renommes,*
> Tout *l'espoir* de *l'honneur* seroit de son costé.
>
> (ll. 25-30)

The words that I have italicized emphasize the fame that is his, because of his bravery and prowess as a soldier. The poem ends with the poet predicting a superb military future for de Guise, whose exploits will be praised more than those of the Battle of Lepanto. The hyperbole and periphrasis combine with clear and forceful lines to make this a very effective example of a baroque heroic poem.

One additional encomium worthy of discussion is "La Gloire, à Monseigneur le duc de Guise" (LII, 213-215). Tristan, rather than praise the Duke himself, relinquishes his laudatory duties to an abstraction, Gloire, who is addressing the Duc de Guise.[15] Fame tells de Guise that his ancestors desired renown as much as he does now. To obtain that fame, he must distinguish himself in war with the Spanish:

> Si toujours vostre coeur pour mes faveurs soupire,
> Tournez vers les Estats que defend le Lyon,
> Et venez prendre part au debris[16] d'un Empire
> Qui sera plus fameuz que celuy d'Ilion.
>
> (ll. 9-12)

---

[15] *Gloire* is used here in the sense of *renommée, réputation,* and *célébrité.*

[16] Débris: n. m. Destruction, écroulement (Dubois et Lagane).

The laudation of de Guise proceeds in the usual manner of the Malherbian encomium until the eighth strophe, when Fame turns her attention to Suzanne de Pons. Calling her a rival, Fame is not jealous or envious of her, because:

> Aussy j'ay de la joie à louer ma rivale,
> Pour mille qualitez je l'ayme avec raison.
> A ce divin chef-d'ouvre il n'est rien qui s'égale,
> Et mesme le Soleil craint sa comparaison.
>
> (ll. 41-44)

At this point in the poem, Tristan reverts to the conventional language of the love lyric and praises Suzanne's beauty in the next twenty lines. Nymphs and naiads are seen in a pastoral setting, extolling "ses beautez." The poem ends with a clever request by Fame to the Duke:

> Il faut qu'un promt retour,[17] grand Prince, nous assure
> Que nulle autre beauté n'ébranle vostre foi ;
> Elize vous en prie et je vous en conjure,
> Ou revenez pour elle, ou revenez pour moy.
>
> (ll. 65-68)

Tristan, writing here at the request of Suzanne de Pons, praises de Guise in the conventional Malherbian mode and Suzanne in a more Petrarchan style. Tristan shows his *acutezza* in the stanza quoted above, when Fame urges the Duke to be faithful to his mistress and to return from Italy either for her or for Suzanne. The blend of styles and the use of an abstraction to narrate the poem, make this an original and very successful encomium of the two lovers.

As he did in *La Lyre*, Tristan included many *précieux* epigrams and sonnets, as well as some longer endeavors that are clearly in the mannerist tradition. The epigram had been used extensively in *Les Amours* and *La Lyre* and Tristan deemed it important to appeal to the *précieuses* by means of this short, witty, verse form. His subjects and tones are either burlesque or slightly obscene. "Pour un jaloux d'une belle femme" (XCVII, 279) is typical of the genre:

---

[17] The Duke was away at this time on his mission to free Naples from the Spanish.

> Jaloux du bel objet dont je suis amoureux,
> En vain ta vigilance à le guetter s'atache ;
> Argus avec cent yeux ne sceut garder sa vache,
> Crois-tu garder ta femme et tu n'en as que deux?

Another amorous epigram, a madrigal, "Pour une belle gorge cachée" (CXIX, 317), will serve to demonstrate this type of verse:

> Les plus beaux ornemens qui soient en l'univers
>   Ne paroissent point sous des voiles,
> Le ciel et le soleil nous sont tous découvers,
> Et nous voyons l'iris, l'aurore, et les estoilles.
>   Pourquoy donc cacher d'un mouchoir
> Ce beau sein composé d'une nege si dure?
> Faut-il par ces rigueurs nous empêcher de voir
>   Les merveilles de la nature? [18]

A good example of the burlesque epigram is "Pour un chirurgien qui espousoit une vieille femme" (CIII, 282). This poem is in the same vein as "La Gouvernante importune" in the *Amours* but it is considerably shorter and more to the point:

> Si tu prens ce squelete antique
> Pour le pendre dans ta boutique,
> Je tiens que tu n'as point de tort.
> Mais quoy, beau joueur de guiterre,
> Tu veux avant que d'estre en terre
> Te coucher au lit de la Mort.

These short witty poems were much in demand in the salons and Tristan showed that he could master the genre. They are mannerist because of the usual reasons, aristocratic audience, imitation of the epigrams in the *Anthologie grecque, acutezza,* refinement, and com-

---

[18] Tristan had written a similar *Lettre meslée,* also of dubious taste, to Mlle de Beaumont:

Mademoiselle,

Il faut que je vous avertisse en secret d'une vérité qui est publique. C'est que vous avez mille apas dans l'esprit et dans le visage, mais parmi tant de beautez qui sont differentes on en aperçoit deux sur votre sein qui sont égales, et que l'on peut apeller en particulier Beaumont, comme vous. (Letter XXXVIII, 88)

plete lack of seriousness. These ludic poems, like their counterparts in *Les Amours* and *La Lyre*, were nothing more than intellectual games enjoyed by a very appreciative audience at court or in
the *ruelles*.

The Tristan of the *Plaintes d'Acante* and the *Amours* appears in
numerous love lyrics in the *Vers héroïques*. These early mannerist
works reflected Tristan's infatuation with Petrarch at first, and later
with Marino. Three sonnets will serve to illustrate his range in the
love poetry found in this volume. Very mannerist is the second of
Tristan's "Belle Matineuse" sonnets. [19] This sonnet (XXXIX, 197)
was one of two entered by Tristan in an unofficial competition with
Malleville, Voiture, and others. [20] In late afternoon, Elize passed by
in a chariot which shone through the sole splendor of her divine
beauty:

> Mille apas éclatans qui font un nouveau jour
> Et qui sont couronnez d'une grace immortelle,
> Les rayons de la gloire et les feux de l'amour,
> Eblouissoient la veue et brûloient avec elle.
>
> (ll. 5-8)

As the sun set, there was a sudden brightness:

> Mon desordre fut grand, je ne le cele pas.
> Voyant baisser le jour et rencontrant Elize,
> Je creus que le Soleil revenoit sur ses pas.
>
> (ll. 12-14)

This version of the Belle Matineuse theme was written for the Duc
de Guise to give to his mistress, Suzanne de Pons, the Elize of several poems. It is very clearly in the mannerist style and it is typical
of the many ludic poems written for the elite coterie to whom Tristan addressed much of his work.

Another sonnet is more in the tradition of Marino and is an imitation of the "Bellissima Mendica" of Claudio Achillini, published
in Bologna in 1632. It is in a group of sonnets that deal with beauty in places or in people where one would not expect it. Like the

---

[19] The other is in *La Lyre*, XXXIX. See the preceding chapter, 129-130.
[20] For an excellent history of the "Belle Matineuse" motif, see Chauveau's *Noti-
ce* in his edition of *La Lyre*, 150-151.

"Belle Esclave More," or the "Belle en dueil," the "Belle Gueuse" (LXVIII, 244) is a person who would not have been celebrated by the Petrarchan poets until the genre was revitalized by Marino and his followers. The Marinism of Tristan is very evident here as he blends it with Petrarchan language in a sonnet that is remarkable for its concluding conceit:

> Ce rare honneur des orphelines,
> Couvert de ces mauvais habits,
> Nous découvre des perles fines
> Dans une boeste de rubis.
>
> Ses yeux sont des saphirs qui brillent,
> Et ses cheveux qui s'éparpillent
> Font montre d'un riche tresor ;
>
> A quoi bon sa triste requeste,
> Si, pour faire pleuvoir de l'or,
> Elle n'a qu'à baisser la teste.
>
> (ll. 5-14)

Tristan overwhelms us with allusions to precious stones and metals and makes it a point in the first quatrain to describe the Gueuse's beauty. The nearest he comes to a real description of her poverty and wretched condition is line six where he says that she is "couvert[e] de ses mauvais habits." The poem is simply a variation on the mannerist love poetry that Tristan has written since his youth; it is well written, witty, and totally ludic.

The final sonnet to be considered in this group of poems is entitled "L'Extase d'un baiser" (XLVII, 206), another poem written for his patron, the Duc de Guise, for Suzanne de Pons. Elize's kiss has very definite effects on the narrator of the poem:

> Mais tout mon sang s'altere, une brûlante fievre
> Me ravit la couleur et m'oste la raison ;
> Cieux ! J'ay pris à la fois sur cette belle lèvre
> D'un celeste nectar et d'un mortel poison.
>
> (ll. 5-8)

This is not a description of baroque passion; it is simply hyperbole within the conventions of seventeenth-century love poetry. The first tercet is laughable in its comic expression of passion:

Ah ! mon ame s'envole en ce transport de joye !
Ce gage de salut dans la tombe m'envoye ;
C'est fait ! Je n'en puis plus, Elize, je me meurs.

(ll. 9-11)

He then closes his sonnet with a metaphor that is found quite often in his poetry, the flower/snake, or thorn figure:

Ce baiser est un sceau par qui ma vie est close ;
Et comme on peut treuver un serpent sous des fleurs,
J'ay rencontré ma mort sur un bouton de rose.

(ll. 12-14)

This delightful sonnet, especially in its concluding *pointe*, demonstrates Tristan's ability to make use of the traditions of the love lyric in a poem rich in images and rhetoric.

There are several long poems in the collection that are not easily characterized, such as the very long ode "La Maison d'Astrée" (XXXIII, 173-187),[21] a poem of 410 lines. It is occasional poetry celebrating the recently remodeled estate of Charlotte d'Estampes-Valençay, Marquise de Puisieux, at Berny. The general theme of the poem is that art imitates and surpasses Nature. It is an encomium of the Marquise coupled with a fanciful description of the construction of her château by thousands of *putti* who surpass Nature in their building and in their art. The exaggerated descriptions of the estate are laced with mythological allusions, resulting in that prettiness that characterizes mannerism:

Les uns dans quelque char leger
Qui fend l'air plus soudain que l'aisle de Zephire,
Guident un cygne et viennent décharger
Des cubes de cristal, d'agathe et de porphire ;
D'autres dans la nue elevez,
Conduisans des pigeons privez,
Ameinent du jaspe et du marbre ;

---

[21] Tristan's letter that accompanied this poem is in the *Lettres meslées*, 142-143. The recent discovery (see next chapter) of six stanzas of the poem in manuscript form in a book of emblems by Otto van Veen, was reported in: Alison Adams, "Glasgow University SMAdd.392 and the printed versions of Tristan l'Hermite's Poetry," *Glasgow Emblem Studies* 2 (1997): 141-147.

Et d'autres pour construire un superbe plancher
Traînent des pieces de quelque arbre,
Où le phoenix peut-estre a dressé son bûcher.

(ll. 51-60)

The unusual combination of baroque encomium within a decidedly mannerist setting lends credence to Warnke's definitions: Baroque, the period, and baroque and mannerism, the dominant styles of the period.[22]

Another interesting poem is a fanciful account of a voyage that Tristan made for Madame, Marguerite de Lorraine, whose escape to Brussels in 1633 had been a subject of great admiration among the French exiles living there.[23] Its full title is: "Les Terreurs nocturnes, Ecrites pour le divertissement d'une grande princesse, sur le sujet de quelques voyages perilleux que l'autheur avoit fait pour son service" (LXXVII, 255-261). The first fifty lines of the ode are a sort of prelude in which the poet celebrates, in Petrarchan terms, the virtues of Madame and tells of his efforts to save her from the slander of those who do not really know her. He invokes the "Grands dieux" to help her and is assured that all will be well with her:

Car l'esprit que je dessers
Se rend les demons dociles ;

(ll. 45-46)

The tone changes with line 50 as the narration of his adventure begins. It is nightfall and as Tristan is riding his horse through a gloomy forest, he begins to be afraid:

Je vay voir mille fantômes
A me faire évanouir.

(ll. 69-70)

Par un triste changement
Que produisent les tenebres,
Les bois et les elemens
Ont pris des habits funebres.

(ll. 81-84)

---

[22] Frank J. Warnke, *Versions of the Baroque* (New Haven: Yale UP, 1972), 12-20.
[23] "Sur la venue de Madame," *Plaintes d'Acante*, 91-94.

The usual elements in a scene of baroque horror appear: wolves and owls; and the darkness of the forest is underscored. The poet blames the gods for his troubles that he is sure will lead to his imminent death:

> Des hyboux chantent là-bas
> C'est fait, il faut que je meure ;
> Sans doute de mon trépas
> Ils viennent m'anoncer l'heure.
>
> (ll. 121-124)

In a return to the theme of love that was so dear to Tristan L'Hermite, he assumes that this misfortune is due to his constancy and suffering in love:

> Mes voeux n'ont point merité
> Que vostre courroux m'oprime.
> J'ayme avec fidelité,
> Et c'est là mon plus grand crime.
>
> (ll. 131-134)

Due to the skill of his horse, he gets through the forest and sees a house that he goes to in order to receive hospitality. At first, no one answers his call; but after dawn has arrived, he ends his narrative with these words to Hylas, his host:

> O brave et charmant Hylas !
> Qu'on me donne en diligence
> Des oeufs frais, un matelas,
> Et trois heures de silence.
> Soulage un peu mes travaux
> Par un secours si celeste,
> Et fay seller des chevaux
> Sans craindre rien de funeste ;
> Hylas ! je n'ay pas la peste,
> Mais j'ay cent fois plus de maux.
>
> (ll. 191-200)

Tristan has taken an encomium of a grand person, along with a very conventional, Petrarchan love motif, and placed them around a description of fear of the dark and the unknown. Love's trials are reflected metaphorically in the nocturnal terrors, and suffering in love is made to be far more serious than being lost in a forest at night. While one might see this poem as depicting "baroque horror," a better interpretation would be that Tristan has again appropriated elements of the baroque style and placed them in a mannerist poem.

The final category of poems to be considered in the *Vers héroïques* is that of personal poetry; that is poems in which Tristan expresses his true feelings about life, freedom, servitude, poetry, and death, or in which he engages in social criticism. An outstanding example of this type is Poem XXIV, "La Servitude" (155-160). The poem was written in 1645 as Tristan reluctantly left Gaston for the Duchesse de Chaulnes. It is a rare example of personal lyricism in Tristan L'Hermite and it is certainly one of his best and most moving efforts. The poem begins with an apostrophe to night in which he asks for its advice concerning leaving Gaston for the service of the Duchesse de Chaulnes:

> Nuit fraische, sombre, et solitaire,
>   Sainte depositaire
> De tous les grands secrets, ou de guerre ou d'amour,
> Nuit mere du repos, et nourrice des veilles
>   Qui produisent tant de merveilles,
> Donne moy des conseils qui soient digne du jour.
>
> (ll. 1-6)

He then launches an attack on the star that has been cruel to him – a Fate that has caused Gaston to cast him aside:

> Je vois que Gaston m'abandonne
>   Cette digne personne
> Dont j'esperois tirer ma gloire et mon support,
> Cette divinité que j'ay toujours suivie,
>   Pour qui j'ay hasardé ma vie,
> Et pour qui mesme encor je voudrois estre mort.
>
> (ll. 13-18)

He attacks the perfidy in Gaston's entourage and reasons that he must give up any hopes with Gaston, for whom he would still die. He then goes to a discussion of servitude, which he graphically describes with very strong metaphors and very vivid images:

> L'image de la Servitude,
> Errant dans mon etude,
> Y promeine l'horreur qui reside aux enfers ;
> J'oi déjà qu'on m'enrôle au nombre des esclaves,
> Je ne voy plus que des entraves,
> Des jougs et des coliers, des chaînes et des fers.
>
> (ll. 61-66)

He invokes reason to advise him and he concludes that he should enter the retinue of the Duchess because of her many fine qualities. The poem ends with eight strophes of praise of his new patron – he will serve her loyally and immortalize her in his verse. If he must bow down to anyone, it should be to her because of her divine qualities:

> Suivre ce digne objet qui n'eut jamais d'exemple,
> C'est servir, mais c'est dans un temple,
> C'est un peu s'abaisser, mais c'est devant les dieux.
>
> (ll. 136-138)

This outstanding poem is an excellent example of Tristan's baroque or serious side. He deals with significant issues in a lofty style, he praises virtues such as loyalty and sincerity and he condemns the hypocrisy and mendacity that was prevalent in the higher echelons of contemporary society. Tristan's very effective use of enjambment is certainly not classical; it is very typical of a baroque poet.

A second personal poem in the volume is "Sonnet" (CXXIX, 28) in which the poet tells us of his fears concerning the onset of old age:

> C'est fait de mes destins ; je commence à sentir
> Les incommoditez que la vieillesse apporte.
> Déjà la pâle Mort pour me faire partir,
> D'un pied sec et tremblant vient frapper à ma porte.
>
> (ll. 1-4)

Death is inevitable and the poem concludes didactically with Tristan's reflections on death and the best way to prepare for it:

> Il faut éteindre en nous tous frivoles desirs,
> Il faut nous détacher des terrestres plaisirs
> Où sans discretion nostre apetit nous plonge.

Sortons de ces erreurs par un sage conseil,
Et cessans d'embrasser les images d'un songe,
Pensons à nous coucher pour le dernier sommeil.

(ll. 9-14)

The sonnet is baroque in its use of rhetoric, its didacticism, and its stoic treatment of death. It is a very serious reflection on death by one who was about to face it.

The final personal poem in the volume is "Prosopopée de F. T. L.," a four line epitaph of *François Tristan L'Hermite*:

Elevé dans la cour dès ma tendre jeunesse,
J'aborday la fortune et n'en eus jamais rien,
Car j'aymay la Vertu, cette altiere maistresse
Qui fait braver la peine et mépriser le bien.

This little poem is typical of Tristan's stoicism and it is certainly true to the facts of his life as we know them. It is serious and is an example of the classical baroque, the *baroque dompté* that Tristan used on occasions.

The *Vers héroïques* contain a variety of poems in the heroic style of Malherbe, the *précieux* style of Voiture, the erotic style of Marino, and the personal style of Théophile de Viau – all poets to whom Tristan turned for inspiration in composing his poetry. The baroque appears very strongly in "La Servitude"; it is toned down in the heroic poems as a whole and becomes almost classical. Mannerism can be seen in the many *précieux* and Petrarchan lyrics, and the influence of Marino is seen in such sonnets as "La Belle gueuse." The volume, like *La Lyre*, is divided into several styles and is a virtuoso's presentation of some of his finest works.

CHAPTER IX

MANNERISM AND BAROQUE IN THE RELIGIOUS
AND MISCELLANEOUS POETRY

I N 1646 Tristan published a volume of religious poetry and prose
entitled *L'Office de la Sainte Vierge* which evidently did not sell
very well because, in 1653, the unsold copies appeared with a new
title, *Les Heures dédiées à la Sainte Vierge.* The volume is certainly
not one of Tristan's better efforts; it does, however, contain a few
poems worthy of our attention. The majority betray hasty composition and a lack of interest on the part of the author. The poems are
very much in the baroque style that was prevalent in the first half of
the seventeenth century. He later translated forty-two hymns from
the Roman Breviary that are much less baroque than classical. In
1997, a group of poems by Tristan was found in a book of emblems,
the *Amorum Emblemata* by Otto Van Veen (Antwerp, 1608), which
was recently acquired by the University of Glasgow. The texts were
published in *Glasgow Emblem Studies,*[1] and were later reproduced
in part in *Cahiers Tristan L'Hermite.*[2] The poems, all of which deal
with some aspect of love, serve to illustrate further the theme of the
emblems to which they are juxtaposed. They were written early in
Tristan's career, and they reflect much the same mannerist style that
we have seen in his other love poetry. In 1654 he wrote and had
published a long poem, *La Renommée,* his last major work, which
reveals a great deal about his evolution as a poet. This chapter will

---

[1] Laurence Grove, ed., "Emblems and the Manuscript Tradition" (Glasgow:
Glasgow Emblem Studies, 1997), 101-192 contains detailed information about the
thirteen previously unpublished poems that are attributed to Tristan. The analyses and explanations contained in this volume reflect the very highest ideals of
scholarship.

[2] Laurence Grove, "Glasgow University Library SMAdd.392: Treize poèmes in-
édits de Tristan?," *Cahiers Tristan L'Hermite* 20 (1998): 29-47.

discuss the religious poetry[3] first, then the thirteen previously unpublished poems in the Glasgow *Amorum Emblemata*,[4] and will
conclude with *La Renommée*.[5] Tristan's religious, early love, and
heroic poetry represent the three principal styles of his poetry—
baroque, mannerist, and Malherbian or *baroque dompté*.

L'Office de la Sainte Vierge is a collection of devotional poetry
and prose, in Latin and French, based on the liturgy of the Church,
the meditations of Saint François de Sales, and the prayers and
meditations of Loyola.[6] I have chosen five poems in the aggregation
which are representative of the collection as a whole: "A Saint Lau-
rent" (199), "Prière à la Sainte Vierge pour obtenir de son Fils nostre Sauveur, la remission de nos Pechez" (135-139), "Méditation sur
le Memento homo" (216-222), "Paraphrase Sur le Miserere mei
deus secundum, etc." (129-134), and "Sur la réception du Saint-
Sacrement" (140-143). The poem to Saint Lawrence is relatively
short, ten lines, and consists of a conceit built around fire and the
Saint's martyrdom at the stake:

> Ménager qui là haut assemblois un Trésor,
> Phoenix entre les Saincts, celeste Salamandre,
> Ta constance et ta foy s'éprouvent comme l'or
> Au milieu du brazier qui te reduit en cendre.

---

[3] Tristan's religious poetry has not been published in a modern edition. It has,
however, been edited and compiled in a dissertation by Ruth Ann Gjelsteen (directed by Claude K. Abraham), "The Religious Poetry of Tristan L'Hermite: A Critical
Edition," Diss. U Cal. (Davis), 1977. It is this edition that will be the source of all
references to Tristan's religious poems. The poems are presented in a diplomatic
format with nasal and missing letter symbols and no attempt to distinguish I, J, V,
or U. I have modernized the text to eliminate confusion between I&J;U&V; and
have replaced the symbols for nasals and letters missing with the complete word.

[4] All quotations from these poems will be from the diplomatic text established
by Alison Adams in *Glasgow Emblem Studies* 2 (1997): 119-139. Since this is a recent discovery, I believe that the diplomatic text would be of interest to the reader.

[5] *La Renommée* exists in the 1654 version at the Bibliothèque National and was
modernized and reprinted by Bernardin in an appendix to his *Un Précurseur de
Racine: Tristan L'Hermite, Sieur de Solier (1601-1655), sa famille, sa vie, ses oeuvres*
(Geneva: Slatkine Reprints, 1967), 616-621.

[6] For an excellent study of Tristanian religious poetry, see Grisé, "The Poetry
of Tristan L'Hermite," 236-271; see also Abraham, *Tristan L'Hermite*, 69-77. I am
deeply indebted to them for my understanding of the religious poetry of Tristan
L'Hermite. Another study of the religious poetry is: Henri Gerbaud, "Au sujet de
l'Office de la Sainte Vierge," *Cahiers Tristan L'Hermite* 18 (1996): 55-59.

Tu sou-ris aux douleurs sur les charbons ardans,
Car la divine ardeur qui t'embrase au dedans
Tourne tous-jours tes yeux vers le Sauveur des ames.

Il semble que le feu soit ton propre element;
Ton esprit & ton corps bruslent egalement,
Tu vis, chaste Laurens, & meurs parmy les flames.

Saint Lawrence is compared to the Phoenix, a symbol of the triumph of eternal life over death, and is given the epithet, "celeste Salamandre," a symbol of fire, which provides a link to the main image of the poem, fire. Because of his constancy and faith, Lawrence is capable of rising from his fiery death as the mythological bird did. Besides the two allusions, Tristan uses many words that suggest flames and fire: *brazier, cendre, charbons ardans, embrase, feu, bruslent,* and *flames.* Tristan continues the metaphor throughout the poem, using the symbolism of fire as transmutation, regeneration, and, in this poem, mysticism, purification, and spiritual energy–all of which are attributes of a saint. The *métaphore filée* and the antithetical final line are baroque traits in this poem because of its subject. The marinistic conceits and plays on words are more appropriate in a mannerist love lyric than in a panegyric to a saint. His skillful use of Christian and traditional symbolism, however, places the poem among Tristan's better religious poems–he has graphically painted a picture of Lawrence and his martyrdom and he has given his readers a vivid picture of why they should venerate this saint.

"Prière à la Sainte Vierge . . ." is a long prayer of confession and contrition asking the Virgin to intercede for him with Jesus for the forgiveness of his sins.[7] The poem is of the meditative type as taught by Saint François de Sales and by the founder of the Jesuit order, Saint Ignatius Loyola. The meditative prayer consists of self-examination, admission of sin, and remorse for sin. Though the poet has grievously sinned, he seeks and finds intercession through either a saint or the Virgin Mary. The poem is filled with strong

---

[7] The narrator in these poems could certainly be Tristan speaking his deep-seated religious beliefs as Carriat and Abraham have claimed. He could also be the anonymous *je* of many poems of the epoch. For the sake of clarity, Tristan and the narrator of the religious poetry will be considered one and the same.

baroque images, especially when describing past sins and death. It begins with a direct address to the Virgin, "O mere tout ensemble & fille de mon Juge" (l. 4) and continues with a meditation and confession of his sins: "J'ay tous-jours vers le vice abandonné ma course" (l. 28) and:

> Des meschans j'ay suivi la troupe ;
> Beuvant dans une mesme coupe,
> Je me suis enivré du vin des voluptez ;
> Et l'habitude prise en ce desordre extreme,
> M'a reduit à tel point, que l'iniquité mesme
> Devient le chastiment de mes iniquitez.
>
> (ll. 31-36)

He continues to use the arsenal of rhetoric in describing the effects of sin on him:

> Aussi ce grand amas d'ordure
> Est prest à combler la mesure ;
> Je sucombe aujourd'huy sous ce pesant fardeau ;
> Mes pechez ont produit ulceres sur ulceres,
> Ce ne sont que defauts, ce ne sont que miseres,
> Et mon corps à mon ame est un vivant tombeau.

He is repentant and asks Our Lady for intercession with Jesus for the remission of his sins, making a rather odd statement urging her to do so:

> Employez le credit de vos chastes mamelles ;
> Ces vierges ornemens, ces deux sources jumelles,
> Dont avec tant d'amour Jesus fut alaité.
>
> (ll. 64-66)

This is obviously one of his Petrarchan conceits that made its way into an otherwise serious work. He ends the meditation with an encomium of Mary, which is a paraphrase of the *Ave Maria*:

> Et vous Source de Grace, Advocate des Ames,
> Vierge soyez beniste entre toutes les femmes,
> Et le fruit soit beny que vous avez porté.
>
> (ll. 82-84)

The poem is a clear example of a baroque religious poem because it seeks to reveal universal truths and it is written for the advancement of the Faith. Its intense images and its stately movement are further examples of the baroque in the poem.

One of the outstanding baroque poems in the *Office* is entitled "Méditation sur le Memento homo." It is based on the Ash Wednesday liturgy in which the priest places ashes on the forehead of the congregants while saying: "Memento, homo, quia pulvis es et in pulverem reverteris." In the tradition of seventeenth-century meditative poetry, the poem is a long discussion about death and what happens to body and soul as a result of it. The opening stanza summarizes and graphically reiterates the message of the *Memento*:

> Souvien toy de l'heure derniere,
> Et de l'horreur du monument,
> Où ta despoüille prisonniere,
> Ne sera plus rien que poussiere,
> Et n'aura plus de sentiment.
>
> (ll. 1-5)

Horatian commonplaces concerning the inevitability of death follow and recall the sentiments expressed in Tristan's poems and letters of consolation:

> Ta vie est fresle comme verre ;
> Chaque jour te meine au trespas:
> [. . . . .]
> Elle [la mort] prend un grand personnage
> Ainsi qu'un pauvre Laboureur.
>
> (ll. 16-17 and 24-25)

A procession of illustrious historical and mythological personages who have met death follows, including Caesar, Alexander, Henri IV and Louis XIII, as well as Hercules (Alcide) and Paris. In a very baroque stanza reminiscent of Sponde or Chassignet, Tristan describes the ultimate end of the body in the grave:

> Là ce corps qui se difficile
> Demandoit tant de mets divers,
> Descharné, relant, immobile,
> N'est rien qu'une charongne vile,
> Qui repaist & loge les vers.
>
> (ll. 51-55)

Beginning with line sixty-six, attention is diverted from the body and placed on the soul which is "plus malade que ton corps" (l. 70). The soul must leave the body and appear before God for His judgment, which for the sinners that Tristan is addressing, is the condemnation of the soul to hell:

> Dieu de ses crimes void le Rolle,
> Et d'une tonnante parole
> La précipite dans des feux.
>
> (ll. 88-90)

The tortures of hell are listed in the last part of the poem before the final stanza, which returns to the *Memento Homo* theme and begins, as did the first, with the imperative, "Souvien toy," thus giving the poem closure and reemphasizing his main theme. The poem is a very serious religious meditation which aims to move the reader into an acceptance of the Christian religion. It contains many baroque images and is a good example of baroque religious poetry.[8]

Tristan paraphrased two psalms and the *Stabat Mater* and achieved success with his paraphrases of the fiftieth and hundred twenty-ninth psalms and complete failure with the *Stabat*. The fiftieth psalm begins in the Vulgate with the words: "Miserere mei, Deus, secundum magnam misericordiam tuam ; Et secundum multitudinem miserationum tuarum, dele iniquitatem meam. Amplius lava me ab iniquitate mea, Et a peccato meo munda me."[9] Tristan, as Grisé has pointed out, converts each verse of the Latin into a sizain resulting in a poem of 102 lines. The poem is marked by "clever yet judiciously used metaphors, antitheses, and oxymora consecrated by biblical and patristic writings; yet these do not convey a feeling of artificiality of artifice. On the contrary, they contribute to an overwhelming impression of dedication, of peace, and of harmony."[10] The poem begins with an expanded paraphrase of the Latin original and continues with, for the most part, restrained images that cause the poem to be baroque in the sense of "classicism" or *baroque dompté*. Though written in the first person, it

---

[8] For an excellent analysis of this poem see Grisé, "The Poetry of Tristan L'Hermite," 244-247.

[9] The quotation is from the Vulgate Bible (Madrid: BAC, 1994), 493.

[10] Abraham, *Tristan L'Hermite*, 76. For an interesting discussion of this poem, the reader is referred to Abraham, 76-77. It is also discussed by Grisé in "The Poetry of Tristan L'Hermite," 251-253.

deals with universal truths about man and his relation with God in perfect, dignified alexandrines that are nevertheless very forceful and have the vividness expected in a baroque composition:

> Je reconnois ma faute, une sourde tristesse
> Qui me pique à toute heure & me ronge sans cesse
> Est un bourreau secret qui me comble d'effroy :
> Mon coeur incessament en reçoit quelque atteinte :
> L'horreur de mes forfaits me tient tous-jours en crainte,
> Et tous-jours mon peché s'esleve contre moy.
>
> (ll. 31-36)

The obvious didacticism of the poem is seen in such lines as:

> Si dans mon repentir vos bontez nonpareilles
> Des termes d'un pardon remplissoient mes oreilles
> Quel doux ravissement couleroit dans mon coeur?
> Se degageant soudain de l'ennuy qui le tuë,
> Il tresailliroit d'aise, & mon ame abatuë
> Reprendroit aussi tost sa premiere vigueur.
>
> (ll. 43-48)

This is one of Tristan's best religious poems because of its subtle procession from negative to positive, its communication of deeply held beliefs, and its judicious use of tropes. I would agree with Abraham (77) that sincerity, or at least the impression of it, pervades Tristan's better religious poems such as the "Miserere."

"Sur la réception du Saint-Sacrement" (140-144) is a joyous affirmation of Christian teachings on salvation and God's love for mankind. The first word of the poem is an imperative, "rejoice," and the poem maintains the joy of the morning prayer cycle from beginning to end:

> Réjoui toi mon Ame, & chantons des cantiques
> Tous esclatans d'amour, d'esperence & de foy ;
> Le Monarque de ciel & ses choeurs Angeliques
>   Daigne venir chez toy.
>   [..]
> Cette bonté, Seigneur, dont la grandeur insigne
> M'offre encor vostre grace au lieu du chastiment ;
> Cette haute bonté que je ne suis pas digne
>   D'invoquer seulement.
>
> (ll. 1-4 and 57-60)

The tone of joyous celebration of God's triumph over sin and the emotional descriptions of God's mercy and love make this poem clearly baroque. It uses rhetoric to convince or persuade, it presents its ideas as transcendent truth, the author believes and wants his readers to believe his message, and the strong emotion of joy that pervades the poem make it an excellent example of the *discours baroque*.

Late in his life, Tristan translated the hymns from the Roman Breviary but they were published in 1665, ten years after his death as part of the *Exercices spirituels*. These paraphrases or translations are more classical than baroque because Tristan seems to have grown tired of Marinism and, as in his heroic poetry, sought simplicity and clarity in his verse. These translations are much the same as Tristan's paraphrase of the fiftieth psalm, discussed above, but with more restrained imagery and with greater simplicity. The translations are good, and Tristan seems not to want to outdistance his models in prosody. Claude Abraham has succinctly and correctly evaluated Tristan's religious poetry:

> It is apparent, then, that, while most of Tristan's religious po-
> ems fall far short of his usual standard of quality–and it may be
> surmised that Tristan sold his pen for pecuniary considerations–
> there are notable exceptions. Penury has nothing to do with sin-
> cerity, a sentiment that pervades the better poems such as the
> "Miserere." To fill the pages of a manual, Tristan had to produce
> a given number of poems, and some do seem like the work of a
> hack; to satisfy himself, he penned some of his best lines for in-
> clusion, poems that are well-crafted and deeply moving. There is
> some sifting to be done here, but great benefits can be derived.[11]

The *Offices* is a collection of many different poems but they are primarily baroque for the reasons given above. The *Exercices spiri-tuels*[12] are translations of hymns and are less likely to exhibit strong baroque tendencies; they are more *baroque dompté* or classical, as are the translations of the Breviary by Corneille and Racine.

Through the years many poems by Tristan have been found that were not included in the volumes studied above. Many of

---

[11] *Tristan L'Hermite*, 77.

[12] Marcel Israel has published four of these hymns in *Cahiers Tristan L'Hermite* 2 (1980): 36-45 and has provided a brief survey of the genre in XVIIth century France.

these were collected by Bernardin and placed in an appendix to his thesis, while some have been published in the *Cahiers Tristan L'Hermite*. The discovery of thirteen previously unknown poems in Glasgow is important because they are early examples of Tristan's love poetry. From the standpoint of style, the lines, written to highlight a very mannerist book of emblems, allow us to see the relationship of the pictorial and literary arts. The great majority of these works are mannerist love lyrics that reflect the vocabulary, metaphors, and tone of the amatory poetry written in France in the late sixteenth and early seventeenth centuries. The poems, along with others by Tristan, Voiture, and Malleville were added to the volume of emblems during the 1620's and serve to illustrate the aspect of love found in the emblems to which they are attached.[13] I have identified each poem by its first line and the page in the *Amorum emblemata* that it faces and have retained the diplomatic text established by Alison Adams in *Glasgow Emblem Studies*, Vol. 2.[14] The thirteen poems deal with various aspects of love and are mostly conventional and very similar to the amatory poetry in four of the volumes that Tristan published during his lifetime.[15] Indeed six selections from the "Maison d'Astrée," nine from the *Plaintes d'Acante*, and ten from the *Amours* are found appended to the same volume.[16]

"Quelqu'autre d'une humour commune" (facing p. 3) is a sonnet that has as its thesis the constancy of the poet and the impossibility of love surviving a long separation. Tristan compares the spring, which splits into various streams as it flows, to the love that cannot survive separation. The theme is a common one but Tristan's metaphor is witty and effective:

> Ainsy la flame separée,
> N'est jamais de longue durée ;
> Nous en voyons bien tost le bout ;

---

[13] I am indebted to the articles in *Glasgow Emblem Studies* for the discussion of the contents and arrangement of this book.

[14] 119-139.

[15] *Les Plaintes d'Acante, Les Amours, La Lyre,* and *Les Vers héroïques.*

[16] Alison Adams, "Glasgow University Library SMAdd.392 and the Printed Versions of Tristan L'Hermite's Poetry," *Glasgow Emblem Studies* 2 (1997): 141-157. This article is a very thorough study of the poems that appear both in manuscript form and in Tristan's published works.

> Et pour dire ce qu'il m'en semble ;
> Aymer en diuers lieux ensemble,
> C'est presque n'aymer rien du tout.
>
> (ll. 9-14)

Petrarchan concepts, such as adoration of the lady until the poet's death and the very conventional use of *flame* to represent love, place this sonnet in the mannerist tradition of almost all of Tristan's love poetry.

"Deux coeurs s'aymans parfaitement" (facing p. 13) is a sententious portrayal of the theme that two lovers become one and share the same fortune:

> Ils partagent egalement
> Et les Espines & les roses.
>
> (ll. 3-4)

The second quatrain develops the theme and states more clearly what the roses/espines metaphor had done in the first verse:

> Tousjours une mesme chaleur
> Rend leur avanture commune :
> Receuant des trais du malheur,
> Ou des faueurs de la Fortune.
>
> (ll. 5-8)

The final strophe deals with the eternality of perfect love, a love that continues beyond the grave:

> Car viuans d'une mesme vie
> Ils meurent d'une mesme mort.
>
> (ll. 11-12)

Tristan has taken one of the commonplaces of love poetry and has presented it clearly and effectively in twelve lines. The poem is an excellent example of Tristan's earlier, mannerist style.

"De mesme que le Cerf, blessé mortellement," (facing p. 29) is a sixain that illustrates its accompanying emblem, which shows Cupid relentlessly pursuing a lover whom he has shot with his bow. [17]

---

[17] This emblem is found in *Glasgow Emblem Studies* 182.

As the wounded stag flees and dies rather than find the *Dictame,* [18] the lover, once stricken by the eyes of the Lady, struggles in vain to escape her dominion. The power of the Lady's eyes, the wounding of the poet and his subsequent death, are all Petrarchan motifs that are found throughout the love poems of Tristan L'Hermite. To his credit, Tristan has condensed his thoughts into six lines with the result that his theme is clearly stated and the poem illustrates the emblem to which it is connected.

The sonnet, "Celuy dont la vertu merita tant de Festes," (facing p. 33), is a poem that has as its theme *amor omnia vincit.* Tristan shows the power of love by alluding to several of the great deeds of Hercules and stating that despite these feats of strength, Hercules: "Se laissa surmonter par un Enfant tout nu." The sonnet is an excellent example of mannerist love poetry as it uses mythology and rhetorical display to eulogize the power of love. "O trop aveugle erreur! ô tourment indicible!" (facing p. 60) and "Philis vous avéz tort de rompre ainsy ma cheine" (facing p. 61) are Petrarchan sonnets addressed to Philis. The first is given a pastoral setting in which the motif of "Amor caecus est" is elaborated on. The narrator tells us that he is unhappy because Philis loves another shepherd but that nevertheless he will serve her despite what his reason tells him. The poem contains many Petrarchan traits that are presented antithetically as the poet proclaims his "cruel seruage" to Philis. Though he realizes his impossible situation, he excuses himself in the rather sententious concluding tercet:

> Je suis honteux de voir comment ie me soumets,
> Mais je croy que le bien d'estre amoureux & sage
> Est un don que les Dieux n'acordent iamais.
>
> (ll. 12-14)

The second sonnet addressed to Philis deals with the lady's rejection of the poet. It is perhaps a sequel to the other sonnet and has the same characteristics and theme. The first quatrain is the pleading of the *amant transi*:

> Je sçay que ie n'ay point merité vostre amour,
> Mais ie n'ay point aussy merité vostre hayne.
>
> (ll. 3-4)

---

[18] Dictame: n. m. Plante à laquelle on attribuait la vertu de guérir les blessures ; et au fig. en poésie, *Adoucissement* (Dubois et Lagane).

The contrast is made in the second stanza between the true devotion of the poet and the cruel disdain of the person that she loves:

> Celuy que vous ayméz, vous tient dans une gesne
> Qui vange asséz mon coeur d'un si perfide tour :
> Il vous donne des loix & ie vous fis la Cour,
> Vous estes son Esclave & vous estiéz ma Reyne.

The use of antithesis, highlighted by the shift in tenses, contrasts the differences between the devotion of the poet and the cruelty of his rival. The two tercets continue the antithetic treatment begun in the octet and the poem ends with a plea to the lady to come back to him. All three of these sonnets reflect the *discours maniériste*, as described in chapter III of this study. They are witty, they are Petrarchan in language, and they are intended for an élite audience capable of appreciating the *acutezza* of the poet. There is absolutely no didacticism in them and they echo the commonplaces found in the amatory poetry of the epoch.

"Beauté la plus angelique" (facing p. 71) is titled "Leale & secreto," and illustrates an emblem that shows Cupid with his finger over his lips. [19] The theme is again the cruelty of the lady and the suffering and loyalty of the poet, who suffers in secret. The same theme is found in "Amour sçait fort bien reprimer" (facing p. 73) and in the sonnet, "Que la grace d'Olinde a de trais rauissans" (facing p. 103). In the sonnet, however, the lover is the slave of both Cupid and the beauty of Olinde. He is incapable of turning away from his love, which will eventually lead to his violent death:

> O Dieux! Ma passion ne se peut destourner,
> Malgré mon jugement ie me laisse mener
> Dans ce nouveau Dedale ou mon ame s'engage.
>
> Et vers le precipice ou ie vais me jeter,
> Je suis comme un Vaisseau que les ventz & l'orage
> Poussent contre des Bancs qu'il ne peut euiter.
>
> (ll. 9-14)

All three of these poems reflect the conventions of Petrarchism and are typical of Tristan's love lyrics.

---

[19] The emblem is shown in *Glasgow Emblem Studies* 177.

The subject of the *stances,* "Canante que'lle merueille" (facing pp. 112-113) is a clandestine meeting of two lovers and the usual protestations of love by the narrator. The emblem to which the poem is appended shows Cupid embracing a woman in a bower where she is waiting for her lover. The theme of the poem, an elaboration of the emblem, is the meeting late at night of the poet with Canante in their trysting place and his desire for a physical sign of her affection. The poem abounds in the Petrarchan vocabulary and conceits that Tristan was so fond of in his early poetry. In the very first quatrain, Canante, like the Belle Matineuse, is said to be another sun:

> Canante que'lle merueille
> Adoucist enfin mon sort?
> Au temps que le soleil dort
> J'en treuue un autre qui veille.
>
> (ll. 1-4)

We learn in the next two stanzas that the lovers have met in their secret place and that Cupid has aided them in their deception. Without Cupid's assistance, their meeting would have been impossible and Tristan, waiting in vain for her, would die of fear, love, and impatience (ll. 15-16). The remainder of the poem is a request for a discernible sign of her affection for him:

> Il faut que dans ce lieu sombre
> Qui recelle nos langueurs[20]
> Je punisse vos rigueurs
> Auec des baisers sans nombre.
>
> (ll. 17-20)

When she does not comply with his demand, Tristan ends the poem with a very graphic request of Canante:

> Dieux! Que vous estes timide
> Vous me sentéz bien mourir
> Et n'oséz me secourir
> D'un baiser qui soit humide.
>
> (ll. 29-32)

---

[20] Langueur, n. f. 1. État d'abattement, de mélancolie dû à la passion amoureuse (Greimas and Keane, *Dictionnaire du moyen français* (Paris: Larousse, 1992).

"Pour moy ie tiens a perfidie" (facing p. 121) is a very short (four octosyllabic lines) poem that is simply a conceit expressing the idea that there is no cure for the *maladie d'amour*:

> Pour moy ie tiens a perfidie
> Tous les conseils de ma raison
> Tant jabhorre la guerison
> D'une si chere maladie.

The message is neatly summed up in the quotation of Saint Augustine that follows the poem: "Deus Deus meus, da mihi donum Continentiae sed non tam cito." [21] The poet is a very willing captive and he enjoys his "chere maladie." [22]

"Olimpe auecque ce poulet" (facing p. 129) deals with the rather common theme of the greed of the Lady, who rejects the lover because of his poverty. [23] He tells Olimpe that he is sending her a *billet doux* in which he has included a very rare opal bracelet, he offers her anything that she might want, and closes with a witty *pointe*:

> Dites ce que vous demandéz,
> Mais ne me faite plus attendre
> Les choses que vous me vandéz.
>
> (ll. 8-10)

The last of the thirteen poems (facing p. 145) is the beginning quatrain of a sonnet. It shows Tristan to be a master at the *jeu de mots*:

> Philis pardonnéz moy si ie ne puis celer
> L'ardeur dont vos regars ont embrasé mon Ame
> C'est en vain que j'essaye a la dissimuler
> Des que l'ouure la bouche il en sort de la flamme.

---

[21] O God, my God, give me the gift of moderation but not so quickly.

[22] The French and Latin texts on this page do not appear to have been written at the same point. Note of Alison Adams, "Manuscript Texts from DMAdd.392," *Glasgow Emblem Studies* 2 (1997): 130.

[23] See the "Plainte à la belle banquiere," *Les Amours* (Camo ed.), 123 and in the *Lettres meslées* "A R.R. Philargire. Reproches d'infidilité et d'avarice" (Grisé ed.), 89-90.

It is likely that he was so pleased with these four lines that he abandoned his intention to compose a sonnet. These last two poems are excellent examples of Tristan's *acutezza* and they reflect very clearly the ludic nature of most of his amatory poetry.

The thirteen new poems found in SMAdd.392 are very much in the same mannerist style as the love lyrics found in the published editions of Tristan's poetry. None of them has any purpose other than that of amusing an aristocratic audience that appreciated *esprit* in a poet and in his work. The poems do illustrate some of the emblems in the *Amorum emblemata* and may indeed pave the way for a more complete study of Tristan and his relation to the plastic arts.

Among the other poems that do not appear in the major volumes of Tristan's poetry, the most interesting one is a small volume of twelve pages published in 1654 by Guillaume de Luyne, *La Renommée à Son Altesse de Guise*.[24] The poem is a long (180 lines) heroic ode written in praise of Tristan's most generous patron, Henri de Lorraine, Duc de Guise. Abraham provides an analysis of the circumstances of its composition:

> As J.-P. Chauveau has pointed out, certain *ancien régime* poets were fortunate enough to be protected by the crown, and their poems thus became apologies for the monarchy as a sacred institution. By choice, or by circumstantial necessity, Tristan was attached to what must be called "the opposition," and he thus became the bard of the aristocratic ethos with all the vestiges of feudal individualism and pride that were to lead to the Fronde and eventually die in the splendor of Versailles.
>
> The heroes to whom Tristan erects his verbal temples are, like those of antiquity, demigods, offsprings of gods or, at least, of other demigods. Such is the basic premise of *La Renommée* . . . .[25]

The poem is a heroic encomium, very much in the Malherbian tradition, of the Duc de Guise, his family, and his martial acumen. The lines are clear and are much less filled with rhetorical display than those of some of his earlier works. As has been seen in other chapters, when Tristan writes a heroic ode, he tends to avoid rhetorical excesses to varying degrees. Here, he has eliminated most of these and has produced a clear laudatory ode in the "grand style

---

[24] Bibliothèque National, Inventaire Ye 34136; modernized by Bernardin, 616-621. All citations are from the 1654 edition.
[25] *Tristan L'Hermite*, 46.

héroïque." It is very much in the classical tradition of Malherbe and shows almost none of the rhetorical excesses that one encounters in his earlier love poetry. The poem begins with praise of de Guise for his illustrious heritage and his heroism:

> Héros charmante & glorieux
> Dont le merite est un prodige,
> Rejeton de cent demi-Dieux,
> Et l'honneur d'une illustre Tige.
>
> (ll. 1-4)

The hyperbolical encomium continues in the second stanza with a comparison of de Guise to Alexander:

> Le Ciel ne t'a rien épargné,
> De la Nature accompagné,
> Qui n'a point pris un soin plus tendre
> Desseignant le grand Alexandre,
> Que lors qu'elle t'a desseigné.
>
> (ll. 20-24)

Stanzas 3-5 praise de Guise's illustrious ancestors, François, Le Bal-afré, and Charles, the Duke's father. As great as these ancestors were, de Guise can surpass them:

> Mais bien que ceux dont tu descens
> Brillent d'une si haute gloire
> Qu'on aura tousjours de l'encens
> Pour en offrir à leur memoire
> [. . . . .]
> Il ne te faut que des matieres
> Pour passer tout ce qu'ils ont fait.
>
> (ll. 61-64 and 71-72)

Stanzas 7-9 celebrate the Duke's military exploits in Italy against the Spaniards and make an excuse for his failure (taken prisoner by the Spanish):

> Tu l'aurois fait par des efforts
> Surpassans la creance humaine,
> Si le Destin par ses ressorts
> N'eust trahy tes soins et ta peine
>
> (ll. 109-112)

In a subtle change of tone, Tristan concludes by saying that Fortune has changed and will now favor the Duke in all his endeavors. The poem ends with an exordium to de Guise, by Fortune, to invade and subjugate Spain:

> Marche donc, Prince sans pareil,
> Et traverse l'onde salée
> Avant le mois où le Soleil
> Visite la Vierge estoilée
> Sous cette constellation
> Il faut qu'une haute action
> Te donne des Palmes nouvelles ;
> Il faut que l'Ibere hâlé
> Par tes armes soit desolé:
> Et que j'aille exercer mes aisles
> Pour en apprendre les nouvelles
> Au climat le plus reculé.
>
> (ll. 169-180)

The classical style of the poem is obvious from the lines quoted above which are clear and harmonious and reflect the *discours baroque* in their pomposity, aphoristic sentences, emotional nature, and serious purpose. The Duke had been a generous Maecenas for Tristan and it was vital that the impoverished writer flatter him and ingratiate himself with his patron. That he was successful is seen in the fact that Tristan died, while in the service of his patron, at the Hôtel de Guise. Since this is Tristan's last published poem, it is interesting to note that his style has become far more baroque in the sense of *baroque dompté* or classicism and that this trend can be seen in his last play, *Osman,* which reminds one of Racine's *Bajazet.*

The poems studied in this final chapter reflect very clearly the three styles of Tristan L'Hermite. The thirteen early amatory poems reflect the youthful exuberance of a poet who delights in the conventions of the love lyric and excels in incorporating them into his poetry. These are very possibly Tristan's first attempts at poetry and they reflect the mannerist style of the Petrarchists. The religious poems are typical of his middle period and are of a usually restrained baroque style. The heroic ode, *La Renommée,* is, like most of his occasional poetry, written in the Malherbian *baroque dompté* that became known as classicism.

CHAPTER X

CONCLUSION

A S has been demonstrated in the body of this investigation, Tristan L'Hermite was very much a part of the literary currents of his era. He wrote tragedies, comedies, tragi-comedies, a novel, some outstanding letters, and more poetry than any other seventeenth-century writer until La Fontaine. His immense poetic output has been classified in many ways: baroque, mannerist, *précieux*, pre-classical, and both Malherbian and Marinistic. As has been established in the preceding chapters, each of these styles is reflected to some degree in Tristan's poetry. The two most important and pervasive styles are mannerism and baroque.

Unfortunately, there has been much disagreement among scholars who have concentrated on the two concepts and have attempted to define them. In the third and fourth chapters of this study, an attempt was made to define, compare, and contrast baroque and mannerism. The basic conclusion drawn was that the intent of the author is paramount in differentiating between the two modes. The mannerist poem is ludic and lacks any monumental or serious purpose–it is a vehicle for the poet to dazzle his readers with his conceits and rhetorical skill. The baroque poet uses many of the same rhetorical devices as the mannerist; but for a serious purpose such as proclaiming the Faith, celebrating events in the lives of the great, and expounding his own deeply-held convictions. The overall impression of a baroque work of art or literature is one of movement, strength, and sincerity, due to the poet's overwhelming use of rhetoric. Mannerism is pretty in its mythologized portrayals of Nature and it is Petrarchist, précieux, and Marinist in its love lyrics.

Tristan is primarily a mannerist poet of love and a baroque poet in his heroic, philosophical, and religious poems. He, like many of

174

his contemporaries, often used both styles in the same work, often toning them down so that they might be called "baroque dompté or classical." The primary focus of this effort was the defining of the two terms and the analysis of Tristan's poetic output for examples of them. This has been done through a survey of Tristan's published volumes of poetry with examples taken to represent each volume and with emphasis placed on his most outstanding efforts. His first two volumes, the *Plaintes d'Acante* and the *Amours*, were found to be overwhelmingly mannerist as were most of the pieces in *La Lyre* and the thirteen new poems found at Glasgow. The religious poetry, *La Renommée* and the bulk of the poems in the *Vers héroïques* are primarily baroque–the subdued, more restrained *baroque dompté* that is often called classicism.

Many poems contained elements of both styles and support the theory of Frank J. Warnke that Baroque is the period style and that mannerism and baroque are the two aspects of the period, Baroque. To this was added the theory of Helmut Hatzfeld and others that French classicism was actually a toned down baroque that was more amenable to French tastes. This style was seen in the heroic poetry where Tristan followed the lead of Malherbe and in some of the religious poems in the *Office* and the *Exercices spirituels*. The study revealed that Tristan L'Hermite wrote in each of the styles available to him, thus revealing a talent that places him in the forefront of seventeenth-century lyric poets.

BIBLIOGRAPHY OF WORKS CONSULTED

Abraham, Claude K. *Gaston d'Orléans et sa cour: étude littéraire*. Chapel Hill: UP of N.C., n.d.

——. "Tristan: Artifice Revisited." *Papers on French Seventeenth-Century Literature* 13 (1980): 13-24.

——. *Tristan L'Hermite*. Boston: Twayne, 1980.

Adam, Antoine. "Baroque et préciosité." *Revue des Sciences Humaines* 55-56 (1949): 205-224.

——. *Histoire de la littérature française au XVIIe siècle*. Paris: del Duca, 1949. 5 vols.

——. *Théophile de Viau et la libre pensée en 1620*. Paris: Droz, 1935.

Adams, Allison. "Glasgow University SMAdd.392 and the Printed Versions of Tristan L'Hermite's Poetry." *Glasgow Emblem Studies* 2 (1997): 141-157.

Arland, Marcel. *Les Échanges*. Paris: Gallimard, 1946.

Baldensperger, Fernand. "Pour une Réévaluation littéraire du XVIIe siècle." *Revue d'Histoire Littéraire de la France* 44 (1937): 1-15.

Barga, Thomas. "Baroque Imagery and Themes in the Theater of Tristan L'Hermite." Diss. Rice U, 1970.

"Baroque." *Oxford English Dictionary*. 2nd ed., 1989.

Battisti, E. "Sfortune del manierismo." *Rinascimento e Barocco*. Turin: Einaudi, 1960.

Bazin, Germain. *Baroque and Rococo*. Trans. J. Griffin. London: Thames and Hudson, 1964.

Belcher, Margaret. "Tristan's Annotations on the 'Plaintes d'Acante'." *Papers on French Seventeenth-Century Literature* 9 (1982): 327-339.

Berdan, John M. "A Definition of Petrarchismo." *PMLA* 23 (1913): 699-710.

Bernardin, Napoléon-Maurice. *Un Précurseur de Racine: Tristan L'Hermite, Sieur du Solier (1601-1655). Sa famille, sa vie, ses oeuvres*. Paris: Picard, 1895.

Boase, A. M. "Poètes anglais et français de l'époque baroque." *Revue des Sciences Humaines* 55-56 (July-Dec. 1949): 155-184.

Bousquet, Jacques. *Mannerism: the Painting and Style of the Late Renaissance*. Trans. Simon Watson Taylor. New York: Braziller, 1964.

——. *La Peinture maniériste*. Neuchatel: Éditions Ides et Calendes, 1964.

Bray, René. *La Préciosité et les Précieux, de Thibaut de Champagne à Jean Giroudoux*. Paris: Nizet, 1948.

Bremond, Henri. *Histoire littéraire du sentiment religieux en France*. Paris: Blond, 1916-33. 11 vols.

Bryant, William H. "A Thematic and Rhetorical Study of Tristan L'Hermite's *Les Amours*." Diss. U of Missouri, 1971.

Buffum, Imbrie. *Agrippa d'Aubigné's* Les Tragiques: *a Study of the Baroque Style in Poetry.* New Haven: Yale UP, 1951.

———. *Studies in the Baroque from Montaigne to Rotrou.* New Haven: Yale UP, 1957.

Carriat, Amédée. *Bibliographie des oeuvres de Tristan L'Hermite.* Limoges: Rougerie, 1955.

———. *Tristan ou l'Éloge d'un poète.* Limoges: Rougerie, 1955.

———, ed. *Tristan L'Hermite: choix de pages.* Limoges: Rougerie, 1960.

Caws, Mary Ann. *The Eye in the Text: Essays on Perception, Mannerist to Modern.* Princeton: Princeton UP, 1981.

Charpentrat, Pierre. *Le Mirage baroque.* Paris: Éditions de Minuit, 1967.

Chauveau, Jean-Pierre. "Maynard et Tristan," in *Maynard et son temps.* Toulouse: UP de Toulouse-Le Mirail, 1976. 245-254.

———. "Un Sonnet inédit de Tristan L'Hermite." *Dix-Septième Siècle* 61 (1964): 31-36.

Chédozeau, Bernard. *Le Baroque.* Paris: Nathan, 1989.

Corum, Robert T. "A Reading of Tristan L'Hermite's 'La mer'." *Papers on French Seventeenth-Century Literature* 9 (1978): 11-28.

Crescenzo, Richard. "Une Poétique de la Galerie? Sur quelques pièces de 'La Lyre'." *Cahiers Tristan L'Hermite* 14 (1992): 46-61.

Croce, Benedetto. *Età barocca in Italia.* Bari: Laterza, 1953.

———. *Storia della età barocca in Italia: pensiero—poesia e letteratura—vita morale.* Bari: Laterza, 1929.

Curtius, Ernst Robert. *Europäische Literatur und lateinisches Mittelalter.* Bern: Francke, 1948.

———. *European Literature in the Latin Middle Ages.* Trans. N. R. Trask. New York: Pantheon, 1953.

Dalla Valle, Daniela. *Il Teatro di Tristan L'Hermite.* Torino: Giappichelli, 1964.

Daniells, Roy. *Milton, Mannerism, and Baroque.* Toronto: UP of Toronto, 1963.

Denzler, Pierrette-Monique. "Mannerisms in Marinism, Gongorism, Preciosity, Euphuism, and Mannerism: a Rhetorical Analysis." Diss. U of New Mexico, 1987.

Donaldson-Evans, Lance. "Two Stages of Renaissance Style: Mannerism and Baroque in French Poetry." *French Forum* 7 (1982): 210-223.

Dubois, Claude-Gilbert. *Le Baroque, profondeur de l'apparence.* Paris: Hachette, 1973.

———. "L'Imitation sans limitation: Réflexions sur les rapports entre les techniques et l'esthétique de la multiplication dans la création maniériste." *Revue de Littérature Comparée* 56 (1982): 267-280.

———. *Le Maniérisme.* Paris: PUF, 1979.

———. *La Poésie baroque.* Paris: Larousse, 1969. 2 vols.

Eustis, Alvin. *Seventeenth-Century French Literature.* New York: McGraw, 1969.

Faguet, Émile. *Histoire de la poésie française,* Vol. III. Paris: Boivin, 1927.

Falicki, Jerzy. *Autotélisme dans la poésie française: époque du maniérisme et le XXe siècle.* Wroclaw: Panstwewe Wydawn, 1974.

Fumaroli, M. *L'Âge de l'éloquence. Rhétorique et "res literaria" de la Renaissance au seuil de l'époque classique.* Geneva: Droz, 1980.

Gerbaud, Henri. "Au sujet de l'Office de la Sainte Vierge." *Cahiers Tristan L'Hermite* 18 (1996): 55-59.

Gibert, Bertrand. *Le baroque littéraire français.* Paris: Armand Colin, 1997.

Graziani, Françoise. "Le Mythe pastoral dans les Plaintes d'Acante: Ovide, Virgile et Théocrate." *Cahiers Tristan L'Hermite* 12 (1990): 23-39.

Grisé, Catherine M. "Italian Sources of Tristan L'Hermite's Poetry." *Studi Francese* 14 (1970): 285-296.

Grisé, Catherine M. "La Vraie source de « L'Ambition tancée » de Tristan L'Hermite." *Revue de Littérature Comparée* octobre-décembre 1967, 585-588.

———. "The Poetry of Tristan L'Hermite." Diss. U of Toronto, 1964.

———. "The Religious Poetry of Tristan L'Hermite." *Mosaic* 4 (1971): 15-35.

———. "Towards a New Biography of Tristan L'Hermite." *Revue de l'Université d'Ottawa* 36 (1966): 295-316.

Grove, Laurence, ed. "Emblems and the Manuscript Tradition." *Glasgow Emblem Studies* 2 (1997): 101-190.

Guichemerre, Roger. *Quatre poètes du XVIIᵉ siècle: Malherbe, Tristan, Saint-Amant, Boileau.* Paris: SEDES, 1991.

Hallyn, Fernand. *Formes métaphoriques dans la poésie lyrique de l'âge baroque en France.* Geneva: Droz, 1975.

Hampton, Timothy, ed. *Baroque Topographies: Literature, History, Philosophy.* New Haven: Yale UP, 1991.

Hartt, Frederick. *Art, A History of Painting, Sculpture, Architecture.* New York: Abrams, 1976. 2 vols.

———. *History of Italian Renaissance Art, Painting, Sculpture, Architecture.* 3ʳᵈ ed. New York: Abrams, 1987.

Hatzfeld, Helmut. *Estudios sobre el barroco.* Madrid: Gredos, 1966.

———. "Literary Mannerism and Baroque in Spain and France." *Comparative Literature Studies* 7 (1970): 419-436.

———. *Literature through Art.* New York: Oxford UP, 1952.

———. "Mannerism is not Baroque." *L'Esprit Créateur* 6 (1966): 225-233.

———. "Problems of the Baroque in 1975." *Thesaurus* 30 (May-August 1975): 209-225.

———. *The Rococo: Eroticism, Wit, and Elegance in European Literature.* New York: Pegasus, 1972.

Hauser, Arnold. *Mannerism, Crisis of the Renaissance.* London: Routledge and Kegan Paul, 1965.

Hocke, Gustave René. *Manierismus in der europäischen Literatur.* Hamburg: Rowohlt, 1959.

———. *Die Welt als Labyrinth: Manier und Manie in der europäischen Kunst.* Hamburg: Rowohlt, 1957.

Humphrey, Peter. "Mannerism." *A History of Art.* Vol. 1 of *The Encyclopedia of Art.* Gen. ed. Lawrence Gowing. Englewood Cliffs: Prentice, 1983.

Ismail, Nahed M. "Tristan L'Hermite et le lyrisme au XVIIᵉ siècle." Diss. LSU, 1973.

Jareno, Ernesto. "Dos casos de la correlación temática." *Revue de Littérature Comparée* 47 (1973): 497-505.

Kronegger, Marlies. "From Fire to Fireworks in Baroque Poetry." *Papers on French Seventeenth-Century Literature* 16 (1989): 211-231.

———. *The Life Significance of French Baroque Poetry.* New York: P. Lang, 1988.

La Fay, Henri. *La Poésie française du premier XVIIᵉ siècle (1598-1630).* Paris: Nizet, 1975.

Lagarde, A. and L. Michard. *XVIIᵉ Siècle.* Paris: Bordas, 1963.

Lapp, John C. *The Brazen Tower: Essays on Mythological Imagery in the French Renaissance and Baroque.* Saratoga, California: Anma Libri, 1977.

Lawrence, Francis L. "'La Gouvernante importune': The Structure of a Pastoral Satire." *French Forum* 4 (1979): 239-248.

Lebègue, René. *La poésie française de 1560 à 1630.* Paris: Société d'édition d'enseignement supérieur, 1951.

———. *La Tragédie française de la Renaissance.* Brussels: Office de la Publicité, 1944.

Leiner, Wolfgang. "Le Promenoir des deux amans: Lecture d'un poème de Tristan L'Hermite." *Papers on French Seventeenth-century Literature* 9 (1978): 29-48.
Lough, John. *An Introduction to Seventeenth Century France.* London: Longmans, Green and Company, 1954.
Mackey, Charles Ruyle. "The Poetic Legacy of Tristan L'Hermite." Diss. Yale U, 1965.
Martin, John Rupert. *Baroque.* New York: Harper, 1977.
Mathieu-Castellani, Gisèle. "La Poésie amoureuse et son commentaire: Les Annotations de Tristan sur ses 'Plaintes d'Acante'." In *Eros in Francia nel Seicento.* Paris: Nizet, 1987.
Miernowski, Jan. "Sur La Mer de Tristan: espace et vision." *Cahiers Tristan L'Hermite* 5 (1983): 30-35.
Minguet, Philippe. *France Baroque.* Paris: Hazan, 1988.
Mirollo, James V. *Mannerism in Renaissance Poetry, Concept, Mode, Inner Design.* New Haven: Yale UP, 1984.
———. *The Poet of the Marvelous: Giambattista Marino.* New York: Columbia UP, 1963.
Mongrédien, Georges. *La Vie littéraire au XVIIe siècle.* Paris: Tallandier, 1947.
Mourgues, Odette de. *Metaphysical, Baroque and "précieux" Poetry.* Oxford: Clarendon, 1953.
Nelson, Lowry. *Baroque Lyric Poetry.* New Haven: Yale UP, 1961.
Nicolich, Robert N. "The Baroque Dilemma: Some Recent French Mannerist and Baroque Criticism." *Oeuvres et Critiques* 1 (1976): 21-36.
———. "Mannerism and Baroque: Further Notes on Problems in the Transfer of these Concepts from the Visual Arts to Literature." *Papers on French Seventeenth Century Literature* 10 (1983): 441-457.
Ors, Eugenio d'. *Lo barroco.* Madrid: Aguilar, 1943.
———. *Du Baroque.* Trans. Agathe Rouart-Valéry. Paris: Gallimard, 1935.
Pedersen, John. *Images et figures dans la poésie française de l'âge baroque.* Copenhagen: Akademisk Forlag, 1974.
Peyre, Henri. "Common Sense Remarks on the French Baroque." *Studies in Seventeenth-Century French Literature Presented to Morris Bishop.* Ithaca: Cornell UP, 1962. 1-19.
Praz, Mario. *Mnemosyne.* Milan: Mondadori, 1971.
Puzin, Claude. *Littérature, Textes et Documents, XVIIᵉ Siècle.* Collection Henri Mitterand. Paris: Nathan, 1987.
Quondam, Amadeo. *Problemi del Manierismo.* Naples: Guida, 1975.
Raimondi, Ezio. *Rinascimento inquieto.* Palermo: Manfredi, 1965.
Raymond, Marcel. *Baroque et renaissance poétique.* 3ʳᵈ ed. Paris: Corti, 1955.
———. "Le Baroque littéraire. État de question." *Studi Francesi* 5 (1961): 23-39.
———, ed. *La Poésie française et le maniérisme 1546-1610(?).* Geneva: Droz, 1971.
———. "Propositions sur le baroque et la littérature française." *Revue des Sciences Humaines* (1949): 133-144.
Reynold, Gonzague de. *Le XVIIᵉ Siècle: le classique et le baroque.* Montreal: Éditions de l'Arbre, 1944.
———. *Synthèse du XVIIe siècle: France classique, Europe baroque.* Paris: Éditions de Conquistador, 1962.
Rizza, Cecilia. "L'Image de l'amant et son évolution entre maniérisme et baroque." *Travaux de Linguistique et de Littérature* 20 (1982): 23-36.
———. "L'Orphée di Tristan e L'Orfeo di Marino," *Convivium* (N.S., 1954): 429-439.
Rousset, Jean. *Anthologie de la poésie baroque française.* Paris: Armand Colin, 1968.
———. *Dernier Regard sur la Baroque.* Paris: Corti, 1998.

Rousset, Jean. *L'Intérieur et l'extérieur*. Nouvelle édition. Paris: Corti, 1976.

──────. *La Littérature de l'âge baroque en France: Circé et le paon*. Paris: Corti, 1954.

──────. "L'Oeuvre de Marcel Raymond et la nouvelle critique." *Mercure de France* 348 (1963): 462-470.

──────. "La Poésie baroque au temps de Malherbe: la métaphore". *Dix-Septième Siècle* 31 (1956): 353-370.

──────. "Le Problème du baroque littéraire française." In *Trois Conférences sur le baroque française. Studi Francesi* Supp. to 21 (1963): 49-62.

Sacré, James. *Pour une définition sémiotique du maniérisme et du baroque: des* Sonnets pour Hélène *de Ronsard à* la Maison d'Astrée *de Tristan L'Hermite*. Paris: Klincksieck, 1979.

Sayce, R. A. "Boileau and the French Baroque." *French Studies* 2 (April, 1948): 148-152.

──────. "The Use of the Term Baroque in French Literary History." *Comparative Literature* 10 (1958): 246-253.

Scaglione, Aldo, ed. *The Image of the Baroque*. New York: P. Lang, 1995.

Scrivano, R. *Cultura e letteratura nel Cinquecento*. Rome: Edizioni dell'Ateneo, 1966.

Serret, Ernest. "Un Précurseur de Racine, Tristan L'Hermite." *Le Correspondant* NS 46 (25 April 1870): 334-354.

Shearman, John. *Mannerism*. Baltimore: Penguin, 1967.

Steadman, John M. *Redefining a Period Style. "Renaissance," "Mannerist," and "Baroque" in Literature*. Pittsburgh: Duquesne UP, 1990.

Studing, Richard. *Mannerism in Art, Literature, and Music: a Bibliography*. San Antonio: Trinity UP, 1979.

Sypher, Wylie. *Four Stages of Renaissance Style Transformations in Art and Literature 1400-1700*. Garden City: Doubleday, 1955.

Tapié, Victor-L. *Baroque et classicisme*. Paris: Plon, 1957.

Triadó, Juan-Ramón. *The Key to Baroque Art*. Minneapolis: Lerner, 1990.

Tristan L'Hermite, François. *Les Amours et autres poésies choisies*. ed. Pierre Camo. Paris: Garnier, 1925.

──────. *La Lyre*. ed. Jean-Pierre Chauveau, Geneva: Droz, 1977.

──────. *Lettres meslées*. ed. Catherine M. Grisé. Geneva: Droz, 1972.

──────. *Le Page disgracié*. ed. Marcel Arland. Paris: Stock, 1946.

──────. *Le Page disgracié*. ed. Jean Serroy. Grenoble: UP of Grenoble, 1980.

──────. *Les Plaintes d'Acante et autres oeuvres*. ed. Jacques Madeleine. Paris: S.T.F.M., 3rd edition, 1989.

──────. *Le Théâtre de Tristan L'Hermite*, eds. C. Abraham, J. Schweitzer, and J. van Baelen. Tuscaloosa: UP of Al, 1975.

──────. "The Religious Poetry of Tristan L'Hermite." ed. Ruth Ann Gjelsteen. Diss. U of Cal. (Davis), 1977.

──────. *Vers héroïques*. ed. Catherine M. Grisé. Geneva: Droz, 1967.

Varga, Aron Kibedi. "Le Poète chante le poète." *Rivista di Letterature Moderne e Comparate* 40 (1987): 317-322.

Veit, Walter. "Mannerism and Rhetoric: Some Aspects of the History of the Concept in Literary Criticism." *Papers of the Symposium "Mannerism and the Manneristic Configurations in the Creative and Performing Arts*, Canberra, Australia, June 1977. Published in *Miscellanea Musicologica, Adelaide Studies in Musicology* 11 (1980): 49-65.

Ventadour, Bernard de. *Chansons d'amour*. ed. Moshé Lazar. Paris: Klincksieck, 1966.

Wadsworth, Philip A. "Artifice and Sincerity in the Poetry of Tristan L'Hermite." *Modern Language Notes* 74 (1959): 422-430.

Warnke, Frank J. "Mannerism in European Literature: Period or Aspect?" *Revue de Littérature Comparée* 54 (1982): 255-260.

———. *Versions of Baroque: European Literature in the Seventeenth Century.* New Haven: Yale UP, 1972.

Wellek, René. *Concepts of Criticism.* New Haven: Yale UP, 1963.

Wölfflin, Heinrich. *Kunstgeschichtliche Grundbegriffe: Das Problem der Stilentwicklung in der neueren Kunst.* Munich: Ackermann, 1915.

———. *Renaissance und Barock: Eine Untersuchung über Wesen und Entstehung des Barockstils in Italien.* Munich: Ackermann, 1888.

CHAPTER XII

INDEX OF PROPER NAMES

Chassignet, Jean-Baptiste, 50, 53, 56, 61, 91, 109n12, 122, 161
Chaudebonne, Claude de, 19, 109n15, 122, 122n13, 123-125
Chauveau, Jean-Pierre, 16n11, 96, 96n2, 106, 109n15, 111n16, 113, 115n4, 116, 121, 121n11, 122, 122n12, 122n14, 123n16, 126, 130, 149n20
Chédozeau, Bernard, 42n6, 46, 46n19, 48, 51, 56-58, 62n39
Cicero, 45n14
Clouet, Jean, 77
Concini, Cosme-Jean-Baptiste, Maréchal d'Ancre, 20
Conrart, Valentin, 35
Corneille, Pierre, 49, 119
Corum, Robert, 137n7
Cousin, Jean, 24
Crashaw, Richard, 20
Crescenzo, Richard, 127n21
Croce, Benedetto, 45
Curtius, Ernst Robert, 27, 29, 30, 45, 45n14

Dalla Valle, Daniela, 39, 60n37
Daniells, Roy, 23n5
Dante Alighieri, 36
Dargan, Edwin Preston, 22n1
D'Aubigné, see Aubigné, Agrippa d'
Debussy, Claude, 93
Denys d'Halicarnasse, 31
Denzler, Pierrette-Monique, 26, 33, 35-36, 60, 62, 62n40
Desmarets de Saint-Sorlin, Jean, 46n18
Desportes, Philippe, 32n37, 36-37, 56-57, 62, 75-76, 81n26, 90n32
Donaldson-Evans, Lance, 53n26
Donne, John, 20, 45n14
Drelincourt, Charles, 56
Du Bellay, Joachim, 31, 34, 65n2, 128
Du Bois-Hus, Gabriel, 56
Duboise, Claude-Gilbert, 32, 52-53, 62, 146n16
Durand, Étienne, 37
Dvorák, Max, 24

Edme de la Châtre, Comte de Nançay, 95
El Greco, 23-24
Estampes-Valençay, Charlotte, Marquise de Puisieux, 151
Eustis, Alvin, 16n15, 36n42

Fénelon, François de Salignac de la Mothe, 54 *chart*
François I, 24
Friedlaender, Walter, 24

Garcilaso de la Vega, 75
Gaston, see Orléans, Gaston de France, Duc d'
Gerbaud, Henri, 158n6
Giraudoux, Jean, 28
Gjelsteen, Ruth Ann, 158n3
Gombauld, Jean Ogier de, 65
Góngora y Argote, Luis de, 20, 54 *chart*, 75
Goujon, Jean, 24
Gowing, Lawrence, 28n32
Grandchamp, Jacques, 20
Graziani, Françoise, 73n15
Griffin, J., 44-45n12
Grisé, Catherine M., 15n9, 15n10, 67-68, 68n7, 73n15, 77n20, 78-79, 86, 86n28, 88n30, 92n35, 92n36, 118, 118n6, 122, 131, 139n8, 139n9, 142, 158n6, 162, 162n8, 162n9, 170n23
Grove, Laurence, 157n1, 157n2
Guichemerre, Roger, 71, 73n15, 73n16, 84, 88n30, 92n37
Guise, Henri II, Duc de, 122n13, 140, 142, 142n12, 143-147, 149-150, 171-173

Hallyn, Fernand, 48, 51, 52n23, 56, 58-59
Hardy, Alexandre, 17
Hartt, Frederick, 23n4, 29n24, 43n7
Hatzfeld, Helmut, 29, 42, 44, 44n9, 47, 53-54, 54n29, 57n33, 59-60, 99, 99n6, 175
Hauser, Arnold, 23n4
Henri IV, 18, 161
Henrietta Maria (consort, Charles I of England), 134, 136
Henriette de Lorraine, 92
Herbert, George, 20
Hocke, Gustave René, 27, 27n20, 29
Homer (Homère), 31, 131, 138
Hopil, Claude, 46n18, 50, 61
Horace, 65n2, 122, 131
Hottinger, M. D., 42n5

Isabella Clara Eugenia (Infanta), 19, 126
Israel, Marcel, 164n12

Pontormo, Jacopo Carucci, 23
Pope, Alexander, 45*n*14
Primaticcio, Francesco, 24
Pulex (Polci), 65*n*2, 127
Pure, Michel, Abbé de, 35
Puylaurens, Antoine de Laage, Duc de, 92
Puzon, Claude, 16*n*15

Quevedo, Francisco, 20
Quintillian, 45*n*14

Racan, Honorat de Bueil, 22*n*1, 50, 65*n*2
Racine, Jean, 44, 49, 53, 54 *chart*, 66, 115, 119
Raphael (Raffaello Sanzio), 28*n*22
Raymond, Claire, 42*n*5
Raymond, Marcel, 24, 24*n*7, 25, 25*n*11, 26*n*12, 29-31, 31*n*32, 32, 32*n*33, 42*n*5, 42*n*6, 46, 46*n*18, 47, 47*n*20, 50, 52, 52*n*25, 53-54, 56, 62, 77
Régnier, Mathurin, 22*n*1
Reynold, Gonzague de, 47, 47*n*20
Richelieu, Armand-Jean du Plessis, Cardinal de, 92
Rimbaud, Arthur, 27
Rinieri, 128
Rizza, Cecilia, 114*n*3
Robinson, Franklin W., 38*n*47
Ronsard, Pierre de, 18, 31, 54 *chart*, 60, 65*n*2, 74-75, 81*n*26, 90, 90*n*32, 97, 128
Rosso Fiorentino, 23-24, 43, 89
Rotrou, Jean de, 49, 57, 60
Rouart-Valéry, Agathe, 45*n*13
Rousset, Jean, 16*n*15, 41, 43*n*7, 46-52, 52*n*23, 53-54, 57*n*33, 68, 77, 126

Saint-Aignan, François de Beauvilliers de, 133
Saint-Amant, Marc-Antoine Girard de, 16-17, 22*n*1, 35, 50, 53, 56, 62, 81*n*26
Saint-Marthe, Nicolas de, 17
Saint-Marthe, Scévole de, 16-18, 74
Sales, Saint François de, 158
Sarasin, Jean-François, 35
Sayce, Richard A., 28*n*22, 47, 47*n*20
Scalion de Virbluneau, *see* Virbluneau, Scalion de
Scarron, Paul, 22*n*1
Scève, Maurice, 60-61, 99

Scherer, Jacques, 118*n*6
Schweitzer, Jerome, 15*n*2
Scudéry, Georges de, 22*n*1, 35, 81*n*26
Scudéry, Madeleine, 22*n*1
Segel, Harold B., 47
Segrais, Jean Regnauld de, 35
Serret, Ernest, 15
Serlio, Sebastiano, 24
Serroy, J., 16*n*12
Shakespeare, William, 34
Shearman, John, 23*n*4, 25, 30, 30*n*28, 30*n*29, 38-39*n*47
Sidonius Apollinaris, Saint, 45*n*14
Spitzer, Leo, 53
Sponde, Jean de, 37, 50, 53, 60-62, 61*n*38, 81, 91, 122, 127, 161
Steadman, John M., 26
Studing, Richard, 26*n*14
Surgères, Hélène de, 18
Surin, Jean-Joseph, 46*n*18
Sypher, Wylie, 29, 29*n*26, 30, 43-44, 44*n*9-11, 45, 47, 53, 59

Tapié, Victor-L., 47, 47*n*20
Tasso, Torquato, 18, 38-39*n*47, 42, 54 *chart*, 65*n*2, 114
Taylor, Simon Watson, 26*n*12
Theocratus, 73*n*15
Théophile de Viau, *see* Viau, Théophile de
Thibaut, de Champagne, 28
Tintoretto, 23-24
Titian (Tiziano Vecelli), 24
Tortel, Jean, 66*n*3
Trask, W. R., 27*n*20
Triadó, Juan-Ramón, 43*n*7

Urban III, 43
Urfé, Honoré d', 22*n*1, 35, 65*n*2, 81*n*26

Van Baelen, J, 15*n*2
Van Veen, Otto, 151*n*23, 127
Vasari, Giorgio, 24
Vauquelin de La Fresnaye, Jean, 18
Vega, Lope de, 20
Ventadour, Bernard de, 36, 36*n*44
Verneuil, Henri de Bourbon, Duc de, 17, 17*n*17
Viau, Théophile de, 16-17, 22, 22*n*1, 35, 37, 46, 50, 53, 56, 60, 62, 65*n*2, 81*n*26, 90*n*32, 91-92, 106, 108*n*11, 124, 124*n*17, 156
Villon, François, 65*n*2

Chapter XIII

INDEX OF POEMS

NORTH CAROLINA STUDIES IN THE ROMANCE LANGUAGES AND LITERATURES

I.S.B.N. Prefix 0-8078-

Recent Titles

THE ALLEGORICAL IMPULSE IN THE WORKS OF JULIEN GRACQ: HISTORY AS RHETORICAL EN-ACTMENT IN *LE RIVAGE DES SYRTES* AND *UN BALCON EN FORÊT*, by Carol J. Murphy. 1995. (No. 250). *-9254-8.*

VOID AND VOICE: QUESTIONING NARRATIVE CONVENTIONS IN ANDRÉ GIDE'S MAJOR FIRST-PERSON NARRATIVES, by Charles O'Keefe. 1996. (No. 251). *-9255-6.*

EL CÍRCULO Y LA FLECHA: PRINCIPIO Y FIN, TRIUNFO Y FRACASO DEL *PERSILES*, por Julio Baena. 1996. (No. 252). *-9256-4.*

EL TIEMPO Y LOS MÁRGENES. EUROPA COMO UTOPÍA Y COMO AMENAZA EN LA LITERATURA ES-PAÑOLA, por Jesús Torrecilla. 1996. (No. 253). *-9257-2.*

THE AESTHETICS OF ARTIFICE: VILLIERS'S *L'EVE FUTURE*, by Marie Lathers. 1996. (No. 254). *-9254-8.*

DISLOCATIONS OF DESIRE: GENDER, IDENTITY, AND STRATEGY IN *LA REGENTA*, by Alison Sinclair. 1998. (No. 255). *-9259-9.*

THE POETICS OF INCONSTANCY, ETIENNE DURAND AND THE END OF RENAISSANCE VERSE, by Hoyt Rogers. 1998. (No. 256). *-9260-2.*

RONSARD'S CONTENTIOUS SISTERS: THE PARAGONE BETWEEN POETRY AND PAINTING IN THE WORKS OF PIERRE DE RONSARD, by Roberto E. Campo. 1998. (No. 257). *-9261-0.*

THE RAVISHMENT OF PERSEPHONE: EPISTOLARY LYRIC IN THE *SIÈCLE DES LUMIÈRES,* by Julia K. De Pree. 1998. (No. 258). *-9262-9.*

CONVERTING FICTION: COUNTER REFORMATIONAL CLOSURE IN THE SECULAR LITERATURE OF GOLDEN AGE SPAIN, by David H. Darst. 1998. (No. 259). *-9263-7.*

GALDÓS'S *SEGUNDA MANERA*: RHETORICAL STRATEGIES AND AFFECTIVE RESPONSE, by Linda M. Willem. 1998. (No. 260). *-9264-5.*

A MEDIEVAL PILGRIM'S COMPANION. REASSESSING *EL LIBRO DE LOS HUÉSPEDES* (ESCORIAL MS. h.I.13), by Thomas D. Spaccarelli. 1998. (No. 261). *-9265-3.*

'PUEBLOS ENFERMOS': THE DISCOURSE OF ILLNESS IN THE TURN-OF-THE-CENTURY SPANISH AND LATIN AMERICAN ESSAY, by Michael Aronna. 1999. (No. 262). *-9266-1.*

RESONANT THEMES. LITERATURE, HISTORY, AND THE ARTS IN NINETEENTH- AND TWENTIETH-CENTURY EUROPE. ESSAYS IN HONOR OF VICTOR BROMBERT, by Stirling Haig. 1999. (No. 263). *-9267-X.*

RAZA, GÉNERO E HIBRIDEZ EN *EL LAZARILLO DE CIEGOS CAMINANTES*, por Mariselle Meléndez. 1999. (No. 264). *-9268-8.*

DEL ESCENARIO A LA PANTALLA: LA ADAPTACIÓN CINEMATOGRÁFICA DEL TEATRO ESPAÑOL, por María Asunción Gómez. 2000. (No. 265). *9269-6.*

THE LEPER IN BLUE: COERCIVE PERFORMANCE AND THE CONTEMPORARY LATIN AMERICAN THEATER, by Amalia Gladhart. 2000. (No. 266). *9270-X.*

THE CHARM OF CATASTROPHE: A STUDY OF RABELAIS'S *QUART LIVRE*, by Alice Fiola Berry. 2000. (No. 267). *-9271-8.*

PUERTO RICAN CULTURAL IDENTITY AND THE WORK OF LUIS RAFAEL SÁNCHEZ, by John Dimitri Perivolaris. 2000. (No. 268). *-9272-6.*

MANNERISM AND BAROQUE IN SEVENTEENTH-CENTURY FRENCH POETRY: THE EXAMPLE OF TRISTAN L'HERMITE, by James Crenshaw Shepard. 2001. (No. 269). *-9273-4.*

RECLAIMING THE BODY: MARÍA DE ZAYA'S EARLY MODERN FEMINISM, by Lisa Vollendorf. 2001. (No. 270). *-9274-2.*

When ordering please cite the *ISBN Prefix* plus the last four digits for each title.

Send orders to: University of North Carolina Press
                    P.O. Box 2288
                    CB# 6215
                    Chapel Hill, NC 27515-2288
                    U.S.A.